HEARTS OF FIRE

11619-FERN

HEARTS OF FIRE

Cult Recovery & Spiritual Transformation

Kara Sorensen, PsyD.

11619-FERN

CONTENTS

DARKNESS STEPS FORWARD

OF SLEDS, CROWS
AND A THREE-LEGGED CAT

THE SOUL'S JOURNEY

ACKNOWLEDGEMENTS

With deepest gratitude, I wish to acknowledge the following:

The spiritual teachers and guardians who have been with me in this healing work, and in the evolution of this book. I am deeply grateful for your presence, protection, and guidance.

Gabe. Thank you for your integrity, perseverance, and willingness to seek the light in the darkness with me. You saved my life, brought healing to my soul's journey, and helped me find my own heart of fire. I will always be grateful.

Richard. Thanks for the patience of Job, humor and the admonition to "just eat real food." What a concept.

Sensei. You taught me to stand my ground when afraid, and fight back when necessary. Thanks for all the years and life lessons.

Pia. For lifetimes of joy, friendship and adventure.

Judith. Thank you for your ceremonies of protection for this work and those involved. Thanks also for your teaching, and for helping me discover my own gifts and personal power.

Jack. Thanks for your support on this healing journey.

Nate and Jennie. For being you. You are a light on my path.

My healing community. For the years we have trained together, partied, disagreed and made up. I am grateful for all of it. Thanks for a place to be myself.

All my teachers. To my native elders, I give great thanks. You have taught me much. To my other teachers, I am grateful for all the lessons you have learned and shared. May this work honor all my teachers.

Anke. Thanks always for your editorial support. Without you, this book would not have happened.

My assorted readers. Thanks for your patience and suggestions. You've been a big help.

Pam and Deb. Thanks for keeping me going on this last leg of the book. You're relentless, and I'm glad.

Survivors of cult abuse, your therapists/healers and those who cherish you. Your plight has kept me working late into the night. This book is for you. May you find it to be a light for your journey. Blessings.

"May the Lord make His face to shine upon you and be gracious unto you. May God give you grace never to sell yourself short; grace to risk something big for something good; grace to remember that the world now is too dangerous for anything but truth, and too small for anything but love. So may God take your minds and think through them; may God take your lips and speak through them; may God take your hearts and set them on fire. Amen."

benediction from the 70s,
attributed to Rev. Wm Sloan Coffin

INTRODUCTION

When faced with personal pain and struggle, we have a choice. We can descend into despair and bitterness, or we can reach for healing, release and peace. It's often a choice we make daily. Hopefully, we will seek the light. Yet, as most know, it is a struggle. As the trauma and pain grow in intensity, so do the possibilities that our world will be turned upside down as we search for hope and light again.

When the trauma is on a large scale, the recovery process becomes even more intense. It can require a deep commitment to recovery and healing, a willingness for profound change, therapists and healers willing to go the distance, and tools that can deal with the extremes of suffering.

As therapists, we continually strive to find the most efficient ways possible to bring recovery and healing from trauma. The more extreme the trauma, the more our abilities are challenged, and the harder we seek for the necessary tools to bring the individual back to the fullness of life.

For those of us with a holistic orientation, we look to include all aspects of the person in the recovery. Thus we strive to find resources which will bring healing to the spirit as well as the mind, emotions and body.

In this case, it was to be my own healing journey. Had I known, I might have fled shrieking over the horizon. As it was, I believe we are protected from ourselves until the time is right. As my own story emerged, I joined the search for the deepest, most complete healing tools we could find.

The harm I experienced was extreme, from sexual abuse to torture, murder and mind control. Such is the life of a child in a cult. My recovery required both the conventional and unconventional resources currently available, as well as a complete spiritual transformation. To give the reader perspective, I wish to identify the primary modalities for recovery and healing which we used.

Traditional psychotherapy provided a stable, strong container for this healing. New models of recovery from the abuse literature were used as the struggle was engaged to find survival, meaning and healing. These were tools which provided a safe environment for the work. Research and findings were also used from the Post-Traumatic Stress Disorder literature as well as that of the Multiple Personality or Dissociative Identity Disorder literature, providing recovery skills and tools not previously available.

Shamanic journeying shared the gift of traveling through time and space to distant experiences. There we were able to recover lost parts of the soul, transform the reality of the past, and bring healing to the present time and state. Soul retrieval, power animals, and assistance from the elemental spirits gave breadth, depth and new abilities to what could seem hopeless. The process empowered me as a survivor to find hope, new life and meaning.

Energy healing addressed the energetic traumas deliberately inflicted by cult leaders, including implants, thought forms, mind control and conditioning. Also known as **energy medicine,** this resource provided avenues for healing traumas which could not be reached with more conventional means. It also provided me with sufficient electromagnetic and physical energy to literally do the "work" of healing.

Homeopathy supported the different layers of healing and transformation, finding ways of correcting the subtle damage that could not be diagnosed or reached by modern medicine. With its minuscule drops of remedy, it assisted in eliminating aspects of =physical trauma. It helped restore functioning to physical systems such as the immune system, nervous system and the endocrine glands. Essences were also helpful in supporting the other layers of my existence, and assisting with emotional concerns.

Spiritual healing addressed some of the more profound distress which cult survivors experience. The spirit realm is often actively employed against the victims. Spiritual programming is common, using mind control to inflict beliefs such as "God will never love you", and "Satan is more powerful than God."

Cultists also frequently use psychic skills in a twisted way to cause spiritual harm. In some cases, it takes a healer who is able to work in the psychic and magical realms to find the path of healing from the spiritual trauma of these cults.

Martial arts was a surprise tool. A sleeper. In my case, imperative. The lessons in martial arts for survival and spiritual combat were immensely helpful, teaching me of personal boundaries, a willingness to "show up" when afraid, to stand my ground, and to defend my own space. I learned a willingness to fight for Life, for healing and for the souls of others as well as myself. Ultimately, I used these tools both in the physical realm of day to day living, and in the spiritual realm to battle the cult on other planes of existence.

All of these pathways were used in this work of healing. Some are known to therapists and found in the literature. Others are innovative and highly unusual, born of necessity. Yet all have been necessary and effective. From their use has come a transformation of the deepest of wounds to find life, heart and soul to live with passion, integrity and completeness.

Ultimately, it was also discovered that there is a loom which holds this tapestry of healing, integrating the threads woven of vast diversity, some coarse and wide, others fine as the purest gold.

That most important pathway, the loom to hold it all, is the realm of the Sacred. An experience of the Sacred not bounded by walls or dogma, rather a wisdom gained which expands life and love, bringing meaning, understanding and compassion to the healing of the self and of the earth.

This, then, is the story of one woman's journey, from the darkness of evil to spiritual wisdom which transforms life. Three unlikely allies came to my aid: a traditional psychologist with an addiction to coffee and a willingness to enter the unknown realms to find keys for healing, a king-sized homeopath with a three-legged cat and a passion for Enya, and a delicate-boned karate sensei who taught me to stand my ground and fight for my life. Each contributed in their own way to weave a tapestry of healing. We hope it informs, inspires and provides hope for healing to others.

DARKNESS
STEPS
FORWARD

The Dawn of Darkness

The heaviness hung in the air, thick like velvet drapes, yet palpable and waiting, charged with energy. I held my breath, waiting with the air itself.

Then it came. Movement flashed to my right as his arm swept down with the ceremonial knife, slashing abruptly past my cheek, splitting the air with an electrical crack.

"I, Wolf Man, with this ceremonial knife, cut this circle, that all evil which was sent out, now be returned to the sender!"

The tautness in the air shattered, reverberating through my body with a shock wave. It's like a tightly-woven web, I realized as the knife flashed past, and the web fractured. Each energy fragment was like a rubber band held taut, then released, ricocheting back to the point of origin.

The significance struck home and I caught my breath. The evil that the cultists had sent out to the innocents, the deep, dark penetrating evil, was returning to them. In my mind's eye, I could see the dark waves of evil. Instantaneously, they were released, flowing swiftly out, searching for home, returning to the original senders. Like dark clouds, the energy flowed. The power of it, and my own surprise, took my breath away. And on its heels, my fear.

Gabe sensed it. "It's all right, Carla." His voice was like softly polished steel, holding the anger at the cultists in perfect sharp-edged control. "All we have done is return to them what they sent out."

"It's reasonable," I thought, now breathing slowly. "And not too much." I would look at the fear later. It was always lurking. Fear of retaliation, over-whelming rage, terror. Carefully, I put it away as I'd practiced, and returned to the work. This was a ceremony, and there was a proper conclusion. Gabe thanked the spirits and guardians, closing the energy. I added my own thanks. Spiritual protection was no small thing, and I was very grateful.

It was done.

As the ceremonial energy ebbed, my breathing returned to normal and my senses cleared. The light trance state shifted. I began to feel my feet again. Gabe moved beside me, and together we stood, companionably, slowly releasing our hyper-alert warrior stances. Wordlessly, we returned to our seats in his office, seen again as an ordinary space.

He seated himself across from me in his black roller chair, his lanky form relaxing as he reached to the bar stool on his left for his ever-present coffee mug. His dark hair curled up at his neck of its own accord while steady brown eyes held me, evaluating. The casual pose belied the warrior beneath, as he watched me with his characteristic alertness and compassion.

Dressed in casual shirt and slacks, his appearance was that of a traditional psychologist. Yet small things hinted otherwise. The Tibetan mala, looking like a wooden rosary just showing at the neck of his shirt, the sage fragrance floating in the air, and the crow feather and stones on the square table to my left. Not the trappings of most psychologists.

Sighing quietly, I sank back into my own stuffed chair, glancing around the office to ground myself, and get further out of the ceremonial trance state. The room was a small rectangle extending away from me, the far left corner holding a modest built-in desk with Gabe's computer and clutter of papers, books and phone.

My eyes roved across from it to the portable massage table, set up with its' sheet folded on the top. Next was the door on my right, the square table to my left and another client chair at right angles to the table completing the sparse furnishings, except for Gabe's chair, of course, and his bar stool/coffee mug holder. The essential ingredient.

The day's work had not been planned, rather evolved from the session with him. He was an excellent therapist, and beginning to show aspects and skills I would never have dreamed existed. The compassion, I had learned to trust. The martial artist, a fact. But this new ceremonial work continued to amaze me, as the power of the ceremony slowly seeped from the space.

The previous thickness in the room continued to fade. We sat quietly, noticing the shifts in energy, each returning to an awareness more focused in the present.

I'd never heard of a ceremony like this, though years later I would find references to a similar one. Tony Hillerman, one of my favorites, wrote of a Navaho ceremony called the Enemy Way—a ceremonial way to return evil to the sender. His books were fiction, of course. But were they? When I read it, I wondered. The Navaho might well have a ceremony that did that. We Anglos were the new kids to ceremony. Not them.

Gabe didn't read Hillerman. He read that heavy, academic stuff. Ceremony was new to both of us. We did our best. Gabe knew energy, and ceremony seemed to come to him when needed.

"OK, Carla?" Seated across from me, he watched my body language and expressions, scanning or searching for any indications of distress. My five foot eight slender form in blue jeans and t-shirt stretched in the chair, black curly hair falling around my features as I leaned forward. A face without make-up, my dark eyes and thick lashes gazed from the depths back at him, while my long fingers held the Diet Coke.

"OK." I shifted quietly in my chair, leaning back once more on the stuffed cushions. I was exhausted now, and with a long drive in front of me. His Chicago office was a long way from my suburban home. Yet somehow I knew I'd be all right on the drive. I'd done it for so long.

"Pretty amazing stuff," I thought out loud. Again, I worried slightly about causing harm.

He reminded me. "It's Justice, with a capital 'J'. What we put out in this world does return, sooner or later. Across time and space."

"I know. It still just takes my breath away. And you know what?"

He waited quietly while my eyes flickered, evidence of the thought processes going on below the surface.

"Part of me is really glad. Something had to be done." I thought of all the evil the cultists had done and to so many. Sending their evil energy back to them was fair indeed.

Shortly afterwards I left the office still turning the experience around in my head. The five hour drive home would pass easily as I pondered our work.

Monday morning came early. Some days I wondered why that was. Saturday didn't come so early. It didn't take a rocket scientist, I reminded myself.

Driving through the early morning traffic, I turned right onto Front Street, then a left at the Six Mile Inn to the hospital. Forty-two, married, with a teen and a pre-teen, I was also a clinical psychologist with more responsibilities than I cared to think about. Although I loved my clinical work, I also especially enjoyed my teaching schedule with medical residents. This was a teaching day, and I had to be particularly alert. Those young, getting younger, minds never stopped, I thought as I pulled into the doctors' lot. The good news/bad news about them, depending on which resident was asking the questions. Who would be interested today? Who, combative and skeptical? Only time would tell.

Three hours went quickly. "So, was that clinical or personal?" one resident quipped to another, amidst good-natured laughter as medical charts closed with a clatter around the large wooden conference table, and beepers began going off again. The residents scattered as my teaching session closed, and I began gathering my folders.

I loved the hospital and the intensity, with the intellectual challenge that the teaching provided. But it was clearly a two-edged sword. Not all the residents valued the psychological aspects. Kidneys were certainly easier to treat than souls. And much less personal.

On my way out, I made sure to stop at Ben's office at the end of the hall. A faculty member of the residency, Ben and I had been friends for a long time. Stopping just outside the door, I waited until the conversation inside was finished and the resident stepped out, then peeked my head around the corner, eyes glittering with mischief.

"Carla!" Ben laughed with pleasure, lumbering his large frame to his feet to bend over me for a welcome hug. His thatch of white hair, doctor's coat and stethoscope made him look intimidating to some, but I knew him as a gentle giant. One usually full of tall tales to lighten the load of misery he dealt with daily.

"Been teaching?" he asked, motioning to the chair in his office.

"Yep. All your darlings. How's the new group of residents looking?" Together we caught up on news, then I had to move on.

"Appointments waiting, Ben. But it's been good to see you." He stood again for a hug, and then I had to go, leaving the warm island of pleasure behind as he returned to his desk.

Leaving the building, I passed by the glass wall leading to the exit. Catching a fleeting glance of myself in the glass wall, I ran my habitual check. Did I blend into my surroundings, look inconspicuous? Was I well enough hidden? Living a life in hiding took attention to the details. The reflection showed me that secrets were undercover, and I looked the part of a traditional psychologist.

I recognized that I was in hiding for two reasons, one known and one unknown. From as early as I could remember, I was cautioned to blend in, don't stand out, don't let others know. Know what? That part I couldn't remember. Just that there were substantial and dangerous secrets to my identity, and I had to maintain them. The best way was to blend into the surroundings. I could be competent and professional, but don't stand out from that group either. It took great care and considerable energy.

The other reason for caution was obvious, at least to me. My conservative blue dress and uniform earrings hid a rebellious soul. I had capitulated to customary dress code to increase my reception at the hospital. And minimal makeup was common there. I fit in. But back in my office, I preferred to wear casual slacks or skirts with soft flowing blouses, easy shoes and fun jewelry that spoke of my more informal nature. A small thing, yet it felt daring in my rather stuffy professional world, particularly paired with my subconscious awareness of a need to hide my dangerous identity.

My reflection had also shown a moderately athletic looking woman, which for me meant some natural ability and a lot of daring. Rather, in childhood, I had thought it daring. Now I understood it was counter-phobic. See a fear, head for it. Otherwise, the bigger fear was that being afraid would stop my forward motion in life. I'd done a lot of crazy things in those years to prove I wasn't afraid, hiding the terror even from myself. Now I was a runner. More reasonable. But I missed those fun days. Racing horses bareback along the steep cliff edge, or clinging desperately to a thin ledge on a vertical mountain face. Or even being hauled unconscious from the Warrior River in Alabama following a trick water skiing accident. Challenge. Adrenaline. Wonderful so long as I didn't remember the consummate terror. At least it gave a target to my fears, holding the unreasonable terror at bay.

Walking briskly towards the parking lot, I reflected on the end of those wild days. That bright sunny morning in a Rocky Mountain ranch yard, the velvety brown horse I had just mounted rising up into the air. Straight up. Stunned, I froze, terrified, as he continued his ascent. The screams of my companions jerked me out of my shock, and I slashed the reins down just before the final moment when his weight would topple us both backwards, crushing the new life just stirring in my womb.

That was the moment I became a mother, I'd often thought. The daredevil, willing to risk all, had receded from sight. Caution replaced foolhardy, but on its heels, anxiety had stolen the heart of daring. I wondered if it were truly a good trade.

Walking to my car, I saw the approaching dark suited figure, jolting me out of my reverie. A doctor. One I knew? Would I recognize him? He appeared to recall me, and wanted to greet me. Panic hit me like a wave, gripping my stomach in a tight fist, forcing my breathing almost to a stop.

"Hey, Carla!" Andy waved, his smile filling his face, flowing to the depths of his intense eyes, complimenting the casual dark hair. With the wave and voice came recognition.

Grateful for small favors, I paused in my trek. "So how are you, Andy?" A medical resident from years past, the pieces fell into place once more and my breathing resumed. My disguise was still intact.

Years later I tried to convince Gabe that I was really fairly all right in those times. His astonishment erupted.

"Carla! You were a fucking mess!" As in, how could I forget?!

I'd rather believe the disguise.

But that day, driving back to my office, part of my mind was on traffic, yellow lights, and cars cutting in and out, while the other part was on the complicated path that had brought me to this place. Friday, a ceremony to return evil to the cultists who had sent it out, a weekend with my family, Monday teaching residents, and now a quick drive to my office to see private clients. A full life, complicated and still holding mysteries.

In that abstract state of driving on automatic pilot, I let my mind wander once more. Here I was, a successful professional, knowing how to be competent and do a good job. And yet.

I'd nearly always known that something was terribly wrong. I just had no clue what it might really be. I only knew that my life didn't seem to be like others. There were parts of it that seemed wildly out of sync. Remembering again, I realized that I had truly lived in hiding. Even from myself. Turning back onto Front St., I let my mind float back over the anomalies and secrets. The hidden scent of danger that followed me everywhere.

An image of myself as a four-year old sprang to mind, as I saw myself curled alone on the cabin's back bed, wrapped painfully around the inflated plastic whale. Even then I extended my awareness, past my wrenching pain and stifled gasps for breath, to the room beyond where my father raged, insisting that I could not be taken to a strange doctor in this vacation town.

I'd wondered why, hearing the rage and knowing the terror that supported it. I knew the fear wasn't for me, as I lay alone with the paralyzing pain, feeling for his emotions. It was fear for himself. Why?

Slowing in traffic to slide past Stewart's Market on my right, I paused at the light, my place in line dictated for me. I saw other oddities of my life flit by. My 12 year old self in a middle America small town, a hidden switchblade, fighting in the night streets under garish streetlights. The thirteen year old who didn't talk outside the family. Why not? When the school began to ask, my father lectured, reminding me of the importance of being invisible, and silence didn't do it. You had to blend in. I made myself say "hello" and use people's names. The school officials kept watching, but quit asking. I was assigned to work in the counselor's office. They observed. Discussed. There was a problem, but what was it?

Doodled teardrops traced the pages of my life, decorated with faces, arms and legs to hide even their true nature. But they couldn't tell me what we were hiding. Basketball championships kept me active and aggressive, but standing in a half circle in choir caused fainting spells. The pieces didn't fit together.

Late one fog-draped night in college, the injunctions and control nearly slipped as I inexplicably walked into two thick lanes of traffic. The counselor who followed said it was disappointment over a boyfriend. I knew that wasn't it, but what was it? I had successfully hidden it even from myself.

Meanwhile, the risk-taking had satisfied something deep within. By giving the fears a concrete reason for their existence, I had a way to exorcise them. When I stopped the risk-taking, the pressure had begun to build.

Turning left off Front St. onto Russell, I drove slowly as the road curved down the hill, leading towards my office parking lot. Drifting, I remembered the early days of marriage, my uncontrollable shaking when a repair man came to the house, the alcohol required to get me through taking small children trick-or-treating at Halloween. Other people didn't have to do that. It didn't make sense. I continued struggling to look as if everything was all right, like burying a time bomb deeper in hope it wouldn't explode.

A shaky marriage took me back to therapy. A small memory peeked through. A closet. My sister had locked me in it. I could hear her walking away, feel the terror in my soul, the conviction that I would die.

"That can't possibly be. You're making it up," my therapist decreed. The secrets receded, to wait their time. The marital dilemma was solved with graduate school. Jack became a father to the children, and things got better. My pain and loneliness were pushed aside by the demands of school, a career and family.

Yet I'd nearly always known that something was terribly wrong. The pressure from holding something at bay began to take a toll. I scheduled my clients first thing in the morning so I had to stop the unexplained tears from the night and get out of bed. There were those occasional terrifying plunges towards the freefall of despair, nightmares that taunted me with menace. Unexplained phobias and anxieties. I was mostly a loner, so no one would guess. When I was in my professional mode, I was respected by the community and clients alike. Yet there was a hidden turbulence which suggested much more.

Therapy with Samuel had helped. A world-renowned and respected therapist and teacher, I'd stayed with him a few years. Until the first memory surfaced. An unmistakable hint of incest and severe family dysfunction. He'd gotten very quiet that day. His lean form, white beard and receding hairline seemed to focus into his folded hands in his lap. Finally he'd looked up at me.

"Carla, I want you to go see Dr. Gabe Michaels."

"Why?"

"I think we have a real problem here. And this is his area of expertise. He's quite good at this."

"I don't want to. I know you, and I like you." We discussed it for several sessions. Or, more accurately, I sulked and argued, and he persisted. I lost. Not a surprise. In the end, I reluctantly agreed to check out this Gabe Michaels.

I first met him at a training institute where he was teaching. "I'm checking you out," I announced, hand on hip, head tilted cockily to one side.

"Oh?" One eyebrow raised, holding his papers after a lecture.

"Samuel said I should see you as my therapist."

"Then I guess we'll have to see, won't we," and he smiled as he shifted his load to walk into the hall. "I expect we'll know by the end of the weekend."

Later he'd led a meditation. Already shaken by having to sit in a circle, I tried to keep myself from relaxing too much. I didn't want "it" to show, the pain that was again pressing against my controls. Quietly our bodies calmed while he guided us. Somewhere in the middle, he first used the phrase: "This is my existence." I lost it.

Fighting for self-control, I felt my body shake and the tears begin to flow freely down my face. Just the thought of my existence was causing a flood of grief. Opening my eyes to escape the light trance and regain control, I found his eyes on mine. He knows. The thought terrified me. What does he know? I couldn't even get clear about that. Again I slid back into trance, and again he said the phrase, with the now predictable results. Clamping my jaws against the sob, I opened my eyes again, furtively checking the room. All other eyes but his were closed. Solemnly, he watched me.

I avoided him after that. This Gabe Michaels knew a piece of the hidden part of my life, a part I couldn't explain. Danger signs were flashing all over my life.

Yet at the end of the workshop, he found me. "I'd be glad to be your therapist." What was the man thinking? Ashamed, I ducked my head, nodding in agreement, murmuring something about calling him. It had begun.

Gabe had been good. The memories had slowly come into focus. My brother and sister did confirm that she'd locked me in a closet, leaving me for hours alone in the house. I didn't know for another ten years that our father had done the same to her.

Memories came up of being tied spread-eagled to the bed, and they too were confirmed. Then memories of the "little house", my uncle's on a farm, and childhood gang rape. All were confirmed by extended family, my parents now long dead. And in the process, I'd learned substantial coping skills from Gabe, enabling me to live a better quality of life.

We had gotten back everything that. as two professionals, we could imagine had been causing my distress. Nothing else new was coming up from the past, and my symptoms were certainly better. Not gone, but definitely better.

I went back into hiding. Hiding now from Gabe. I was tired of being in therapy. Maybe he had done all he could. Perhaps this was the level of distress I would have to tolerate. No more memories surfacing. No more causes for my remaining distress. I was doing the best I could. Time to quit therapy. I would go on a weeklong healing retreat to put closure on all of it. A retreat in the midwest for healers, it would confirm that I was done.

That fall morning at the retreat had been startlingly beautiful. Cold, crisp with a clear blue sky. I sat with Jeff, my best friend at the retreat, in the living room. The fire crackled behind us with the wonderful smell of wood smoke, while we looked out the enormous glass windows reaching from the floor to the ceiling, disclosing the countryside rolling gently away. There were several bird feeders which were full of colorful diners, some on the feeders and even more on the ground, providing a bright counterpoint to the white snow in the brown fields. Even wild turkeys wandered through, suggesting a peacefulness that was only illusory.

With this as the end of the retreat, Jeff and I had relaxed, stretched out on the long sofa with the large pillows. The rustic table in front of us was handy for his everpresent boots as he stretched his lean frame out over the end of the sofa.

"It's been a good retreat," he reflected and I agreed. I had put closure on my incest work, feeling relieved about that. And it was a great place. Quietly, we enjoyed the late fall day. There was only one unfinished piece of business, and finally I gathered the courage to mention it.

As prelude, I slid down amongst the pillows, hoping to hide my anxiety. Jeff looked over at me, suddenly more alert. "What, Carla?"

"Well, there's just one thing I don't get."

"And that is . . . ?"

"When I was meditating this morning. I got these really clear, vivid images. There was a bonfire and candles, and it gave me the creeps really badly. It wasn't like a normal bonfire or candles. There was something terrible and cold about it."

My chill returned as I remembered, and even the fire couldn't keep me warm. I huddled under the red wool throw on the sofa, my face white with anxiety.

"It really scared me. I don't know why. That fire and the candles just gave me this sense of terror, like something sinister following me, tracking me." By then I was shaking.

Jeff had looked at me as we both became very still. His eyes were somber, quiet, sad.

"Oh, Carla." That was all he said. That scared me even more.

"Jeff, I've worked so hard. I want to be done with all the trauma and pain. This worries me. It makes no sense."

"I know. I know." We both stood up, and quietly he held me.

"What's it mean?"

"You'll have to go find out."

"And if I don't want to? What if I'm not strong enough?" I was trembling again.

He held me to stop the shaking. "You're strong, Carla. You're strong. Look at all you've been through and the work you've done. You just need to find out what it means. That's all."

The dinner bell rang then, calling the group together. A delicious turkey dinner, and I could barely taste it. Soon I was on my way, driving home. I knew there was only one direction I could go. Forward. I had to find out where my terror was coming from. What it meant.

I saw Gabe the next week. Shaking again as I sat in the familiar black stuffed chair, I explained. Gabe's reaction was similar.

"I don't want to do this, Gabe. I don't want to open up anything more."

"I know, Carla. But look at you. I don't know if we can keep it down, whatever it is. Looks like it's starting to come forward. Remember when Samuel sent you to me to do your incest work? This is how we began. The memories just started coming, whether you wanted them or not. Then we had to do the work."

"I know, and look how long that took. Years, Gabe. It took years. I **do not** want more ugly work to do. More memories coming up. It messes with my life!" Temporary anger gave me more energy, then it dissipated as he just sat, waiting. There was no answer.

Gabe's voice softened. "You know that there are still symptoms we haven't been able to get, Carla."

Numbly, I nodded. "Symptoms that make no sense," I grumbled to him.

"Like your real terror in group settings. Of sitting in circles. Your fear of doctors. Jack has to take the kids to the physician. Unanswered pieces that don't fit anywhere."

Still shaking, holding my hands between my knees, I relented. I needed to face this. Something was going on. Something intense. And I really still didn't want to know. Yet I knew I had to. The anxiety was following me again, like a ghost covered with ice, coming close at unexpected times, chilling the air and my soul.

This could put my professional life at risk, and my family life, I knew. Yet I had to see what was there. Like a fire smoldering, the delicate wisps of smoke were warning me of a possible conflagration below. I had to know before it erupted, throwing me into panic and worse. The work was before me. I hated it.

I thought about my family. Jack, my husband, and Nate and Jennie, the kids. I had told them only minor amounts of my incest work. They knew that my family had abused me. I had never seen any reason to tell them details. It was mine to deal with, not theirs. Jack and I kept the kids away from my family. That didn't take much explanation since my brother and sister were the only living family I had. As they lived hundreds of miles away, I just made sure we didn't visit. Or if we did for a few hours, the kids were never out of my sight.

Other than that, it had been my recovery and my healing. My responsibility. I hadn't wanted my kids to have the responsibility of parenting me. "Parentified child" we called it in therapy. I wanted to stay in a parental role and let them be kids. A mistake? Who knows. What to do now? An avoider at heart, I put off the decision. I always did like Scarlet O'Hara. I would wait to see what this terrifying feeling was about. Maybe there wasn't much at all to it.

Denial is great.

North Wind

The snow was falling lightly as I walked into the warmth of Gabe's building. Brushing myself off, I headed for the ancient elevators, letting them creak their weary way to the sixth floor and his office. He was waiting, his lanky form leaning up against the waiting room door, watching as I walked in.

"I'm feeling just a tad cautious," was my warning as I threw my coat on the spare chair, aware of the smell of a warm cinnamon bun and coffee. Smelled good. My stomach growled in response.

"Caution sounds appropriate," Gabe responded, sipping the hot coffee from a blue mug lettered GREEN EARTH.

"The fires and candles are coming in my dreams now. Nothing is happening with them, but they keep showing up. And dark forms that don't take a clear shape."

"How've you been feeling emotionally?"

"I always wake up anxious from the dreams. Sweating. And during the day, the anxiety seems higher than it's been for some time. I try to deny it, but it's there. Afraid people will recognize me. Other odd fears."

I nervously pulled on the edge of my royal blue sweater, watching his responses, trying to hide my anxiety, hoping he didn't think this was too bad. It was clearly too bad for me to handle, though I didn't know why. Like bats lurking in your cupboards, ready to hurtle out the moment you opened one. I was feeling very afraid we might open a cupboard.

"What other odd fears?" He looked all right. Not overwhelmed or turning away yet. I'd tell him more.

"Realizing that I never put a drink down and then drink from it again because I'm afraid it will be drugged. That's a life pattern that I'm more aware of right now. I recognize it's not the norm in our culture. Those kinds of things."

"Hmm. How are things at home?" He leaned back in his chair, one foot up on the stool rung, sipping his coffee, watching me closely as I still tried to hide my anxiety.

"They're OK. Stable. Kids are their usual selves. Jack's working hard. I'm working hard . . . using it to distract myself from my anxiety."

Leaning forward, he put elbows on knees, looking right at me. "So, I think we need to look into this some more. To go after some of the images and just see what happens. That way we'll get a better idea of where your anxiety is rooted. Are you all right with this?"

The bats were banging inside the cupboard doors, demanding to get out. Fly in my face. Terrify me. Maybe we could crack just one door. To take the pressure off.

"Yes," reluctantly. "I know it's the only way to get these symptoms really gone. We got a lot of it before, but it's pushing on me again."

Mentally I flinched against those shut cupboards. I think they were meant to stay shut and locked, but the racket was getting too loud. The pressure was pushing on me. There had to be a way to release some of it. I minimized my distress to Gabe, but knew we had to release some of it. My anxiety was too high again. We had to go forward. Fortunately, at some part of my depths, I was aware that he knew this was so very serious. I wasn't fooling him. We both felt the danger signs flashing. No way but ahead, I thought to myself.

He nodded grimly. "I know. Let's get to work."

Getting up, he went to his desk in the corner, taking out a sage stick and matches.

He carefully lit the sage, inspecting it as it caught. I knew the smell from our previous work, the scent of the sacred from his Native American tradition. Gabe had learned about it in his years studying with the elders. The Medicine people. Used for clearing negative energy, sage returned a space, and the individuals, to a sacred state. I loved the aroma, a comfort to me now.

As Gabe moved slowly around the office, I watched him, remembering that this was now sacred space. We were working with spiritual assistance. It helped me center myself in the sacred, calm down and breathe. The world was a bigger place than my fears. I had to remember that. I steeled myself, forcing the calming breath. The bats were creating a ruckus again. I had to stay in control. We had done scary work before, uncovering my incest background, and I'd survived.

Besides. We would just go exploring and take the edge off the tension. And maybe prove there was nothing really to this. Maybe I was just being overly sensitive. The sage reminded me again of my spiritual focus, my belief in the power of Spirit to help me.

Gabe resumed his seat in the roller chair, and moved slightly closer to me, reaching for the table beside me. Picking up an old, wooden rattle with a dark feather hanging from the end of the handle, he began swirling it, starting a gentle rhythm, swaying and repetitive. I'd never seen him use a rattle before, but it had a good sound, reassuring, reminding me again of his appreciation for the Native American traditions.

Slowly, rhythmically, he began to sing. It was a song, but soon became a soft chant. A language I didn't recognize. A gentle rhythm, it's beauty slowly filling me, calming my breathing as I slid into a light trance, my breath becoming slow and even.

"We're going to go on a guided meditation, Carla. Just pay attention to what you notice. We're starting on a path." He waited a short time, gently swirling the rattle as I slid just a bit further into full relaxation.

"What do you notice?"

I took a deep breath so I could respond. "The path is dirt, firmly packed under our feet. We're walking side by side. There are a few trees, seems like pine trees. That clean fresh pine smell." I took a deep breath, loving the scent.

I had done this before with Gabe when he helped me with my incest recovery. Some call it "journeying". Together we went to other times and places to create healing. I had created a "safe place" for wounded child parts who had been traumatized.

When we did the abuse work, I followed what was ahead of me, reporting my experience. Sometimes he clarified things, and sometimes he didn't. But I felt safe with him as we did this. Occasionally, it was terrifying, but he had taught me how to manage my fears.

"The pines do smell good, don't they." We paused, then he continued. "We're going down a hill now, and turning a corner to the right. Are you with me?"

"Yes. This is a different place than we've ever been before, isn't it."

"It is. It's a new place where I've been working. There are Native Elders waiting for us. They know we're coming. Look for them by the path."

Watching, I could see them. It was always reassuring when Gabe and I saw the same thing. "They're there, on both sides of the path. I can see the buckskin clothing, and they have drums and rattles. Why are they there?"

I felt the rhythm of the drums deepening my trance state, a common use of drumming. Soothing, filling me. I relaxed even further, watching the elders as we drew closer, noticing the fringing and beadwork on their garments, and their leather moccasins and boots. The drums and rattles continued, keeping a rhythm as we walked closer.

"They are the Old Ones. These are the Guardians of the Sacred Fire. They are allowing us to pass through the gauntlet."

To my surprise, I intuitively knew exactly what he meant. Carefully I looked again at the elders, noting their advanced age and quiet strength born of deep wisdom and growth. These men and women had been the Elders of their respective tribes, leaders of their people, renowned for their wisdom and judgement, known for their spiritual depth and truth.

Now, after death, they had come together to guard and protect the spiritual pathways and sacred places. They helped those of us on this plane who searched for spiritual truth, healing and wisdom in a sacred manner. Guarding this old and sacred pathway in the spirit realm, their chants, drums and rattles wordlessly welcomed us on our quest. Knowing our intent was pure, they allowed us passage. My heart opened in awe at their reception, the moistness in my eyes a tribute to my appreciation for being allowed in such a sacred and guarded place.

Together we walked, the Old Ones on both sides of us, chanting, drumming, rattling. I felt the rhythm inside as my breathing matched it, vibrating with them, creating a sense of spiritual presence and acceptance. Gabe's voice came to me.

"There are two hills ahead, one on each side of the path. Do you see them?"

My attention reluctantly left the elders as I looked ahead. "I do. They're small, but close to the path. Right?"

"You got it. They are also Guardians."

I understood that more than the spirits of humans could guard a sacred place. We crossed between the hills as I felt a slight sense of resistance, as if we'd just gone through an invisible shield. So subtle, it was almost like a breath, but clear enough for me to feel it. Interesting. Gabe's laugh interrupted my concentration.

"There he comes. See him?"

I looked ahead, just in time to see a magnificent white horse race from behind a cluster of pines. Fully muscled, an almost iridescent white, he galloped our way, mane and tail flying as he shook his head majestically. A rider myself, I was immediately in love. Forgetting entirely the purpose of our journey, my breath burst forth in an appreciative gasp. Gabe laughed again.

"Meet White Wind. The final Guardian." He was upon us then, rearing at the last minute, his intelligent eyes searching us as he whirled in a spin, racing away with dirt spraying behind him.

"Wow."

"Beautiful, isn't he." And after a pause, "We're allowed to pass." Gabe's attention refocused. I followed his look.

A large plain stretched out before us. Not far away, I could see a fire, and as we walked closer, I began to realize its immensity. The flames reached hungrily for the sky, taller than two or more of us, while the heat seared my face, taking my breath away. Sparks rained down around us, although I never felt their sting.

Startled, I stepped back, aware of the vacuum created by the fire. The wall of heat was so intense that it was creating a pull of air into the base while it burst through the top to the heavens, sparks and flares dancing, throwing even more embers.

"Don't be afraid. This is a Sacred Fire, used for sacred purposes. You won't be burned. It's for protection and purification. Within it, nothing can harm us."

I liked the idea of protection, and sacredness. I just worried about that little line of his. Within it. What's that supposed to mean? He caught my concern.

"Trust me, Carla. We've always been all right before. Take my hand, and together we're going to step into the fire. Remember, it's for protection."

Remember, faith is a verb, I reminded myself. Time for verb stuff. "OK. Whatever you say." Easy to say, I thought and held my breath, like that would help somehow. Not.

Gabe took my hand and we stepped right into the middle.

I waited for certain death. Trusting, but certain death. Nothing happened. Maybe he was right. Again.

Letting my breath go, I realized that the flames were flaring and flashing all around me, but I wasn't feeling heat. I felt calm and clear inside, protected from any danger outside.

"This is great." Protection is a good thing.

The flames rushed up through each of us, purifying and cleansing any negativity. Indeed, a Sacred Fire, I calmed even more as I realized I was feeling fresh, strong and sheltered.

Gabe had been quiet while the fire purified us. Now he spoke.

"It's time now, Carla. You're protected here. Nothing can harm you. It's time now to see what the bonfire and the candles meant, and why you're so anxious. I want you to look out from the safety of the fire and tell me what you see."

Frightened again, my breath caught, and then I remembered that he was right. I understood that I was safe in the fire. I could risk looking further. Pulling myself together, I looked, surprised that I could see outside the fire.

"There. I'm beginning to see some shapes over there."

"What do you see?"

I watched while they became clearer. "Another fire. It's the bonfire." My heart lurched. I forced myself to calm down and look.

"There are candles around that fire. In a circle. But it's strange."

"Why's that?"

"Well, they don't move. They are just there. Perfectly still. Not like regular people near a bonfire holding candles or anything like that." Relieved, I realized that the terror of the first glance wasn't with me. I could look and see, and even become curious. Gabe looked where I pointed. A slight pause, and then he understood.

"Those are votives."

"OK. And?" That still didn't explain it to me.

"The votives are on the ground. In a circle, that's true. But they aren't moving because they are just placed on the ground."

"Oh, I get it. That seems right. But why would anyone do that, do you think?"

"Look more closely. Tell me what you see again."

Slowly the scene became more and more clear. It's as if the emotional part of me detached, to tell him the story of what I saw.

There wasn't any terror. I was watching it from far away. And my insatiable curiosity was probably my saving grace.

"It's a ceremony of some kind, Gabe." I saw a child tied on the ground, cold and shivering, and realized it was myself as a very young child. Two? Three? Somewhere in there. There were animal sacrifices, symbols drawn in blood. I'd never seen those kinds of symbols. Quietly I told him what I was seeing. Beside me, I could feel his presence and acknowledgement.

"What are they doing? And why?" I didn't understand. Still protected by my observer perspective and wondering, I could continue to look, although I realized that some feelings were beginning to break through for me. This would be tough later.

He paused, considering. "It's a marriage ceremony, Carla. Look around and tell me who and what else you see."

"Well, I see my father. He's wearing a black robe with a hood that's fallen down around his shoulders. I don't get it. They are all dancing, this frenzied sort of thing. A sort of maniacal energy. Torches. They're whirling around wildly. Pretty weird, don't you think?"

"Um hmm." He was unusually quiet. The significance wasn't hitting me yet. "What else?"

"There's a **meanness** about them. A perversion feeling. It makes me feel cold and sick inside. This is **not** good." The understatement of the century.

"Anything else?"

"No. Just my awareness of what it must have been like for me as a child. It's so strange. And so **mean**. That's my father there. What are they doing? What do you mean, a marriage ceremony?"

"We'll process later. Anything else that you are aware of before we leave?" His voice was soft, yet firm, keeping me on track.

"Just an awareness that I learned to not recognize faces as a child. And trust people. Some of those people are relatives. I'm sure they are. No wonder I didn't trust. Who could live with that? Especially a kid?" Now I was getting mad. Anger covering fear.

"OK. You've learned enough. Time for us to leave. What do you say, let's take your child self with us."

"Really?" Hope stirred, pushing away my settling despair. "All right." Then I paused. "How do we do that? She's tied down."

"You've used a knife before in some of your incest healing work. Take that knife now. Do you have it?"

"Yes." This part was familiar. We had worked with creative imagery before. As I called the knife to mind, immediately I could feel it in my hand. Reassuring.

"Now walk over to the little girl." I thought about it, and realized that we had left the Sacred Fire, watching instead from near the ceremony. I could move around here, and had as I'd observed the figures dancing. Quietly I followed his instructions, walking over to the child tied to the ground. My feet crunched on dead grasses and plants, releasing the dry, brittle smell of fall.

"Cut the ropes where the little girl is tied down. Then take her hand. She's frightened. You're going to have to reassure her."

"What if the others see us?"

"They won't. That part of the ceremony is over. They're too busy with their frenzied dancing."

I looked at the child, wild-eyed with terror, and knelt down beside her for reassurance.

"Come on, don't be afraid. We're going to get you out of here." I began to cut on her ropes. Seeing that, she calmed, if only a little.

"It's all right. I'm going to get you free." She watched, fear turning to surprise as I cut her ropes and pulled her small, body to her feet. The ceremony went on around us, as Gabe had predicted, with the adults in robes dancing wildly, crazed looks in their eyes. Were they on something? Finished with the child, they didn't notice as the three of us slipped away, then ran quickly through the night. The safety of the Sacred Fire was just ahead.

"Run!" Gabe urged us. The adults were beginning to shout, screaming curses as they finally realized the child was gone. Quickly we three neared the fire.

"Hold her hand, and tell her about the safety of the fire. I'll go in first, so she'll know it's all right. Then you follow with her."

"All right." I turned to her, explaining. Gabe stepped forward, quickly immersed in the safety of the fire. We held hands and followed. Turmoil was erupting behind us as we disappeared from view. I watched as the robed figures raced chaotically, searching vainly for her.

"Pay attention to what you feel, Carla."

Again, I could feel the energy as the flames raced through and around us. A cleansing sensation, relieving after the sick feelings of the ceremony. The child smiled shyly up at me, calm with her hand in mine. A strange place, but she knew me in her own way, and trusted this adult self. She was safe with me.

"This Sacred Fire is also purifying you, Carla. It's clearing away any evil you and your child self still have from this experience. Really feel the flames flowing through you and purifying you from that time."

I paid attention again to the cleansing sensation. Pure and clear, the fire raced through us. Dark residue left from the fear and the ceremony flowed up and out with the fire's burning embers as the flames raced heavenward. Relaxing, I felt the cleansing sensations replace the degradation and terror of the experience.

"Look!" Gabe's voice compelled me to follow his gaze back the way we had come. "Carla. What do you see?" I looked.

"It's a huge wind." Amazement was in my voice. "Which direction is that?"

"That's the north."

The North Wind came, dark and fierce, swirling and gusting, sweeping all before it. Gathering strength and power, it howled ferociously as if it had teeth, devouring all in it's path. One minute the ceremony was in chaos, and the next . . .

Gone.

The bonfire, candles and figures had all disappeared. In the deep still darkness, it was as if it had never existed. A forest. A meadow. And silence.

Stunned, I watched, then turned to Gabe. "It's almost as if Nature was on our side. They're gone."

He just smiled.

Slowly we left the fire. White Wind watched from a distance as we led the child toward the Guardian Hills and through. The Old Ones were waiting, with quiet smiles of approval, drumming and chanting. We walked between the two lines once again, while the child watched, eyes big. They smiled and nodded to her, seeming pleased to see her. As we walked, they blessed us and our work.

I couldn't believe it, and yet I could. The Old Ones knew of our journey, our work, the rescue of the child. And with their knowledge, came their blessings. Too soon, we left them behind.

"There's a fork in the path up here, Carla. When we reach it, take the child to the healing meadow you developed in our work before. I'll meet you in my office."

I nodded. I knew. It was a great place, where I had previously left wounded child fragments to heal from our incest work. A beautiful mountain meadow, it was crafted after those wonderful Rocky Mountains meadows I had experienced and loved in years gone by.

This place was special, protected on all sides by high snow-capped peaks, giant ponderosas and tender, quaking aspens. The meadow was temperate, lush green grasses of all varieties and textures covering the expanse, with berry bushes sprinkled in closer to the bubbling stream that coursed gently through the center. The children played, picking berries and splashing in the shallows, a small cottage nearby. Older children watched out for the younger ones, with a young pre-teen in charge. No adults were allowed. The children didn't trust them.

Blue jeans, tennis shoes and a gray sweatshirt, the oldest kept a careful watch over the others, with a weather eye attuned to the other spiritual realms for any new arrivals. Wounded children from my earlier experiences who needed rest and healing had been brought here, to be met and cared for as they healed. This new wounded child part of my self would find healing there.

Reaching the fork in the path, I told her of the meadow. Looking where I pointed, she saw it, delight filling her eyes. Moving closer to the meadow, she saw the oldest girl reaching out to welcome her, offering a huge chocolate chip cookie. Tentatively, she took it, as other children came forward with flowers and greetings. The child in good hands, I allowed myself to back slowly away, watching as she merged with the group of welcoming, compassionate children. Slowly I turned my head and looked towards Gabe. A sigh escaped my lips, telling Gabe I was done.

"Now come back to the office, Carla. That's right. Take a deep breath. When you're ready, open your eyes. You'll be completely relaxed."

I opened my eyes to his somber gaze. Relaxed, yes. Confused? Also yes. I moved slowly, mentally as well as physically, to bring myself back to the present time and place in a good way. I didn't want to rush this, and end up disoriented for the whole day.

Gradually my senses adjusted to the office, his chair and Gabe's form in front of me, the feel of cushions under my body, the aroma of cooling coffee mingling with Xerox odors from next door, the sound of a fax ringing. I was back. The real world. Well, which was real? No, don't go there. My attention turned to Gabe.

"So, talk to me. What the heck was that?" My voice had an edge. Fear? Anger? Both.

"What do you think it was?"

"It's what has been described to me as cult abuse. And I'm sure I don't want it to be that." Panic lurked around the edges.

"I don't want it to be that, either," he agreed, getting himself some coffee and handing me my Diet Coke. Slowly he settled in his black chair, placing his coffee on the bar stool beside him. I leaned back and slid down, resting my head on the back of my chair.

"I don't like this."

"I know. I don't either. Let me check in."

He'd only been doing that recently. I'd just discovered that he'd become clairvoyant, able to see things other people couldn't. It seemed pretty weird, but I was getting used to it.

He could also talk with what he called his spirit guides. That was new. Spiritual guidance. From dead people, as far as I was concerned. But seemingly dead people with a bit more experience and perspective than we had. Dead people who were evidently operating from the knowledge of their many lives.

These spirit guide dead people seemed smarter than my dead Aunt Ruth. Once in a reading, someone told me that my Aunt Ruth, deceased some twenty years, was there and thought I was too thin. She wanted me to eat more cookies. She had loved to bake cookies, I remembered. Her solution to most problems. Eat cookies! She and the Cookie Monster would have made great pals.

But I figured there were levels of ability in dead people too. Just like us. This work requires a sense of perspective, I reminded myself. Gabe seemed to be in contact with a number of these advanced spirits, and he could call in ones who would understand what we didn't.

Maybe some were angels, too. I wasn't sure at this point. But their perspectives were often helpful, and solved problems troubling us, so it was fine with me. Whatever works.

I waited while he checked in.

"Well, at this point, my guides aren't too impressed with this crew. They are cultists, but so far seem to be primarily dabblers, practicing the forms they've been taught. It doesn't look, at least now, like they have a lot of substance to them."

I sighed. "I suppose that's the good news."

"Well, there has to be some." He smiled ruefully.

I thought some more. I didn't want them to be skilled, and dabblers sounded about as good as I wanted them to be, at their strongest.

"Maybe what we saw is the worst that happened." Hope burns eternal. "And this will take care of my anxiety and these wild swings into despair. I can see now why I'd have the symptoms I've been having."

"They certainly do make more sense," Gabe agreed quietly.

I thought some more. "I'm grateful for the fire, the healing that it gave, clearing me of the evil from that time. When we left, it was as if it had never happened."

"That should help you with any residual feelings you may have after you leave here. It's really been taken out of your system, your energy field, so you shouldn't be overwhelmed. A healing experience like this changes the trauma forever for you. I expect you'll grieve, but it should be manageable."

Without the incest work we had done, I would not have understood at all. But that had been my experience with him. If we healed it, or took it out of my energy field, the trauma was gone. I would remember it, but the overwhelming feelings were reduced. As if it were truly a long way away. A moment in my history, among many moments. What a concept. As a profession, we needed more of this kind of work available to us. I thought about what he said, the sick feeling of the ritual, and it's now being manageable. I certainly felt better than when we first saw what was happening. And better than the anxiety I'd experienced before we started. Seemed as though healing was indeed taking place.

"Good. I need this to be manageable. Let's keep it that way. This could get out of hand in a hurry."

Gabe just nodded in agreement.

"What was the marriage ceremony?" I didn't like the sound of that.

"In their minds, they were marrying you to the cult or to their dark power. It was their way to make you one of theirs."

A shiver ran down my back. One of the bats had gotten out of the cupboard before I had gotten the door slammed. The rest rattled their wings. Or was it my imagination? Maybe there were no more.

"I hope that's it. Maybe I just got in on the end of that craziness." I clearly did not want more. Get real. I didn't want this much. Let's call it quits while we're ahead, even though this doesn't qualify as ahead. Let's just assume this is all. Wishes took form in warp speed as I settled back into my preferred denial. Or tried to.

"We both hope so, Carla. We'll just have to see." He was hedging, of course, and had to, but I went with the wishes. Maybe this really was all there was to it. This would be enough to handle, anyway.

Our session ended then, and we said our good-byes. Gabe gave me a bigger hug than usual. We had entered a new territory, frightening and intense, and it had affected both of us, drawing us closer. It reminded me of war veterans from the same unit. We were bonded by our experience, each affected by the work we'd done and what we'd experienced, and closer for it.

At home, I was subdued. I did my job, saw clients, taught residents, cooked dinner. But in the down times, I was quiet. I treasured time to process the events of my visit with Gabe, to journal, draw, and let myself drift. It was a healing way for me to process my therapy work. But I was also worried now. Was there more to this cult business?

I tracked my dreams. What did they have to teach me? I didn't remember all of them. Never would have gotten any sleep if I had. One night I dreamed of a house under major renovation. There were no working bathrooms, the bedrooms were full of dismantled drawers, and clutter was everywhere leaving little room to step around, and no way to find order. My life was under renovation. I had the feeling nothing would ever be the same, and wakened disoriented.

The next day flew by in a haze, appropriate to reconstruction, I suppose. As I was cutting the peppers for chili that evening, Jennie walked in. Twelve was still a good age. Most days.

"Want to cut the onions?" I asked, my right eyebrow cocked up towards her.

"Nope. No way." She plunked her slender form, clad in jeans and a soft, emerald green sweater topped with ash blond hair, down on the white stool, elbows resting on the counter to watch. "Makes me cry."

"Um. Me too." I waited, knowing she had come to talk. Those times were becoming more rare as she moved towards the teens. Some days I wished I could back up with her.

"When will dinner be ready? Will Nate be home? Are those enough peppers?" Jennie had a unique capacity for picking up emotions, yet didn't have the clarity to understand what she was feeling. Her questions signaled anxiety, but she didn't know the cause of her feelings, much less being able to discuss them at that age. I knew better than to probe, remembering that defensiveness lay just below the surface.

"Dinner will be ready at six, your brother should be home, and do you want more peppers?"

"No. Did you see Bobby across the street today? He was chasing that dog again." She was starting in on what I called chatter. Meaningless to me, talk that went on and on. Someday I would decode it, but I doubted I would have the energy today.

Quietly she talked and I listened with periodic response, the rhythmic chopping of the knife on vegetables keeping cadence with her monologue. It was better than no contact at this fragile age.

The session with Gabe weighed heavily. Strange symbols drawn in blood were not my idea of a good time, much less the rest of it. The Sacred Fire and North Wind muted my grieving, giving me hope, yet I was restless, increasingly aware of a strong need to be able to protect myself.

Tuesday morning I headed to the dojo, hopeful of a way to work out some of my frustration. Wanting to learn to defend myself, I had asked any martial artist I could find to recommend a school for being able to protect myself. All roads led to Parkman's school. That was the place to learn street fighting. I really didn't know what I was asking. Parkman, I later learned, was retired Special Forces, the student ranks full of cops, detectives and armed service personnel. A rough school, demanding, military. Could I last? Only ten percent remained past the first three months. Four classes into it, I was still determined.

The neighborhood was rough, matching the school. Not a suburban dojo. This school was in a deteriorating neighborhood down by the river. A former warehouse district, upgraded to rowhouses, downgraded by crippling poverty, the connected buildings' decaying forms were surrounded by neon-lit bars, broken whiskey bottles, drooping sparse vegetation, and loitering residents, watching suspiciously.

I parked on the one way street between an abandoned car with a broken windshield and no tires, and a pickup listing dangerously to the right. Locking my doors, I walked briskly through the broken glass and around the corner, slipping through the gate in the wooden-stake fence. It was another world.

The fence hid a delicate oriental garden. A path of stones led to a raised wooden bridge, arching over a small stream which emptied into a pond on my right. A waterside dwarf red maple swayed in the slight breeze. The water bubbled while the earthy fragrance of small hidden plants filled my senses as I crossed over the bridge, enjoying the miniature beauty.

Soon I was entering the glass doors of the converted warehouse, bowing and walking down the narrow hall to the upper deck. The smell of sweat and dirty gym socks assailed me as I approached the smaller deck where a dozen students warmed up, stretching out on the polished wood floor. A quick change in the locker room, a few stretches on the upper deck, and the directive came.

"Line up!" Sensei commanded from the lower and larger deck of the training hall. Immediately, students jumped to their feet, bowing to Sensei. I watched him, wondering about the man who commanded such quick response. Watchful, we lined up for meditation facing the kamiza in the front. Bowing again, we knelt while I secretly enjoyed the light splashing in through the rice paper covered windows at the end. I absently watched it reflecting onto the warm, polished wooden floor and bouncing off the mirrored walls. I was new. My concentration was nil.

Practicing forms and stylized movements carefully, I worked out tense and sore muscles, trying to get my arms and legs coordinated, still in some awe at the higher ranking belts and their smooth movements. Then seated with the white belts at the side, I watched sparring practice.

"Yami!" the halt command cracked the air like a whip, penetrating to every corner of the room. The fighters stopped mid-strike, hands cocked back ready for the blows, trigger tempers flaring. The white-uniformed figure leapt across the polished hardwood floor and between two practicing warriors, forcing them back from each other. Their eyes glared, anger sparking, tension seething close to the exploding point. Sensei stood firm between them, challenging them with hard eyes.

"Control! Control first, power second!" he reminded them. Corrected, the fighters all began again, more carefully this time. All thirty fighters had taken the reminder as pertinent to them, watching their moves and those volatile tempers.

"I don't have a temper," I thought to myself. A small voice inside disagreed, and I argued with it, these days only aware of my fears. We'd see. I watched the figure who had asserted his control over this wild-looking group.

Sensei. He taught all the day classes, and many of the night ones. Small, compact, muscled, his delicate bones disclosed only in his face, he moved with the grace of a dancer and the quickness of a hummingbird. The class silent and still again, he demonstrated a technique, swiftly moving out of danger while experienced black belts shook their heads in wonder.

I watched him carefully, noting the senior students' respect and distance. This was a complicated man, and I wanted to use common sense. Class over, I rose to line up for closing meditation, muscles already sore from the workout.

Earth Spirit

Christmas was approaching, and the chaotic wave of the season was beginning to overtake me. Clients, teaching, and dinners competed for presents, wrapping and holiday celebrations. Meanwhile, my kids were restless; mutiny was drawing near.

"Where are we going for Christmas?" Jennie demanded, one hand on her hip and the other holding the phone, snacks piled on the table. "And when will we be back?"

Her brother, Nate, backed out of the refrigerator, mustard balanced on top of the tomato which was on top of the lettuce keeper. "I'm going carolling with our instruments, don't forget," he reminded me, getting his two cents worth in. "We do that every year." His statement came with the crash of the mustard jar mixed with Jennie's shriek.

Overwhelmed, I invoked Jack. "We'll figure it out. Your dad and I will talk." I fled the kitchen. They often overwhelmed me, escape my only route.

It was bewildering how overcome I could feel at times, life getting ahead of me like a tornado rushing past and hurling me along with it. Then I would retreat into denial. The kids really were all right, it was Christmas, my client load was full. I could live a "regular life."

It only took three more days for me to realize again, this was not a typical life. That third night I woke, in the deepest part of the night, sitting bolt upright in bed, heart pounding frantically in terror, sweat rolling off my body. Stark images saturated my soul, compelling but without order or understanding.

An overpowering sense of vulnerability pervaded me as the terrifying impression returned—the dream image of a dark man rising up in front of me, over me. Visible from the waist up, he was naked. My eyes fixated, paralyzed, on the huge muscles, rippling with power. In horror, I saw the right arm rising above me, then saw only the knife in that hand as it plunged unerringly towards my chest.

Suddenly awake, I was gasping for breath, sitting rigidly, every muscle tense, my body drenched in sweat. Jack stirred beside me, mumbling, restlessly responding to my sudden movement. I stilled my breathing, forcing it back to normal, and willed Jack back to sleep. A reaction. I still didn't understand that I was acting out the injunction: don't let **anyone** know. It was automatic, reflexive. He rolled over, mumbling and I laid down, breathing evenly while the images flashed through my mind.

What did it mean? What could it possibly mean? Sleep was gone for the night. Exhausted from the fright, I rested quietly so as not to disturb Jack further. As he slid back into deep sleep, I lay silently wondering, waiting as dawn slowly slipped in through the blinds and church bells rang of the Christmas season. The good and the terrifying, wrapped together like tangled ribbons, unsure of their proper places.

Christmas came and went, leading into January and my long drive to Gabe's office, the distance dictating monthly sessions. In a way the time lag was good since it gave me time to process our sessions. I'd also had to learn to compartmentalize things until I could get to him. Like the nightmare I'd had. On the drive, it came slipping back, filtering in around the edges like a fine fog filling the deep woods, covering each branch before slipping on to the next. It was all right. This was the time to deal with it.

His familiar office brought the comfort of a place where healing had occurred. This time his desk was a bit less cluttered, and the bar stool standing near the massage table held scribbled notes. His coffee smelled good, as did the package of peanuts he'd been munching. A meditation chime sounded from another office, telling tales on another therapist in for the morning. All was in order. We were ready to work.

I sat carefully, trying to still my nerves, yet betrayed by my jiggling foot. He watched me quietly as he always did. Although, this time he seemed more alert than usual. And I was more nervous. I really didn't want to talk about the dream. My fingers nervously worked the edges of my jacket, until I caught his eyes on them. It was hopeless. I was nervous, and it was showing. So much for being hidden around Gabe.

"Hi," he greeted me steadily.

"Hi back." His presence was calming. I quit fiddling with my jacket, and my foot relaxed. Being with him gave me a feeling of peace and safety I rarely had anywhere else.

Silently, he lit the sage, letting it burn as it spread the familiar and sacred scent. Again it had a sacred feel for me, and gave me that sense of spiritual presence and clarity. I watched as the smoke curled fragrantly around the room, encircling me with a sense of the sacred and protective. Then he sat with me again, giving me some time.

"What's worrying you?"

"I don't want this to be anything."

"I know."

"I had a nightmare."

"You know we have to look at it. If we don't, it will just come back another way."

"I know. And I hate it."

"I understand that. I really do."

He was good. And I knew he did understand and was compassionate. Leaning back against his chair, black hair framing his concerned eyes while long fingers wrapped the coffee mug, black this time, he observed and listened. There was no judgement or blame in him. Carefully, he paid attention as I began to tell about it, especially taking in my body language. That always spoke volumes to him, particularly my eyes. Movement, breath, eyes, words . . . he read it all. Listening and watching, he let me finish, then sat quietly, face serious, eyes turned inward, fingering the Tibetan mala around his neck.

"It's memory fragments, Carla. Sometimes they come this way. You remember that happening some with your incest work. Come on, let's get to work."

He rose to pull out the massage table, while I got the sheet to cover it. We had started to do energy work, an essential part of my healing. The oriental word for it was chi or ki. Whatever it was, old to the oriental culture or new to me, I worked better with it.

I laid on the table, sunny side up as we liked to call it. In English, it meant facing up, lying on one's back. Every field of work has its own humor. Some more warped than others. Gabe looked at me, evaluating again my level of energy, looking for blocks, energy leaks and anything else he could find.

Grinning sheepishly at me, he pulled on the bottom of my pants' legs, straightening out the wrinkles. "Easier to see you with," he commented, teasing and at the same time apologizing. "I still seem to think that I see clairvoyantly more clearly when there are no wrinkles."

I chuckled up at him. We all have our glitches. His humanity and growing edges were one of the things that relaxed me about him. He didn't have to pretend to be perfect. Serious again, he turned to his work.

Placing his hands on my major energy centers, or chakras, in a systematic pattern, he was able to increase my energy which also heightened my calmness and emotional strength, giving me the assets I needed to do this kind of work. It also showed things more clearly to him, so he was able to work with more precision and clarity.

"How are you doing, Carla?" He had noticed my breathing slowing and becoming regular. I loved the feeling, noticing my muscles letting go of the tension as I relaxed and filled up with the chi.

"I'm feeling calmer, fuller in my body, maybe denser too, if that makes any sense."

"That'll do. It's a lot easier to work with you full than empty."

I smiled as he worked. He had a ready sense of humor, reminding me actually of the medical field. A humor that was used to relieve too much stress. I could feel it around the edges, waiting if needed. Fuller and more confident now, I watched him as he moved onto his bar stool, resting one foot on the lower rung, ready to work with the nightmare.

"This time we're going to take you back in time, to the place of your nightmare. We'll go straight there. Just ask your unconscious to take you there. Are you ready?"

"You'll be with me?" I didn't want to do this alone again. Once as a child was enough.

"Yes, I can track you." His psychic abilities were opening in ways I didn't understand.

Moving into trance, his office slipped into the background, leaving me aware of a dark mist, hiding what I was reluctantly seeking.

"Keep going, Carla. Ask yourself to go to the place that will give you the answers to your nightmare. Remember, I'll track you there." His voice felt distant, disembodied. Yet I could follow the directions.

"OK. I can do that." Another minute passed while I got oriented. The dark mist was thinning. I could see more.

"Doing OK?"

"Yes." And more reluctantly, "Those people are coming into view. The cult." The scene gradually became more clear. "I see the candles again, low on the ground."

"I see them." He was with me.

As the scene cleared, I could see slowly moving shapes. I had expected something different after the frenzied movements of the last time. But these figures were moving quietly. They seemed to be positioning themselves. I felt like a spy as I watched with a sense of detached curiosity.

"How are you doing?"

"OK so far. It doesn't look too scary yet."

What was happening with these people? All I could see were a few dark robes, moving in the night within the circle. There seemed to be hoods too, as I couldn't see faces. The fire in the center roared, sending out sparks. Interesting. A fire that seemed to throw off cold instead of warmth. Was everything reversed in this world?

"Who do you see, Carla, that you recognize?"

I hesitated, then moved into the scene before me. "My father is there. He's moving within that circle. He seems to be doing something rather purposeful. And my mother is in the outer circle with the women. The women are seated on the ground outside the candles, watching and waiting. She seems numb, as if she's in trance. And in denial about all of this."

My curiosity allowed me to look, and more importantly for me, to sense into the scene. With vision partially obscured by the night, my sensing gave me a path of knowing, and I traveled it carefully.

"Where are you seated, Carla?" His questions helped me fill in details, and continue to sense into the place and time. Together we searched for my child self.

"There she is." We found her, sitting alone in that outer circle, as a three year old little girl. Others were nearby, but the child sat by herself with no one touching her or talking to her. I was aware of the little girl and her isolation. Her child self was cold. The grass hard and prickly. Alone, she waited, huddled with her arms around her drawn-up knees, in horrified anticipation. My eyes shifted from the child. Something else was calling for my attention.

"There's a woman, Gabe. Do you see her? She's blond, lying on the ground near the fire."

"Yes. I see her."

"Something's wrong with her. She's not moving at all. She's not right. And there's a man on top of her."

"Yes."

"He's all black. Can you see that?"

"Yes. I'm with you." His voice was there, yet continued to be from a distance.

"But it's weird. There's something not right about the blackness of him. I don't get it. What's not right?" My frustration was making my voice begin to rise, increasing my anxiety. I fought to stay objective and be the observer, to know the difference between then and now, the office and there, as we had practiced.

"Take it easy. I'm looking." He paused. "Oh, I get it, Carla. Is he African American?" He wanted me to get it for myself.

Looking, I began to increase my clarity. "No. He's not. But why, then, is he black? And it's not a normal black. It's oily and shiny."

"Yes, it is. That's because it's grease paint. They are using that to heighten the ritual."

He paused as he listened to his guidance for clarification. "The grease paint enhanced the contrast between the light of the blond woman and the darkness of the cult. This was about the power of evil to overcome the light." His explanation made sense of this, and again helped me to stay the observer.

"That makes a lot of sense. In a crooked sort of way. What's wrong with the woman? She's not right." My voice tensed again with worry.

"She's drugged. That's why you're getting such an odd sense of her. She doesn't know what's happening."

"Well, at least I'm glad for that."

Together we watched the scene unfold, the man raising the knife, it's plunge towards the woman's body. I jumped in my seat as the knife drove forward, jolted from my observer view.

"Gabe!"

"I know. I know." His voice shook at the edges. "Back up a bit, and get back into your objective view."

I did as he said, pulling myself back in the scene to watch more from a distance. Gradually my heart slowed it's erratic pounding and resumed a quick, stressed rate.

"Breathe, Carla." His voice sounded even again. "Good. Keep breathing. Remember, it already happened a long time ago. That's good."

He coached me through my panic. Finally I felt more stabilized, but my senses were on red alert.

"What the hell were they doing?! Why did they do that?!" Shock turning to mad.

"I'm sorry, Carla. It's tragic, and I had hoped we wouldn't come to this. They have evidently sacrificed this woman. We'll talk about it when we're done."

I sat back in my chair.

"But right now, you need to understand what happened for you, too. Can you go on with that for now?"

"I think so." I was feeling shaky again, but recognized the wisdom of following the rest of this while we were in it. Didn't want to leave the session and not have it. Hey, God, how about a new life. I nodded at Gabe.

"You were well-experienced at dissociation by that time. But you just made one real big mistake there."

"What?" I was feeling cranky again. The man was stabbing the woman to death. I hated it.

"You dissociated into the woman's body. That's how you experienced the knife coming into your chest, which was the memory fragments from your nightmare. Because you went into her, you experienced it from her vantage point. Clearly very traumatic for you. If you're going to dissociate, that's the wrong place." Now he was chiding me, bringing me out of my frozen horror.

"Guess so," I mumbled, reflecting on the scene.

Again, we returned to the scene, to see what we could learn to help my healing. "Oh, now I see what happened, Carla. Look, see how terrified you were when you saw that knife coming down."

"I was. I was only three years old. And all by myself."

"Exactly. It was too much for you. So you dissociated first into the woman in your terror, then when the knife came down, you dissociated straight down into the ground. Better than being there when the knife hit. Does that feel right to you?"

I thought about it, and tuned into my own feelings. It was pretty strange, but it sure felt accurate. With my child self, I felt like I was four to five feet underground, and actually, it felt great. It was dark, cool, and above all, safe. No naked ladies, and no knives.

"What's it like down there?" I think he was curious how I'd describe it.

"Actually, this is really interesting. It's kind of dark, yet it's as if I can see through the earth, just as people see through the air. And it feels so much safer than being up there."

"I'm sure it does." He thought about it for a while, then shook his head. "But Carla, we can't leave you down there."

"But I kind of like it."

"I know it's comforting. But remember our prior experience with your healing work. You need all the parts of you to function well in your day to day life."

"Well, bummer. I know you're right. I just don't particularly like it. I guess we have to retrieve the kid, huh. Then she'll be scared again."

"It'll be all right, Carla. We'll take good care of her. We always do." He was moving now to perch on his stool on my right, his hands on either side of me.

"OK. I know you're right about that."

"I'm going to bring you out, Carla. I want you to hold onto my arm. You may experience some quick-moving sensations. Just stay with it." I did as he suggested, and held onto his arms. There was a pause. It lengthened.

"Carla . . ."

"Yes?"

"Is there anyone else down there with you?"

I thought about it, and then began to feel around me with my senses. Son of a gun. There was. There was a presence with me down in the warm, protective earth. "Yes," I said with a smile.

"Where is it?"

I sensed again into the earth around me, paying attention to how my body felt and the space around me. I knew.

"On my right."

"That's what I thought." Another pause. "Are you holding hands?"

I considered again, checking in, then smiling to myself. What a wonderful feeling.

"Yes, we are." This with a large smile.

Gabe was smiling, yet serious. "Carla, this is an elemental with you. Kind of like an earth spirit. It's been holding your hand, your child hand, since you escaped from the knife and into the earth. And it's been keeping you there, so you couldn't come back up and be traumatized, perhaps into psychosis. If you'd come up, you'd have been in her body and experienced the stabbing. It would have been too much."

"So, it's been comforting me and keeping me safe."

"Exactly."

I knew it was true. There was great comfort in the hand I was holding. And protection. Along with an unspoken warning about the dangers of going up any higher. The spirit knew what I would encounter. Here I was safe, protected and comforted. The down side was, I needed that child self now.

"I can only bring one of you up, Carla. I'm not strong enough to bring you both up. You're going to have to let go of its' hand."

Now that felt like a problem. I found myself amazingly attached to my earth spirit protector. I didn't want to let go, even though I knew I needed to bring this child self up.

"Gabe, I don't know what to do. I mean, its been helping me all this time. I can't just drop it, and bust out of here."

"I think you need to thank it for this time and protection. The comfort it's given you. And also explain why you need to bring your child self up. We're here now, and it is time. We'll keep your child self safe."

I knew he was right. It was just difficult. I talked to my spirit friend for a while, and we both seemed to agree that it was time for me to go. But it was hard letting go, and I became afraid when I tried.

"It's all right, Carla. Keep at it." Slowly Gabe talked me through the process.

I turned to my earth spirit friend again, and sent my thoughts of gratitude. I felt the response come back, natural and warm. "Of course," it seemed to say. Almost as if I were one of theirs. A response full of love and compassion.

"I have to let go now. I have to go back to my people."

"I know. It's time," the spirit sent back. "You'll be all right now."

A space formed between us, one full of peace and completion, as we gradually let go. It was time to go back up, back to the physical world. We'd take care of my child self. There was a soft spirit kiss, and the time had come.

"All right."

"Good. Hold on tightly now."

I was stunned at the swiftness of the motion; the similarity to a rapidly-rising elevator. Swiftly Gabe brought me up through the earth, then through the woman's body and out, into an arc through the air which made my head swim and my stomach lurch. Finally and still very quickly, into the child's body. It startled me to realize that I was now seeing the scene from the vantage point of my little girl self.

As the child, I was terrified, breathing rhythmically and spasmodically. Isolated within the group, I was silently hysterical, with no one to calm me or protect me. The moment had been frozen in time.

"There's nothing else to be learned here, Carla, and no reason to leave your child self in that terror. Time to get you back into your adult self and out of there. Bring yourself back to the office. You know how to do that."

He paused while I worked, although I became aware of my lack of willpower. Then I realized I was back, feeling the massage table supporting me.

Gabe, meanwhile, asked for spiritual guidance. It still made me wonder. The God of my church wouldn't be in a place like this. Then Gabe chuckled, and while running energy for me, told me what he was seeing psychically.

"The guides are trying to get you back in. There's one at your feet, pulling. And another at your head, stuffing. Seems you need some extra help today."

It felt true. The dissociation and the trauma had eroded my willpower for coming back into my body. I just didn't much care at that point. But I did need to get back in. I couldn't stay in trance. These spirits had evidently come to assist.

Pushing and pulling, Gabe helping, they all worked. "Got to get you in, woman," he kidded. "Stuff you in, if nothing else works."

"Try to feel the inside of your fingers. That's it. Now your toes. When you feel them from the inside, you're in. Good. How's that feel?"

"More like me. Not quite right, though."

"I know." He went to my head.

"What are you doing?"

"Following orders. The guides told me to work on your medulla." His hands cradled my head while he searched with energy fingers.

"There it is. I'm to stop the neurons from continuously firing. The trauma set off the spasmodic breathing which initiated the neurons firing. We need to get them stopped."

I felt into his work. The uncomfortable pulsing was going away. He moved to my diaphragm.

"Now what?"

"The diaphragm needs to be cleared from the breathing problem. It's the physical plane residue from the trauma. The part that so often doesn't get cleared when people just do talk therapy."

"How do you know to do this?"

"I haven't known. The guides are showing me as we go, probably pertaining particularly to your system and your physical reaction. It's new to me, too. Kind of like paint by number. I keep asking for a fuller picture, but, no dice."

He continued working. I'm really grateful, I thought to myself. Without the spiritual guides and energy work, I don't think we could have done this. At least not this thoroughly.

"Carla, we're done now with the work. While you are still there on the table, I'd like to give thanks for our spiritual help. Are you all right with that?"

"Um hmm." Still too groggy from the energy work to have much of an opinion, it sounded good. I was beginning to get more oriented to the room again, focusing on the oriental wall hanging over my right shoulder.

I watched him get the sage, all his attention concentrated in his movements, focused inward on his intent. He stood straight beside me, match in hand, quietly lighting the sage. Walking around the room, the smoke from the sage lightly flowed around objects, filling corners, and finally floating over me.

"Clearing?"

"Um hmm."

Then he stood alertly next to me. I watched carefully, trying to remember what he was doing.

"I give thanks to Earth Mother. To Sky Father."

His resonant voice filled the room with power and warmth. A gentleness and calmness filled me, while the vibration of his voice carried a feeling of love and peace.

"I give thanks to the Spirits of the East, to the Winds of change and healing that have filled this space, giving us guidance and wisdom for this time." I watched as he turned each way, giving thanks to each Direction.

"I ask that the sweetness of this smudging stay with Carla, filling her and reminding her of this healing, of the sweetness of Spirit's presence." Softly, he concluded. "A ho. So be it." In my heart, I added another "a ho," and with a small smile, I heard an echo from the earth far below.

"Easy, Carla. Let's get you up and to the chair to get reoriented."

It took some time. Sitting up helped. We only had a few minutes to process any more of the incident.

"What are you aware of, Carla?"

"My sadness and grief for the woman right now. And for my child self who had to endure the experience. The sweetness of Spirit is with me, but those things, too."

"Of course. It's an experience worthy of grieving."

"But there's something else. I think what I'll take most from this is the Presence of Spirit. Especially the presence of the earth spirit. It was so precious. And it stayed with me all that time. The trauma was terrible, all around, yet the spiritual presence is a balance when I see it from here."

He smiled. He knew. That's what was keeping us going. There had to be a balance in this for us to keep going, and that seemed to be what it was. We weren't alone in the work. And there were other forces besides evil. Hold that thought.

"Time to go, Carla." He smiled with that sweet look, one I came to associate with coming out of the strong spiritual energy. "I know. Thanks. And take good care."

"You too, kiddo. Drive safe." I smiled and let myself out. Thank God for good healers and therapists.

I was grateful for the long drive home, taking the opportunity of the mesmerizing miles to help me slowly process the incident, and come out of trance more fully. Along the way, I thought of the woman who had been drugged, remembering my fear of someone drugging my drink. Even that fell into place now, another reaction grounded in an absurd reality.

The miles rolled rhythmically under the tires. Some days I wondered who really drove my car. I seemed to get from one place to another with only thoughts of other worlds and places. Good thing it was almost all interstate.

My karate was still coming along, though I was clearly a new kid. I had myself on a tight schedule, fearing that if I missed a class, I wouldn't return. But it was tough.

Thursday class was smaller, and I was sore, favoring my right leg. Out of the corner of my eye, I watched the brown and black belts. They didn't have the bruises I had, and they weren't limping. And how did they move so smoothly? I was discouraged, limping slowly through my forms.

"Don't favor that leg. Walk on it," came the familiar voice cutting across the floor. Sensei. Watching while correcting two green belts, he had caught my limp. Dang. Steeling myself, I forced the leg to work. No limp. Done with the green belts, he walked over to me.

"This is not an injury. It's just pain," he informed me.

How did he know? Maybe it was an injury. Tentatively I took another even step, realizing then that I could. And another, sighing with some relief.

"One of the many lessons here is that you can work through pain. You'll learn to tell the difference between pain and discomfort, and genuine injury." Snappy today, he moved away, crisply addressing another student.

Gingerly, I walked, then moved back into my forms, realizing he was right. The difference wasn't something I'd ever really thought about, though it could come in handy. The back of my mind superimposed another picture, cultists dancing madly in the dark. That, too, was painful to consider, but it wasn't life-threatening. The very real danger was over. I wondered if I could tolerate the continued discoveries about the cult, then thought of the karate lesson at hand. The important difference of discomfort versus pain which could harm in the present. A distinction to remember.

The next morning, I was out running at dawn, practicing for my 5K race. The beginning was painful, sore muscles and labored breath beleaguering each step, but soon I was moving smoothly. My route led through our midwestern suburban neighborhood, streets lined with a mixture of home styles from old mansions to modern bungalows. Thinking of my work with Gabe as I ran, I remembered the earth spirit, aware of my steps and the earth below.

The world was a fascinating place. What if spirits were everywhere. Maybe they were. I had to keep a perspective in this work. A trauma survivor was not my whole identity. I couldn't let it be. I was a professional, training in karate, had a family, friends and hobbies. And I honored earth spirits.

The half-light of dawn with its fading stars greeted me as I began my first-ever ceremony. A ceremony of thanksgiving to the earth spirit who had been my companion those dark years, comforting me and keeping me safe. In the early daybreak, brisk winds tumbled the bare branches above me as I stood shivering, icy fingers holding the sage stick while I raised my prayers to the Divine.

Gently I laid gifts of remembrance for that spirit and all spirits of the earth, placing them on the decaying ivy-covered stone wall at the back of our property. The wind rustled bony shrubs in acknowledgement of my closing prayer while I completed the ceremony, thanking the spirits of each direction, then hurried back to the house for warming tea. Solace was a gift, and expressing thanks helped complete the circle of offering and gratitude.

The morning at the office had been hard, the air still saturated with the tears of the young girl and the sorrow of her mother. The sadness clung to me like a heavy envelope. The ringing of the phone broke my melancholy drifting.

"Carla!"

I smiled into the phone, grateful for the relief. "Hi, Ben." Hearing the residency intercom, I pictured him in his office, leaning back in his swivel chair as he talked.

"Lunch?"

"Sure. Where shall I meet you?"

"Mickey's Bar and Grill, ten minutes." The phone was dead. That was certainty. And trust in our relationship. Gathering my purse and locking my desk, I hit the light switch as I walked out. A playful gentle giant was a good antidote.

After work I headed home, pulling into the old-fashioned two-lane driveway. Our brick home dated to the 1920s, one of the older houses on the block. The homes on our street were varied, with small houses, big houses, apartments, falling down houses, rehab houses. The transitional neighborhood.

The back door off the drive led to the kitchen, our real entrance and center, where I tossed my papers on the old oak table, one of the multitude of family antiques I'd inherited. Heading left through the dining room with its cherry dining table, family china and crystal, I passed through the end of the living room to the porch looking for mail, finding only the usual array of circulars and junk mail.

Back inside, trashing the mail, I walked to the stairs, pausing by the fireplace while Kanji, Jennie's new black kitten, staged an attack. Bending, I played with her a bit, then went on up to change clothes, check bedrooms for hidden teens, then gratefully opened the door to my healing room.

Home alone gave me time to relax, stretch out, look out through the skylights and enjoy the solitude. I loved this place over the garage, trees beckoning at the windows on all four sides. A place of peace, I retreated here when I could. Relaxing, my mind drifted. The woman. I wondered if her family ever found out what had happened to her? Someone should let them know. Maybe then I could put closure on it. How could I help them? I considered the dilemma, the police entering my consciousness. Maybe they could help. Maybe I should contact them. A door slamming downstairs was followed by a shout. Time was up.

That night I dreamed. A bitter, frightening dream. A warning. I was a small child in a meadow at the edge of a woods, a stream behind me. Other children were there. I was in a small group, standing by a large rock, trying to make myself invisible. This felt incredibly dangerous to me, though I couldn't have said why. I shook in fear as I waited, watching the children furtively out of the corner of my eye. Be invisible. I knew it was critically important as I faded back against the rock.

Adults came. A child was chosen. My child self hid in the tall grasses by the rock, sliding back further into the background, merging with the rock, terrified. The adults, laughing, gave the young boy to some men to hold until time, whatever that meant. Suddenly I startled, surprised from the dream to an awake state. The men had worn uniforms. They were police. The police were in the cult. The truth was clear, untenable, and etched in my mind like burning acid. I had to find out.

Morning finally made an appearance. Waiting impatiently hadn't hurried it. Hours more for the time change, and finally I dialed. My older brother picked up the phone.

"Hey, bro." I envisioned him holding the phone, his six-foot frame casually draped over a chair. Straight black hair contrasted with my curls, while his soft-contoured build reflected his lack of activity.

"Hi, baby sister!" He was cheerful. But then he was always cheerful, no matter what was happening. New York City could be in flames, and he'd be cheerful that it wasn't L.A. That just seemed to be his nature, something that grated on me with my struggles to maintain in spite of my fears and depression. How did he get off so easily? I put those feelings aside while we chatted, finally asking the questions I'd spun in my mind in the early morning light.

"Remember when we were kids, staying over at the farm?"

"Oh, yeah. That was always quite a time. We were sure over there a lot."

"Who lived there?"

"Our aunt and uncle, dad's side. They were really strange ducks." No kidding.

"Were there any other kids there?"

"Oh, heavens yes. They had migrants in there all the time. They were always moving in and moving out. No one could keep track of them. And we all ran in little packs. It was great fun." So now we knew where all the children came from.

"Do you remember much about the police there?"

"Funny you should ask. That was really a strange place, but a great adventure. And yeah, our family knew the police. I remember when we big kids blew off a great big cherry bomb one night. You were probably too small to be along. But we dropped that sucker right down into a storage tank. Just behind the police station. Did that ever blow!"

"Didn't you guys get into trouble?"

"Oh, nah. The police knew our family, and our aunt and uncle. Everyone was just one big family over there. Whenever we did anything, they looked the other way. They didn't care. So we got to do all kinds of things. Great place to grow up."

His blind cheeriness grated again. Blessed are those who don't remember their dysfunctional families . . . until they do. I hoped he never would, actually. And as a professional, I knew that it was the way it happened for many survivors. They only remembered if something specific triggered the memories, or their own child became the age they had been when molested. Or, or. There were so many reasons for memory recall, or lack of it, that we didn't understand. Professionals even had hospital documentation of abuse. Medical records of care. And the child or adult would swear they'd never been abused. Denial can be very important. My brother was not unusual.

A substantial part of me was glad he didn't remember. In a meditation once, I saw him as a fragile porcelain doll, riddled with cracks. I was pretty sure he'd never survive the recollections. Many people didn't, either through deteriorating mental health or suicide. No, I didn't want my brother to be a statistic. Still, his total lack of recall continued to grate. Our family was not the Waltons, no matter what he wanted to believe.

Our conversation moved to other things. He remembered a lot. Just not the dark side. But I had places to go and things to do, and I wanted this healing. Unfortunately, it was already crystal clear that the police were not a part of my recovery. First rule: don't be stupid. But who takes care of the law when the law is crooked?

Sing

Nightmares were becoming more frequent, launching me out of sleep, hurling me against the walls of my denial, shattering any semblance of peace. In the daytime, I tried to recreate calm, keeping the intruding demons of fear at bay.

Journaling was a way of distancing myself from dream fragments, putting them on paper to make them objective. And then to leave them. But the images often stayed, imprinted on my reluctant mind. Images of contact lenses the size of dinner plates, cracked and covered with blood. I couldn't get them in.

Scenes of frozen empty landscapes where I walked a slight trail, insufficient supplies in my meager backpack. Of cars parked, covered with snow, freezing air and driving snow keeping me from finding the safety of my car. Frightened, I sought more resources, calling Gabe for a brief connection.

"There are safer ways to investigate the **cold** than alone in the dark and without proper supports," he reminded me. "The cold is about how scary this is and about ritual abuse. You need to ensure proper support as you investigate it."

Another reminder to amp up my support system, as well as my coping skills. This was getting harder.

Karate was increasingly becoming a place of support. Hopeful, I went to the dojo the next day, dressing for class in fear and lethargy, yet determined to get stronger. Bruises lined my arms and legs from the hits I was taking, while I looked again at the black belts, wondering about their secret. I needed their strength, their resilience.

Frightened of sparring, I welcomed the work on the kata or form. I liked mine, the smooth movement (on a good day), the turns, blocks and strikes. Sensei had run us through drills, then turned us loose to practice kata. Smoothly I worked, trying to maintain the slippery pig of concentration while moving arms and legs in the proper direction.

Sensei's quick, sharp eyes took me in, my pleasure at moving and my soft, gentle style. Merry eyes, contemplating mischief. I caught the look, my eyebrow raising in question.

"You couldn't fight your way out of a paper bag!" I heard brown belts Peter and John snickering, and flushed red. A glare from Sensei silenced them, but not my embarrassment.

My blood boiled, and my scowl met his laughing glance. You won't always laugh, I thought to myself. I'll show you. I'll learn how to do this. Gentle moves gained focus. Each step had more power, more clarity. Only at the end, did I catch his look once more. Softer now, pleasure and satisfaction. Eyes twinkling. He had challenged me to be better, and I had met the challenge. I'd been had.

Nightmares struck again, a hand reaching for me from behind, taking me down and holding me to the ground. A left hand came across my forehead as I struggled. Something hard was placed across my neck, pinning me down while I felt my feet being bound. Terror rose in my body, racking me with sobs as Jack shook me awake.

Driving north to Chicago and Gabe's, I reflected on the month. I had stayed the night at Jack's sister's house about an hour out of town. It gave me a needed break in the long drive. Now, approaching the office, my anxiety set in once more. Trembling, I said my prayers as I drew closer. What would today bring?

Crows called in the office parking lot, reminding me of the feather in Gabe's office. My black curls blew in my face as I dashed into the eight story building, fleeing the March wind and shaking myself back into order. Stopping at the pharmacy, I got a candy bar. Nutrition for stress.

I sighed as the elevator creaked its ancient way upwards. It had to be the slowest, if not oldest, one in the city, I grumbled once more to myself. Finally I exited, turned right and walked past the lawyers' office, the stale odor of cigars seeping out under the door. The antiseptic pediatrician's office echoed with the cries of a frightened child. I walked on.

Gabe's office was at the end, a list of six psychologists on the door. Dr. Gabe Michaels. I read it each time, my routine reminder that he really was there and could help me. The waiting room had another couple talking to each other, and I uneasily sat myself at the opposite end. Finally he came, wearing a softly blue-striped shirt and jeans, watching me as I rose.

In his office, I sat down, eyes flashing, tears brimming.

"What's the matter, Carla."

"I **hate** being kept waiting. I know it's immature and lots of other things I can think of, and I hate that part too, but it makes me too incredibly nervous. I'm sorry, Gabe. I just hate it so much, get mad at you for keeping me waiting, and then kick myself for my reaction."

He looked at me solemnly, eyes steady and large.

"You know, Carla, it makes perfect sense. And you don't need to apologize to me, or feel ashamed. Think of the things that you have had to wait for."

I thought about it. Rituals. Murder. God knows what else. My deep sigh expressed acknowledgement of the truth.

"But other people don't know that I have any reason to be afraid."

"No," he sighed, "they don't. So you can either tell them, or be more patient with yourself and your assorted symptoms. Hopefully, over time, we will get many of them reduced."

I nodded in agreement, noticing again that he was looking more serious than usual. Perhaps even sad. I looked at him, the question in my expressive eyes.

"I've been doing some reading about cults. A book called *Out of Darkness.*"

"Good?"

"Yes." His eyes clouded over. "But at one point, it hit me. I got just how tragic this all is, and it went right to my heart. I have to tell you, Carla, that this impacts me, too. I was enraged, and then I cried and cried. For you. For all the others. For the senselessness of it all. For the tragedy of it."

I was quiet, taken with his grief, knowing that I was a part of it. "I'm sorry."

"Not for you to be sorry. I have my feelings, too, and it's only fair that I share that part with you. It doesn't lessen my ability to work with you. It's just important for both of us that you know that I have feelings about this, too."

"You know, I'm glad you do. This is pretty awful. I try to ignore it, dodge it, compartmentalize it. But there's no escaping the fact that it's a tragic thing. Scary too."

"I know. And we'll make it. I'm here with you. All the way."

"I know. And I'm **very** grateful. It just is hard."

We sat for a moment longer, sharing the grief of what we faced. It was good to know that he had feelings about it too, and to know that those feelings would inform him, temper him, but never stop him. We could go after the healing, together.

"So, catch me up, Carla." To work. He knew my style. Lay out everything in the first five minutes, then we'd sort it out and see what we needed to do. I filled him in on the nightmares, my hip pain, difficulty seeing clearly. Anything I could remember, even if it seemed unrelated. We never knew.

"All right. Let's check it out. Sounds like we need to start on the table." We both got up, moving the massage table to the center of the room, covering it with a sheet.

"I sure wish you wouldn't do an orange sheet. I hate orange." He just smiled. A reserved smile, today.

While I laid face up on the table, he pulled up his bar stool and settled himself, tuning in to his guides. I was getting used to it. I could have had a normal therapist, but no . . . Then again, this was light years better.

"They want me to *Sing* you, Carla. I'll be singing a Medicine Chant. It's to raise the level of energy in the room. It will also raise my energy, and get you in a place that's needed."

"OK. Sounds different, but whatever you guys think."

At first quietly, then with building cadence and power, he sang. A chant in a native language, the rhythm mesmerized. I could feel the energy raising to a higher level in the room and in my body. It was stunningly beautiful. A small vibration built within me, ebbing and flowing with the unknown chant, while a peacefulness filled me, replacing my tension and uncertainty. Slowly the chant came to an end, leaving a sort of echo without sound as we paused in the silence.

Finally it seemed that I could breath again. "It was beautiful. I had no idea you could do that."

His smile was almost shy. "It's something I've been working on. Now, let's take a look." He began to scan my body, looking for the energy clues of problems.

Other healers looked for hot or cold spots to indicate trouble. Gabe seemed to use another way of sensing along with his increased clairvoyance. Stopping, he looked at me.

"What do you feel in your hips, Carla?"

"It's really uncomfortable. A tightness, like I'm being squeezed. Lack of fluidity, freedom of movement. Does that make sense?"

"Yep. There seems to be a band around your hips. Does that feel right to you?"

Surprised, "Yes. It does. That's exactly what it feels like. I just couldn't imagine what would create that sensation. It's very confining. But how could that be?" My mind began swimming again. This made no sense at a rational level.

He laughed at my incredulity. "When something happens in our lives, it leaves an energy imprint. That imprint can be seen or experienced later when and if it begins to create a problem on the physical level. The imprint tells us what the cause of the physical problem is, and then we can work on it. That then, relieves physical distress."

"Serious?"

"Carla, would I kid you?"

"Absolutely, but probably not about this." He was working now, seeming to hold something, grasping it carefully. I was quiet while he concentrated. Carefully, he lifted it, turned to his side, and placed it on an invisible tray.

"Great. What did you just do? Where did you put that sucker?" Again he smiled at me, eyes laughing.

"I asked a guide to come with something for me to put it on. He had a tray and then took it away. Now, let's see what else is here." Again, he scanned his hands over my body.

"You do much of this sort of thing these days?"

"More and more. I had never planned on it, but this work seems to be evolving for me. Things do leave an energy imprint, and it's good to get that out. Relieves a lot of distress."

"Oh, man." I was going to have to think about this.

"So how do your hips feel?"

I sensed into that area, searching for the discomfort that I had been experiencing. It was gone.

"I can't believe it. It's really all right."

"Hey, whatever works." Finishing with his scanning, he put his attention on my sternum. "Any sensation here?"

Working together, we found and released restrictions at my sternum, then shoulders. My eyes were still blurry as he continued with the energy scanning.

"Oh, I get it. It's like they had something over your whole head. Does it feel like there is anything over your eyes?"

I sensed into that area again, aware that my vision was blurred as I focused there. I couldn't see. "Yeah, but I'm having trouble telling what."

"What's the texture? What does it feel like?"

I sensed again, feeling a thickness, a little stiff. "I'm not sure. Maybe like leather? It is all around my head."

"Um hm. Seems to be like a hood. Does that sound right?"

Reluctantly. I didn't like this. "Yeah," I grumbled as he worked. Using a cutting motion, he released it. I blinked, looking around. Things were definitely much clearer.

"I can see."

"Handy. Now pay attention to what you are feeling. And any images that come up."

A really deep sadness was beginning to fill me. I didn't like this part one bit. Slowly, I let images float through my mind.

"This was all part of a sexual abuse ritual, I think. My sensations are a lot of sexual stimulation, confusion from not being able to see, pain from being held down like that. I just don't know." I didn't want to look further.

"It was, Carla." Gabe confirmed it, watching clairvoyantly at the activity associated with the bands and hood. "It was sexual stimulation and abuse, combined with violence, for the perverse pleasure of the cultists."

"I don't like this. I know it's an understatement, but it's feeling real, and I don't like it one bit." A numb shock was taking over.

"I know. I don't either." He tuned in to his guides to find direction.

"They want me to *Sing* you again. Only this time will be different. Is that all right?"

"Yeah. Whatever." I was beyond caring, lost in grief for what had happened. Images and sensations were coming up. I was trying so hard to be rational about all this cult stuff. To keep it at a distance. A sort of denial, I'm sure. Maybe part of the shock of finding this out, and having to consider that it's real. I was still struggling to compartmentalize it, but just at the moment, it was impossible. Reality broke through, and sadness filled me.

Whatever had happened long ago felt very present and immediate. It could have happened yesterday, the feelings were so intense. I felt lost, numb, sad, cotton in my mind and pain in my heart. I didn't care what Gabe did.

He moved to my hips as I lay on the table, placing a hand on each side of me. Quietly at first, then rising in strength, he Sang. Immediately I recognized the words. Even the tune seemed to feel familiar, though I had no memory of ever hearing it sung.

This was the Beauty Blessing. First at my hips, then sternum, then shoulders, then head, he moved slowly as he sang each verse. The resonance increased, deep and powerful, as the vibration moved through my body like a cleansing rain, purifying all that was in it's path.

"Beauty before me . . . beauty behind me."

The vibration increased, pulsing with warmth and clarity and beauty itself. "Beauty beside me."

Slowly I relaxed, letting the sound completely fill me.

"Beauty above me. Beauty below me."

The powerful yet soft sound washed through, leaving nothing of the sadness and grief behind. "Beauty within me. May I walk in beauty."

Slowly and gently he closed the song. Quietly we sat together. Images had come to me as he was singing, surprising me. First I had seen my uncle's farm, the rolling hills with the meadows and the woods at the side. The cultists were in a meadow, and I saw my child self as part of the ritual, struggling, surrounded by a dark haze of some kind. My spirit was struggling to free itself from the bonds and the trauma, while frenzied, dancing figures whirled around me in deeper chaos and darkness.

I noticed the land also. A land devoid of the spark of life, the earth and trees looking empty, with no glow of spirit or energy. It was as if Life itself had left this evil place, leaving only a skeleton in its place.

Gabe's voice had sung on, clearly, deeply, penetrating through the depths of the darkness. Like small threads of light, I could see the singing wrap around one cult figure, then slide up behind another, quietly creating a slender web of light slipping into more and more of the darkness, pulling it apart strand by strand, like cotton candy being pulled apart by one who was patient and willing to do so with beauty and grace. On and on the singing went, as more and more light threads slipped here and there amidst the frenzied cultists, diluting the darkness and the evil, the child surrounded now by a glowing orb of light, comforted and protected. Confused and disoriented, the cultists began wandering uncomfortably away in what was now light and peace.

My attention was drawn, then, to the land itself. The desecrated, barren land, poisoned by the repeated evil use of energy. As the threads of light wove their tender web, the grasses slowly turned vibrant green, the cultists faded from view as the bushes returned to life, and flowers began to appear, drawing butterflies. Birds flew in, landing in now fertile ground, seeking for life and sustenance. A stream flowed, gurgling and laughing as it danced over small rocks. The land was alive, vital and whole, while the cultists and evil were gone, pulled apart until they disappeared. Now, in that place, child Carla was standing alone and free, at peace with Beauty all around and within. The incident was healed and the land healed with it. I let the images soak in my mind and soul, aware of their healing power.

The hands-on part of the session was over. Quietly I got up and we rolled the massage table over to the corner, taking our seats.

"Talk to me." I needed clarification. "What was all that about?"

"The guides told me that you needed to be reminded of Beauty. That's one of the reasons why they told me to *Sing* you. It was also a way of transforming what had been done, so that it is no more."

"What do you mean, 'is no more'?"

"It's taken out of the permanent energy field of that place. It's as if it never happened." He relaxed back, sipping on cooling coffee.

Still thinking about the implications of what he'd said, knowing I would process that further on my drive home, I told him about my imagery.

"It was amazing, wasn't it." He too, had seen the change in the scene and in the land. "When the trauma is healed, the earth is healed, too. We heal Mother Earth by healing ourselves. At least, that's one of the ways. One of the best."

"It was beautiful." That, almost reverently. I was still in a state of awe about the beauty of the land and place.

"My guides said that you need to continue to remember Beauty. To remember that Beauty is the antidote of Evil, Carla. Beauty is an equal and opposite force. Whenever you get too sad or overwhelmed by the evil or pain, you are to remember this song, this Blessing, and steep yourself in Beauty."

I sat thoughtfully, understanding what he meant. The Blessing had cleared all my feelings of despair and grief, as well as transforming what had happened. I'd have to remember. Beauty, the opposite of Evil.

We shifted gears. "What do you think of this cult, now, Gabe?"

"Well, I don't get that they worshipped any particular source or entity, but rather evil itself. Evil was the focus of their rituals, their abuse and their atrocities . . . all in the service of evil. But I think we're becoming more aware of the seriousness of this bunch."

"As in, kids were hurt."

"Yes, and probably even murdered."

"I don't like this."

"I don't either, but we'll take it as we get it, step by step. The guides are with us and helping."

"I know." I let out a deep breath. "Faith is a verb, just like your teacher said."

"Yep. I think so."

He was still pensive, thinking about the cult. "What we saw today was that they used a lot of torture devices. Perhaps from the time of the Inquisition. With your father's genealogy from Europe, I wonder about the thought forms being handed down from torture days, then brought to the U.S. and passed to this group as a continuation."

"What are thought forms?"

"When we think something intensely, it creates an energy form. What that form is, depends on what's being thought, as well as seen at the same time. It all coalesces into what we call a thought form, or an energy form of the intense thought. And they can be carried and transferred. I just wonder if the Inquisition tradition is part of what this cult was about. There are some real similarities."

"At least this is beginning to give me a sense of coherence to all of this. Like these cults are a real thing, and this isn't just an experience free-standing out there in space somewhere."

"No, it all has a history. And there are a lot of cults. There are real explanations for all of this. We just have to see what we can find."

"I think I may do some reading. See what is published about them. Maybe it will give me a more solid framework."

We both noticed the clock. Time to go. We got up, walking towards the door, where I turned. "Thanks."

"You're welcome, Carla." Volumes in that compassionate look. A quick hug, and I was gone.

The first part of my drive home was saturated with my awareness of beauty. The winter sun shone on the cold-frosted earth, while red-tailed hawks circled and swooped overhead. Cows and horses grazed peacefully, winter coats gleaming in the light. My eyes caught a toss of a head as a horse startled and pranced a few feet, only to stop and graze again. The world was full of small pleasures so often lost in our hurry. I soaked them in like a soft spring rain.

The feeling stayed for a long time. Only to be replaced by anger. At God. "**Where were you? Why wasn't this stopped?**" I ranted on and on, coming to peace at last, a deep knowing that Spirit was with me, Gabe was being assisted, and somehow, we'd come through this. Silently I let the miles slide by as the dry roads disappeared under the car, and the winter day fell to dusk.

At home, I was developing a routine, sleeping in on Saturday followed by dealing with household tasks, driving Jennie if necessary, talking with Jack, spending time with my journal and in silence digesting the work Gabe and I had done.

Grief followed my steps, and dreams tracked my nights as I tried to maintain a balance in a shifting world view. Sunday night I laid in the living room, watching the flickering fire to the mixed scents of wood smoke, Nate's incense and the remnants of dinner. Jack sat behind me at the round table, working on a project, while Kanji tumbled over my legs. Turning, I glanced at Jack.

"How're you doing?" I asked. His bent head examined papers and the computer screen as he sorted data. Brown hair fell down across his forehead as he nibbled the end of the pencil, blue eyes focused, brow furrowed. Concentration at work.

"All right. Working on a contract for work. I have a lot to do." That was an understatement. Jack was always busy. I had finally understood that. Flames dancing while Kanji jumped off my left leg, my mind drifted to our relationship.

We'd married in our twenties, but in retrospect I wasn't sure we'd actually known each other well. I had met Jack in college in Illinois following another relationship breaking up. We dated about a year until I graduated, moving on to Chicago to start my professional life. I'd enjoyed it, but missed Jack as he finished college one year behind me. We were married the following fall, notably without much time together. Seattle was the next stop for Jack's graduate school.

The only stir in the breeze of discontent that I noticed those early years was that we so rarely had anything to talk about. I used to think that if we just spent more time together, or had a shared activity, it would change. I tried a lot of things, but nothing seemed to change. Gradually, two busy people, disappearing into family and work, grew apart. Marriage therapy and three moves had brought us some closer. My graduate school required he become a parent rather than babysitter. That change lasted and was a bonus for everyone. But still we drifted, looking for a mooring in a changing sea.

I thought, too, of the friends we'd had in some of those other locations. Good people. They had been a bond in the early days. Thanksgivings shared with young couples away from home like ourselves. Parties. Young children growing together in our small group of young families.

As we moved and the kids grew, those gatherings decreased. In this location, there were few couple friends. So many changes. Hard on couple life. Maybe we could find another way. Watching the fire flicker and the lights dance their colorful dance, I drifted, remembering those old times and old friends.

Mellow in the firelight, I reached for Jack once more. "Want some dessert?" I rolled over on my side, looking back at him seated at the round table, the lamp shining a centered glow on the stacks of papers, his head bent seriously over them.

He looked up and smiled. "Yeah. Let's."

"Yes! Chocolate. Comfort food." I hauled myself up, dumping a surprised Kanji, and we headed for the kitchen.

Family life continued, in spite of my cult work. Nate developed mono and panic filled me. Doctors. I couldn't deal with them. Jack had to take him in, get the diagnosis confirmed, watch our usually hyperactive son sleep the days away to recovery. It seemed as if everything was setting me off these days.

Aware of my chronic inappropriate reaction to physicians, I put in another call to my brother, leading to a call to our only other known relative who might know anything, my cousin Jared. A Presbyterian minister, he had always seemed a bit odd.

"Just watch out for him, Carla," my brother had warned me. "He's buried himself in his intellect, and I don't know what help he can give you."

"Carla!" Jared's response was warm. We hadn't talked in years. I did the social chit chat for a few moments, then told him I wanted some information. About the farm and his parents.

"My parents really were odd ducks," he replied. "You know, my mother had a live-in lover who stayed at the little house, separate from the main house on the farm."

I hadn't known. That was certainly strange.

"And my father was a sick man. After he died, I found a whole set-up of stuffed animals in grotesque sexual positions down in one of the cabins. He'd thought it was neat, he'd once told me. I think it was sick."

My stomach turned. I thought so too. And it really wasn't surprising. I told Jared about my suspicions about a cult operating there.

"Oh, it wouldn't surprise me, given how bizarre things were there. And my sisters are just so very unhealthy. Something pretty traumatic had to have happened."

"Jared, were there any doctors associated with your family at the farm?"

"Oh yes. There were two men who were there all the time. They did have gatherings at night that I don't remember, but I do know that my parents were very thick with those two physicians."

It all made sense to me. Another fear uncovered, if not healed. I would have to talk with Gabe about this fear. It was crippling me as a parent.

Monday came quickly, and was often a welcome relief from the reflection of the weekend. How successfully could I bury myself in work again? And not think about this distressing cult stuff. Still in denial, I rationalized. Maybe this cult was a sort of passing event in my family. A form of bargaining with the fates, I'm sure.

Putting my personal concerns to one side, I unlocked the door to my office. Friday's mail was on the floor, shoved there by the mailman who knew my routine. Flipping the lights on, I moved from the small waiting room on into my own office, unlocking my desk and hanging up my coat behind the door. Punching numbers on the phone, the answering service messages began playing back. It was another day at work, focusing on others' problems, finding other dilemmas to solve. Fortunately, I still loved my work.

In the evenings, after family dinners, I searched for written material on cults. The university library had the book Gabe had mentioned, and random articles arguing the existence of cults. Reminded me of the early days of incest therapy.

My favorite bookstore, also in the university district, had nothing. Lenny ordered Gabe's book for me and I waited. Patience finally paid off, as I followed a trail of references to obscure articles and self-published material.

Reading, I was struck by how systematic cult life appeared to be. There was a standard calendar, and common rituals on certain dates. It seemed pretty consistent across kinds of cults. Gabe and I would have to talk about this.

It also gave a sense of order to my experiences. I wasn't making it up. There was data. Real, hard data. Data from the FBI and the police. From trauma centers. Patterns were emerging. It wasn't "just me". It had been there for centuries. This was not new. The good news and bad news.

As I searched and read, dealt with homelife and my practice, I continued to try to compartmentalize the cult work. It was hard. I could push it back during the day, allowing myself only small times of sitting, vacant-eyed while my mind wandered in sorrow with the little that I knew.

But night was different. I was at the mercy of my unconscious. Now the nightmares and their meanings were more hidden. Fragments, sounds, blurry sights which left me drenched in sweat when I awoke. No clues left other than my quickened heartbeat and damp skin, the chill of fear seizing me in it's firm grip.

I continued training at the dojo in day class which was smaller with more control. The Saturday class was bigger, my presence due to Sensei's urging. Under his insistent probing, I had told him fragments of my history, supporting my need to learn to defend myself. His serious eyes had followed my story, and his intensity now pushed on my fears. I felt his commitment to my self-defense. The good and bad news. I had support, and he was going to push me. Saturday class escalated my training, mixing in a larger group of students from both day and night classes. More unpredictable, harsher students, but more adversaries for training.

That morning I'd seen Sensei as I stretched on the upper deck, crowded with students of all sizes, shapes and conditioning. He'd nodded abruptly at me, returning to his conversation with the black belt at his side, both on the floor stretching their legs before them. Silently, I followed his example, focusing on loosening tight muscles so I could work out. Tension was making me tight. I breathed deeply to try to relax. Saturday class was a big jump for me.

Class began well, the children dismissed after the first hour as we increased the pace. Another black belt of the many at Parkman's school was teaching.

"Find a partner!" he commanded, and I frantically looked around. Not much of anyone wanted to work with a white belt female. Suddenly I felt a presence before me, looking up to see the most senior black belt. Slightly taller than I, brown hair and solid build, all muscles, he stared wordlessly at me. Rooted to my place in astonishment, I bowed, acknowledging my partner. He had chosen me. Respect demanded that I stay there with him as my opponent.

"Hajami!" Sparring began as he moved silently, throwing punches and kicks, while my peripheral vision took in the increasing ferocity of the attacks around us. Frightened of getting hurt, I punched lightly while dodging.

"Come on," he urged.

I threw a punch. Then another one. I realized belatedly that I was doing the girl thing. Punching at him, and barely repressing an "I'm sorry" if I actually hit home. I tried harder, but it was still a feeble attempt.

Suddenly he stopped full in front of me. In the midst of seeming chaos, the whirling of white-clad arms and legs in constant intense movement, this man created an island of stillness.

"Carla."

"What?" That, with a small voice, totally overwhelmed at this man in front of me, and his stopping us in the middle of controlled chaos to talk. Talk. One never talked during sparring.

He looked very directly at me, making sure I was listening and taking in his meaning. My heart stopped, waiting.

"Being nice is not a good defense."

"Huh?"

"You can't just hit me softly, or mutter that you're sorry, and expect that I will then treat you lightly. **Hit** me. Make each strike count." He started to move, his solid form shifted left, and suddenly the wind whizzed past my face as his well-aimed punch slid by my ear.

"I'm not attacking you as a friend, and your being nice isn't going to make me treat you well. **Go** for it." Steady, serious eyes held me. He shifted again, another punch landing lightly at my solar plexus, the abrupt stop sucking the air from my body. A punch that would have thrown me across the dojo floor if he'd willed it.

"OK," softly.

I started again, beginning to understand. Not hitting him did not mean that he would not hit me. He did. Hitting him gently did not mean that he would hit me any easier. He didn't. If anything, he hit me harder. The blows came back more quickly now, and as I struck more firmly, he nodded his approval. I felt stronger and attacked again, feeling the punch land and stop.

"Change partners!" He was gone. But the lesson stayed. In the deepest part of my soul, I had always hoped that if I were nice to people, they wouldn't hurt me. And maybe they'd be nice to me. A lesson learned in the cult, I was sure, when I examined it. But it never worked, of course. Now I was just learning it in a different, more effective, way. Class continued.

Star

It was a chill, wintry morning, the sky blue with just the faintest wisps of clouds playing tag. Gabe's office was bright with sunlight as I entered, the blinds all the way up, and the view crisp and clear. I always loved looking out his window over the large park next to the office, connecting me once again to the earth and Spirit.

He came in behind me, carrying the attached cup of coffee, smiling cheerfully. It seems we'd both accepted the work, and were ready to go. It was good to see him. I looked around.

"Writing another book?"

"Look like it?"

"Just a step beyond the usual mess." I had noted the papers strewn in a sort of random order, piled around the desk. A few more stones and mementos filled in spaces, along with resource books on the desk. The computer was open, screen flashing. He went over and turned it off.

"Yep. Working on the next one. Always something in the works." He smiled and took his seat, the coffee smell filling the space pleasantly. I settled into my comfy cushioned chair, then turned my attention inward, getting serious.

Looking up at him, I smiled but with more caution. "Ready?"

"Let's go. Tell me what's been going on."

I sighed. "Well, I seem to be dealing with more sadness again recently, and a lot of just internal tension. I can't place it. I'm just nervous and really jumpy a lot, almost like an extra electrical current randomly pulsing through my body. And for no particular reason. Nothing's really going on in my current life to cause it."

"OK. Anything else?"

"No. Not really. Just this diffuse anxiety and sadness. I'm pretty sure it's related to the cult. But I don't know what."

He paused, reflecting. "You know, Carla, I'm reminded of a story I heard recently." Shifting, his eyes got that faraway look, as he heard the story again.

"It was from an Elder. She had been all night in a hogan healing ceremony on the reservation for a sick child. At the end of the ceremony, the Medicine Woman stood in the center of the circle of participants. Waving a beautiful Eagle-feather fan, she looked right at each participant, blessing them and shaking the fan at each. "Always remember to pray for yourself first!" she admonished them.

"This Elder thought she had said it only to her, but the others had the same experience. It was very powerful, and a very important message. One I think you need to be remembering, Carla."

"I say my prayers outside each morning by my Medicine Wheel. I'll have to remember to do that part. I always remember to pray for others, but I forget that. I guess I need to remember to ask for what I need, too."

"You got it." Then getting up and putting his coffee on his desk, he moved towards the massage table. "Let's get to work. You get to put your favorite color sheet on the table."

"Gee, thanks. You're really all heart today." It's a good thing I cherish this man, given what we're going through, I thought to myself, grumbling while I lay the orange sheet over the table.

Lying down, I watched as he got what looked like a new kind of incense out. Lighting it, he put the match on a stone, then began to walk around the room perimeter. Finishing that slowly, he made another circle around me. A sweet, floral scent drifted over me in wisps, as I caught the scent and relaxed with it.

"This is nice."

He smiled quietly, eyes lighting up with soft amusement and pleasure. "I wondered why I brought this incense this morning. But it was really clear that I was to bring it, so I did." He paused as he listened.

"Spirit just told me why. You needed to be surrounded by sweetness."

"And it is a sweet smell. I like it." Taking it in, I let myself relax in the goodness of it. The tightness of my muscles was beginning to let go.

Gabe moved to my feet again, laying his hands on them for the connection, and began to Sing. Once more, it was breathtakingly beautiful, with the melody weaving its enchantment around me, relaxing me even further. A song about Star Maiden and Moon Mother, it wrapped me in waves of loving protection, layer upon layer settling gently yet in strength. The Beauty song was next, filling the space with Beauty in all directions and within each of us. Prepared and supported, we turned to the work.

Working with the main chakras, he again ran energy, filling me up so we could work better. Finishing, he sat on his stool, scanning my body.

"What are you aware of?"

"Mostly the energy flow in my body. I'm not known for my real acute self-awareness, as you may remember." I gave him a sideways look and he smiled back, checking in with his guidance. I waited patiently. I was learning about this guidance thing.

He turned back, a mischievous grin. "Time for school."

"Hm?"

"Remember my telling you about my training with the Elders in Oklahoma? They told me that in an altered state, I could do anything. Well, that includes being able to leave our body and fly."

I cocked an eyebrow.

"In an altered state of consciousness, of course. No jumping off high buildings." That in reply to my unspoken question. I took this man on faith. To get rid of the anxiety twanging my every nerve like guitar strings, I'd do just about anything. My deep sigh was response to him.

"With that as a skill, we can go find the ritual, yet be safe above it. My guides and I can learn about it from there and get a better idea of what's going on."

I thought about it, aware of the table beneath me, yet also looking out and beyond. "You mean that for this to work, you need to be able to see it and learn from it. That means I have to go there, and sort of open it for you and the guides. And this will be a safer way to do it."

"That's it. Sort of like opening a computer file. You open it so we can look and figure out what to do. OK?"

"OK. Sounds reasonable to me."

"Good. Let's play with this. You've had some experience learning to leave your body in some of our other work. We'll just expand on that. So, this first time, just let yourself go out the top of your head a couple of inches. Ready to try it?"

"Ready." I focused, part of my attention with my body on the table, and part of it with my energy body, allowing the latter to rise up out the top of my head. But just barely.

"That's it. Now come back in."

That worked, too.

"OK. Now get completely out, and come back in."

Tentatively, I sensed my energy body edging up and out the top of my physical form. Carefully, I checked to see if I still had control of my energy body. To my relief, I did, tilting my energy form one way, then the other. Experimenting, I floated just above my physical form.

"It's kind of a startling sensation, but fun. A sense of freedom, but I'm also not very oriented."

"I know. It takes some getting used to. All right, clear back in."

Grumbling, I got clear back in. I already enjoyed the sensation of being out. Sort of like strong dissociation on purpose.

"I'm in my toes." Reluctantly.

Gabe grinned. "Good for you. All right, you can go clear out again, and let yourself just play with it, then come back in, and we'll make plans."

Tentatively, I slid back out once more, tilting, floating, then rolling. Finding I could do all that, I tried cautious soaring. I grinned to myself. A new kind of play. Knowing there was serious business ahead, I came back into my physical form, wiggling my fingers and toes when I was back. The sensation was so different, I thought to myself as I grounded and looked back at Gabe.

"Great job. Just don't forget the coming back in part."

"All right. All right. It is fun to be out, though."

"So, this will be similar to what we have done before. You'll just deliberately rise out of your physical body first. Then you'll set your intention on finding the target of your distress and dreams. We'll go together, and we'll stay well above whatever we find. You got it?"

"Got it. I'm ready." At this point, I was still entranced with the adventure part of it. Yet, as we started out, the anxiety filled me again.

"It's OK, Carla. Stay focused. Just look for the source of your distress, and that will take us there. When we get there, you'll feel yourself both on the ground in the child state, and up in the air. Focus on the part that's in the air, so you'll remember that you are safe."

Together we flew into the darkness that always seemed to hide the rituals. The black night deepened as we crossed into a different time and space. The air was thick with menace. Guided by the intention to find the source of my distress, I saw the glow of a fire and candles ahead. I'd found them again.

"Good, Carla. Now stay high up above them. Come close enough to see, though. What do you notice?"

"I see a huge bonfire, and the circle of candles. Some torches too, I think. The circle seems larger this time, as if it's most of the field. There's a ring of people again, but they're outside the candles. Maybe that's why I'm having trouble seeing them."

"Yes, and the torches are partially blinding you. Back up a bit so you can get out of the glare of the torches."

Together we watched the scene as the adults in the black robes, whom I sensed were men, carried torches. The torches were moving in an ever-increasing speed around a star shape.

"Uh oh."

"I know, Carla. I see it, too. Describe to me what you see."

"It's a star shape with men carrying torches. They are moving faster and faster, gathering energy, I think. And there are four small children tied to the ground inside the star. I'm one of them." My heart was beating faster, tension growing in my throat as fear seized me.

"I know." Gabe was quiet as he, too, watched.

"Knives, Gabe. They're all carrying knives!" My voice conveyed my sudden fear.

"Yes." He replied quickly, to calm me down. "But the knives are not for sacrifice. They are to terrorize. The point of this ritual is to terrorize."

Suddenly the knives all came down around one child: the chosen. In fear and relief, I realized that I was not the chosen child.

"What else do you need to know?"

"Nothing. Can we leave now?"

"Are you willing to receive more information later if it comes to you?"

"Yes." I wasn't thrilled about the idea, but I was committed to my healing. I would take whatever information I needed to accomplish that.

"Then, there's one more thing we must do," he explained, preparing me. "Ready?"

"Got it."

As instructed, I came down, invisible to the cult, and sat beside my child-self. Using my willpower, I focused calming energy to the child, bringing down her terror. Quietly, she looked at me. Gabe was on my right, just outside the circle and star. I held her hand, calming her further.

Startled, I heard Gabe's powerful voice with force and vibrancy, announcing his presence to the cultists. "What's he doing?!" He hadn't told me this part.

"I, Wolf-Man, am here to wipe this abomination from the face of Mother Earth!"

The cultists froze in shock and disbelief, barely able to believe what they were seeing and hearing. Stunned, I couldn't either.

Continuing, he announced his protection from the different levels of existence, stopping them from being able to interfere.

". . . to destroy this cauldron of evil," he finished. In his right hand, he held his own ceremonial knife, abruptly slashing down, breaking first the circle, then the star. As startled as everyone else, I jumped with the stroke of the knife.

"Star Maiden, unweave this web of darkness!" his voice was strong and sure. Arms raised, he continued to demand the changes of the powers that be. Energy shifted. Cultists, shocked to immobility, stared, fear beginning to enter their stunned faces.

Quickly Gabe leaned down to my child self, using the knife to cut the bonds. "Hurry, Carla. They'll recover quickly. And they aren't going to be nice about it."

"What are we going to do?" I whispered, as I tossed away remnants of ropes, helping the child sit up.

"See the fire?"

"Theirs?"

"Yes. The purpose of the fire has been distorted and twisted here, but remember, within each flicker is the sacred flame, safe and holy for us. Come on, take her arm and run for it. We're going to the fire, just as we did before."

Quickly we took the child by the arms, raised her up, and dashed for the fire. None too quickly. Cultists were picking up weapons, charging.

"Now!"

We stepped into the fire, finding the sacred flames, entering another reality as that one disappeared in an instant. I became aware of the office, Gabe's hand on my solar plexus, as he ran more energy and strengthened me. I felt exhausted, appreciating the energy boost.

"How are you doing?"

"OK," I replied softly, recovering my equilibrium. "That was intense."

"Um hm." He was busy running energy to help me get really back into my body.

"What about my child self?"

"Where do you want to take her?" He could run energy and talk. Amazed me.

"To the healing place where we took the incest children."

"All right. Bring it to your mind's eye."

Once again I could see it. The meadow, blueberry bushes by the stream, the white-capped mountains in the background, keeping the place safe and hidden. Children played, scattered here and there, yet the leader waited, as always when a new child was coming. I watched them greet her. Reassure her. It was over. She'd be all right.

In a daze, I understood. This was a soul retrieval, bringing back a split off part of myself, as we had done before with other parts split off in trauma. Reuniting that self with the fullness of who I am, I would be more whole and able to function in a healthy way. Welcome home.

We had some time left in the session, and I needed to understand. It would be a long month until I saw Gabe again, and I wanted to ask my questions now. "What was that? Was there also a murder? What were they doing? And why?"

Gabe sat quietly, playing with another cup of coffee as he tilted back in his chair. My left leg crossed over my right knee, I pulled absently with my shoe laces as we considered what we had just experienced. Finally, he began.

"This ritual was not about sacrifice on the physical level; rather, it was about soul loss. They took the chosen child's soul to the Inner Plane."

I was feeling deeply sad for the chosen child.

"Couldn't we have helped that child?"

"Not this time. We are told when we are to specifically intercede for the others. And when we're not to, then we don't. Today's work was for you. But in breaking the energy of the star, we freed the energy for each of the four children imprisoned at the four corners. They now, wherever they are, have more light and energy available for their healing.

"Your responsibility here is to yourself, and to pray for yourself first. You need it now. And the universe will assist the others in the appropriate time and way."

"It's kind of like what we were talking about at the beginning of the session," I added. "The story about 'pray for yourself first.' And then we see if we can help others."

"Yes. I'm sure that's why I was reminded of that story."

I was quiet a moment, then looked at his still form in some wonder. "Just when did you get so gutsy to do something like break that circle. Not to mention the knowing how to do it?"

He grinned, delighted. "You know I'm a martial artist, Carla."

"Well, yeah." And I knew he had an edge. But this?

"I'm also a displaced New York Jew. So, yes, I have an edge and maybe it's also just my nature to walk in. I hate to see things like that. If I get the indication to change something on the energetic level and can, I will."

I sighed. We were probably better matched than I had ever imagined. My mind started roaming again.

"You know, I'll always worry about the other children."

"I know you will. And we'll always do what we can and however much as we're directed."

I thought some more about the tears and fearfulness I had been feeling. "It makes more sense now. No wonder I've been feeling this way."

"Yep," softly. "This ritual was designed to instill terror, to terrorize the children so that they would behave and so they would never know who would be chosen. It's no wonder you've been more fearful, with this memory coming up. The memory was pushing the fear to the surface. Just remember that it was in the past."

"That 'now and then' thing again."

"Exactly. And there were other times for this ritual, too, Carla. And this group has killed before. No wonder you've had times of being afraid of dying and of being responsible for the death of another. I'm sure you felt responsible when another was chosen. That's classic survivor's guilt. You can read about it in the literature. Common with experiences like this, and well documented."

"That's true. I'm familiar with that in the academic sense. Now I have an experiential base for it too. A fuller picture. Well, I sure understand those times when I've panicked about feeling so responsible for others."

We talked some more, processing, grounding the experience in more literature and clarity of understanding. My experience made sense of the symptoms I had been experiencing. My previous therapy had also taught me that this would reduce the symptoms, at least the ones related to this ritual.

"I'd love another way to resolve my symptoms, yet I'm sure learning a lot with this, too. Especially about a larger picture."

"I know. We'll keep going and do what we need to do. You take good care of yourself."

"You, too." That, as I was leaving the office, aware of my gratitude for Gabe. I was blessed to have him in my life.

Back home, the nights were clear, yet the wind held a hint of warmth as spring toyed with us like a familiar game of hide and seek. I loved walking at night, and after a busy day of family, clients and business meetings, I looked forward to my silent walks as a way to sort out my feelings and experiences.

The stars were brilliant as I walked two nights later. It was later than usual, with some of the houses dark. The street next to ours was best, as they didn't have street lights. That made for a darker walk and brighter stars.

For some reason, walking alone at night never frightened me. I remembered the time as a child when I'd stayed at a lakeside cabin. I often walked that road at night. No lights, it would be so dark on a new moon that you couldn't see your hand in front of your face. It had been wonderful, the dark wrapping itself around me like a protective cloak. I merged with the nightlife, hearing things one never heard in the daytime.

Now I remembered that love of night, and merged once again. In my early teen years I'd been taught to walk in the middle of the street for safety, but I'd relearned that lesson. Staying away from the light, danger couldn't find me. The rhythms of the night fascinated me. Which animals were out. And where. What and who moved and what it meant.

I walked the streets, slipping from shadow to shadow. The different hues of gray competing in their soft textures counterpointed by the deep blackness where there was no light, shattered then by the brilliance of an occasional porch light. Contentedly, I moved silently from shadow to shadow.

Lights were on in some of the modest houses. A mixed neighborhood, one house modern, next to another much smaller and older house, next to a rambling huge one. It was fun to walk that street in the day and notice all the differences.

At night though, I enjoyed the stars, the occasional lights in a window, and the moon. Especially after Gabe's singing, I felt close to Star Maiden and Moon Mother, feeling a sense of power and connection.

The pattern to my life was becoming well established. Visits with Gabe, followed by two to three days of grieving, sadness and lethargy, and then a sort of reattachment to my current life, parenting, clients and all the daily concerns. Right now I was still walking off my experiences with Gabe.

It was an odd thing, to be dealing with cult abuse. At this point it was so hidden from public view. The way incest was at one time, twenty years ago. No one believed you then if you said incest was an issue. I'd never forget the professional literature at that time, stating you *never* believe the child. And here we were again.

Yet where do cult survivors go for support? My friends were shocked and horrified, and very clear that they didn't want to hear about it. With the atrocities that I knew occurred in cults, this was in many ways on a par with the political terrorism and even the Holocaust experiences. Yet it was still almost totally hidden. The Holocaust survivors had a museum; Viet Nam Vets had a wall. I seemed to have my isolation.

Oh well, I cautioned myself. In other ways, it's no different from other tragedies. We're all alone in our suffering. Cancer patients. Quadraplegics. All kinds of life tragedies. And no one can walk it for us. Yes, some are more obvious and therefore supported, but that's just the way. As my cancer patients reminded me, you can't look at the sun all the time. I needed to sort this part, and then let go and have a life. That took work, but was necessary.

And there was another part to this. I was developing a real sense of wonder. The reality of the world as I knew it was so much larger. The spiritual aspect to my healing astounded me. And the larger perspective of reality that we were approaching. I understood that most people didn't even acknowledge that Inner Planes exist, and maybe even Soul Retrieval and Moon Mother and Star Maiden either.

But I'd seen all of this. There was no dry, academic debate for me. I'd been experiencing it. Any debate as to the reality of it all was frivolous and a waste of time to me. Not to mention terminally irritating.

I wanted to learn about this larger spiritual reality; not argue about it. We can break an energy circle and star that is harming others. Relieve old, and very old, pain and suffering. Invoke the help of Spirit in many forms. It's all in the Sacred realm. Learning about the vastness, wonder and power of the Sacred makes it worthwhile. Well, almost. On a good day. My walk over, I let my mind return to family as I approached my own house. The grounding of a current life.

The months marched by in precise order, their nature generated by the shape and texture of my work with Gabe. Some were smooth, filled with healing, calming, supporting. Others were sharp-edged, cutting and piercing, muted only by the transformative work with the spiritual realms.

Dreams continued vividly bringing awareness of the changes in my life. One night I dreamed of a flood, water rushing into my house, sweeping it downstream. Helplessly I struggled against the powerful force, waking thrashing in my bed, Jack muttering in protest. I realized how out-of-control I felt with my changes.

Another night I dreamed of a young woman who tried to kill herself. Was I in that danger? Sometimes it felt close. Her father stopped her, calling the physician. She would be all right. Would I? The constant struggle was taking a toll on my nerves, as I found myself looking more drawn and frazzled. Determined, I trucked on.

Gabe and I kept at it. My family experience with the cult was looking bigger each time I saw him. It was March, winter moving sluggishly towards spring, to the accompaniment of changing weather and sloshy streets with melting snow and slush. I begrudged March, not liking the switches back to winter, wishing my temperament would pick up with the spring rhythm.

Our shamanic journeying took us to another ceremony, another rescue of my child self. The tumultuous emotions washed me dry of reserves. I wanted to get it over with, be done with it.

"Pace yourself, Carla," Gabe reminded me, dark eyes serious beneath the rumpled hair. You have to take this piece by piece.

"I know, but I want to get it over with. This is so hard. I want my life back."

"And we want you to survive the process." Was he aware of my suicidal bent? It was subtle. Or was it the obvious stress in my face, the nervous mannerisms I was acquiring, hands shaking as I picked at my clothes.

He continued that day. "Survivors often want to rush the process. It's a way of re-enacting the abuse."

"How? I don't get it."

"Well, with the abuse, you were overwhelmed. It was too much, too fast. If you rush your recovery work, you can re-create that problem. We don't want that. You just have to pace yourself. One step at a time."

Grudgingly, I gave in, sliding down into my chair with my arms crossed in front of me. I was obviously digging my heels in, but so long as I was willing to follow directions, it was all right. He'd let me dig in.

The following Sunday afternoon was warm again, March trying to fool us. I was in the kitchen, trying to recreate the peacefulness I had experienced with baking bread. The smell of rising bread filled the house, as I rolled the new loaf on the aging oak table, my hands full of flour, pressing and rolling again. I loved the rhythm of it. Nate wandered in, drawn by the smell, dropping his lean form into a kitchen chair, legs over the side and long brown hair pushed back.

"Smells good, Mom," he grinned in anticipation. I looked at him and smiled. So often I was anxious about my parenting, worrying constantly about both the kids. I cherished these good moments, as well as his recovered health from his mono.

He settled in, clearly enjoying watching me work the bread.

"Did your mother teach you how to do that?"

"No, honey, she didn't," I reflected. He looked up at me, surprise written on his face, leading me to continue. In my minds' eye, I could see my old kitchen with the rough wooden table and linoleum floors, white walls and old counters. My mother was usually in that room, baking, cooking, creating something that smelled wonderful.

"She was such a fabulous cook that I didn't need to learn. It was clearly easier for her to do it than teach me." I glanced back at him again.

"Then how did you learn?"

I thought back to those days again, seeing her resting, her health slipping away.

"When I graduated from high school, I had one summer before I left home for college. We realized it was too late for her to teach me to both sew and cook. We could only do one of them. We had waited a bit late," I reminisced, glancing at Nate. "We chose sewing, since she said I could learn to cook from a cookbook."

I pounded the flour down one more time, and rolled it into the greased bowl, setting it aside. Nate watched carefully.

"So, how did you learn to cook?"

The question brought me back. "From a cookbook," I grinned at him, sprinkling flour on him as I cleaned up. Laughing we had a small flour fight as he fled the room.

Later I reflected again on my relationship with my mother. She was a kind, passive, overweight woman who developed diabetes which would prematurely end her life. I wondered about her. It was so contradictory. I could see her in that fifties kitchen, cooking dinners and plates of cookies, seemingly content as she worked. Other images reminded me of her vulnerability which showed after my father's death, when she retired to her rocker for the next eleven years, sad and withdrawn.

How did I put the varied pictures together? The nurturing homemaker, the grieving widow, and the woman in the cult circle? Dependency on my father? Total denial? What? No wonder I was so conflicted about "nice" women.

I needed a break from work, tragedy and parenting, and gratefully found my lunch date with Pia in my appointment book had come due. Finishing at the office, I drove the quick mile to the Double Dragon with its huge red doors and fish tank just inside the door. It reminded me that I should study Feng Shui. In my next life.

I didn't have to wait long, gazing at the huge golden fish as they wobbled from one end of the tank to the other, when I heard the stir and turned. Pia walked in, heads turning to watch her. Everyone watched Pia, with her fluid grace, delicate build and glowing smile. She'd put a light blue and purple scarf around her waist as a skirt over her leotard. Earrings dangling and complimenting a delicate necklace, her smile radiated.

"Pia!" I laughed and gave her a big hug, readily returned. Then I pulled back to admire her, giving her another warm smile. "It's so good to see you."

"It's so good to see you, too!" she exclaimed, laughing again, and brushing her straight black hair behind her. From Thailand, small and lithe, I always saw her as gorgeous, partly from the dancing eyes and enthusiasm that went with her everywhere. She'd just come from teaching yoga, and was even more relaxed than usual.

The waitress, a mature Chinese woman, smiled her welcome and recognition. "Same?" she queried. We nodded, still basking in each other's presence. Soon we were at our customary window table where we could watch the street and the weather, and gather what sunshine happened to be in the area.

We already had our heads together, her graceful fingers talking along with her, when the Chinese waiter brought our tea and soup.

"Same today?" he looked expectantly at each of us. We nodded our replies, gleeful in our pleasure at being in a place where our wishes were known so well. We always felt at home here. When I was with Pia, the pain of life went on hold and, I remembered that the sun also shone.

Pia giggled like a young girl with a secret. "Guess what?" as our water came.

"What?" I was curious. Pia always took great pleasure in the goodness of life, no matter what else was going on.

"Eric is coming home tonight. Isn't that wonderful? He's been gone for two weeks, and I've missed him so much." Her whole body was vibrating with her excitement. I loved it. To be that excited to see your husband is a wonderful thing, I thought to myself. Then I reminded myself of their difficult history. His military injuries, and his living in Thailand for two years so Pia could adopt her niece. The child, now called Shara, would have been sold into prostitution at the age of four by Pia's uncle if Pia hadn't intervened. And Eric had sacrificed two years there so they could bring Shara home. No wonder they were so close.

Together we shared news, friendship and our hopes and dreams. Too quickly, the time passed.

"Are you going up to Gabe's today?" she asked, lunch nearly over.

"Yep. I head up after my clients. I'll stay with Jack's sister again, then see him tomorrow morning."

Her eyes got serious, as only Pia could. "How's it going, Carla?"

"I don't like it. I think I'm really going to have to think about this whole picture some day. But so far I've been able to sort of compartmentalize it. You know. That's my life there, and this is my life here. I try really hard to keep them apart."

She nodded thoughtfully. "You know how to find me if you need me."

"I know. Thanks." I knew she knew about hard times. It helped. Time to change the subject. "How's skating?" I missed her in karate. She had come to look at the dojo with me the very first time, then gone on to skating, proving herself a natural.

"Great." She glowed again. We touched in and out of my therapy issues, but I knew she was there for me. That helped.

Soon we were out in the brilliant sun. Midsummer already. How time was flying. A big hug and we were on our separate ways. I edged backwards a few steps, watching her willowy movement to her car. Her natural grace was such a delight. And her friendship a bright spot I cherished.

Soul

The months slipped steadily by, my time constantly shifting between therapy, family, work and friends. My life felt like a club sandwich some days; which layer was I on this time?

We were already drifting into the lazy, hazy days of summer. Those days where you just sit and veg out. The air was drier, and the sounds of the insects were changing. The colors followed their timeless changes from the brilliant hues of spring and early summer to the beginning of the more subdued later summer and early fall coloring.

Late summer produce was coming in. My favorite time of year in some ways, as I pined for home-grown tomatoes and corn. Old habits and small joys which sustain us through the challenges of our lives. I thought of them as I drove north again for another session with Gabe, watching the corn tassels and the roadside stands with their rich, colorful treasures.

The drive was smooth with light clouds playing chase across a clear blue sky. Further north, the first hints of fall colors were seriously showing in the changing leaves. As I pulled into the parking lot at Gabe's, the crows were even more active than usual, swooping and calling from the trees over to the large parking lot lights and back. Soon it would be time for a light jacket, I thought as I walked towards the door. I'd rather have more days like this.

Stepping around the ambulance pulled up at the entrance, I waited as they wheeled an elderly gentleman in a wheelchair past me. He looked frail with his blankets pulled around him, yet his face was kind with a large white mustache and white thatch of hair. The attendant moved him carefully from the ambulance and through the building door. This building was saturated with doctor's offices, waiting for their patrons. Not that anything medical helped my chronic anxiety at all. Especially just before a session.

Gabe greeted me with a warm smile.

"Hey."

"Hey, yourself. It's nice out there," I returned.

"I know. Puts one in the mind for hookey."

"Tell me about it. There are places I'd rather be. And it's not about the company here."

He smiled. "I know. We all have those thoughts." Bantering was our companion, warding off the seriousness of the work ahead.

Settling in, I relaxed in the familiarity, noting his coffee on the desk, along with a partly-eaten bagel on it's wrapper. Traffic sounds were far below us.

"Smells good around here."

"Breakfast on the run. You want anything?"

"No. I'm fine, thanks."

"So catch me up," as he leaned back in his chair, grabbing his coffee while tilting backwards. Suddenly straightening, it was obvious a thought had found a home. He gave me a direct, pointed look.

"How's your therapy at home?" He had insisted I find someone. Once a month with him wasn't enough. He thought I needed more support.

"I don't like him."

"Aw, come on, Carla. Have you tried?"

"I try. I try. He doesn't believe in the spiritual part. And that's what's most important to me."

Gabe sighed. It was hard for me to find someone at home to supplement his work. We'd been together a long time, and I trusted him. My therapy work with Gabe encompassed so much more than traditional therapy. It was hard to find a complementary, supportive therapist.

"You know that I worry about you. I just want you to try some more. OK?"

"All right. But I don't like him."

"Carla." That stern 'you should do what your therapist tells you' tone.

"All right. All right. I know I need support. Maybe he and I can talk about other things. It's just hard to dance around the spiritual when it's such a significant part of my healing. The energetic work that we do, too. I'll be glad when more therapists get a more integrated model of working. He's just not a Dr. Gabe Michaels, you know, and he's committed to being psychoanalytic. Wants to know about my transference. I'd rather punch his lights out. I could out-transference him if I wanted." I was getting hot on the topic.

"I know." Gabe grinned, hands up in mock defeat, the expression wrinkling the corner of his eyes while he tried to keep from breaking into outright laughter. Some days it's tough being therapeutic. I was being more than slightly stubborn. He knew I didn't like this guy. But I'd try. Really, I would. At least sort of. He sat back with a sigh, evidently resigning himself to a partial victory. I'd said I'd try.

"What about your other supports?"

"They're good," I announced proudly. "I see Pia for lunch on a regular basis."

"And Ben? Do you see Ben?" I knew the reason besides support that Gabe wanted me to see Ben regularly was that Ben always watched for signs of my trouble with depression. The unspoken piece of our relationship. I did the same for Ben, knowing he could fall into the pit himself. As professionals, we were clear about the signs, even in our friends.

"Oh, yeah, I've been seeing him for lunches here and there. He tells the most outrageous stories. I've even gone out for faculty lunches with them a couple of times. I think I'm currently adopted faculty."

Gabe grinned, relaxing even further. "All right. "So how's the month been?"

I thought again about the month. It had been all right. Kind of average for this work. Gabe and I had been working on solid, traditional therapy issues of support, pacing, and how this impacted me. Plus the additional work of releasing parts of the traumas from my physical system. It had been long, slow work, but I seemed to be responding to it. Each time, the symptom at hand lessened. And I was continuing to be stronger emotionally as we did the energy work, using the energy to support all levels of my being.

Going slowly was paying off. Even if I was impatient. Pacing, as Gabe insisted. I had other thoughts about it, but we'd skip that. I did know that it was the wisest course and that it was helping. Something about no need to retraumatize me. Going slowly and supporting my work energetically would lessen our chances of needing an emotional ER. I returned my attention to him, coming out of my internal review.

"Physically, I'm feeling pretty good. It's obvious that the energy work that we've been doing, and the energy clearing is helping. I'm not so symptomatic at home." Time to catch up and get serious. I continued.

"I have had some more restless nights, though. Feels like more memories trying to come through, but I don't have a real handle on anything in particular. I'm just more jumpy recently."

"So I want you to remember how I've taught you to bring your own guidance in for protection."

"OK. Do that now?"

"Yes."

I remembered what he'd taught me, and asked for my own spirit guide who protected me to come now. I knew her as Dorothy. Some people called them their guardian angel, and that was true,

too. Dorothy and I had actually met face to face when I was nearly
wiped out in an car accident long years ago. That kind of experience,
when you see your guide in physical form, had a name, but I
could never remember it. The experience was enough.

Now I was grateful to remember her, and trusted her protection.
Gabe had challenged her on that. Was she strong enough to protect
me, knowing now that we were going into cult work?

The result had been humorous. She had replied, more than a
little put out, "Young man! You have no idea what my other past
lives have been." She had merely appeared to me as a sweet elderly
woman at the accident so as not to frighten me. Obviously, that
was but a small part of her full repertoire. Gabe had been chastened
for his lack of faith in her, and we'd learned we could trust her to
be there, no matter what.

"Can you feel her yet?"

"Now I can," I answered him, as I felt her presence against the
back of my neck and then on my spine. That's where I felt her
come in, as did most people, evidently. Settling into the sensation,
I let myself be aware of the protection with me. Always a good
way to start a session, since we didn't know just where we were
going.

"All right," Gabe smiled, taking my left hand. "Now that we
both have protection, we're going to journey today to see if we can
find out what's stirring back in that mind of yours."

I smiled back, a little less confident. But his hand felt firm and
comforting, and with Dorothy as protection, I'd do this.

"Close your eyes, and settle your breathing." Gabe paused,
breathing with me until we both were in a relaxed state.

"Now we're going to an entrance place to another dimension,
an opening between two large rocks. There's a large rock on our
right, and a smaller one on our left. See them?"

"Got it."

"On the count of three, we will step between them. Ready?"

"Ready." I found myself nodding. Not too effective with our
eyes closed, but habits die hard.

"All right," Gabe continued. "One. Two. Three. Now!" and I stepped between the rocks. On the other side there was a path, winding away ahead of us.

"Don't look back, but behind us there is a Guardian of the entrance, which has allowed us passage." I was aware of a strong male presence behind me, knowing without Gabe's telling me that in the absence of that Being's permission, we would never have been allowed to come this way.

The path wound gently through a beautiful western countryside which turned slowly to a flower-decked meadow surrounded by woods on the sides. Reds, yellows and blues peeked their heads through the tall grasses, fallen limbs showing occasionally along with small rocks. Distant snow-covered peaks raised up majestically behind the forest-covered hills.

We followed the path as it rose slowly and saw a divide ahead, the more traveled part of the trail winding down and to the right. Together we walked up a slight rise to where the path parted.

"We take the one on the left," Gabe directed me quietly, as we both took in the beauty all around. The air was clear and crisp, smelling of sweet fresh pine from the woods now around us. Everything sparkled with a brisk clarity, from the mountain flowers to the blowing grasses as we walked higher. Ahead was a clearing, appearing at the top of a small rise. Trees nearby formed a shelter for the clearing as the path opened to it.

"This is a sacred place, Carla. Look, in the center."

I looked and saw a large stone. The ground around it was clear. This was the focus point of the high clearing. Walking closer, I inspected the stone, finding it to be larger than I had first thought, and having a depression in the center. Looking closer still, I found water in the depression, the sun glittering off the surface, reflecting the blue sky punctuated by scattered clouds.

Suddenly aware of a presence, I looked up to see a woman walking towards us. My breath caught in awe. She was beautiful, but more than that, she radiated strength, presence and compassion. I took in her Native American appearance as she approached, knowing her to be an Elder and Medicine Woman. Her dress was made of buckskin with intricate beading on the bodice, hem, and down both sleeves. Simple yet elegant, she walked slowly forward, tall moccasins quietly treading the ground between us. Her energy was that of a very centered and grounded strength, which reached out, surrounded and filled me. She inspired total confidence.

"I'm going to let go of your hand, Carla, so you can go with her. I'll be here when you're done, and will take your hand again to direct you back." As Gabe let go, he stepped back, outside the circle created by the clearing. I was alone with the woman. Still looking at her eyes, I felt calm and peaceful. This was a woman of power. I didn't need to be afraid.

She handed me something, and I looked down, wondering. It was a rattle, clearly the most beautiful rattle I had ever seen. Accepting it from her, I was immediately aware that it was ancient, had been used often for ceremony, and vibrated with sacred energy. The carvings were intricate, the designs unknown to me. Feathers hung gracefully from the handle, completing it's beauty.

"Shake it three times," Gabe directed me from behind, "and give it back to her. Then she will smudge you, and offer a blessing to the six directions. You will go with her," and he stepped back further still.

Smoke filled the air with the familiar scent, followed by her blessing. My senses were alert, following the blessing to each of the six directions, noting her words, energy and power.

The woman motioned me forward, and I followed her to the stone bowl. The water sparkled in the bright light. I knew somehow that it had been prepared in ceremony for this purpose. She pulled out a pouch, sprinkling herbs on the water, and it darkened. Her meaning was clear. I looked into the stone bowl.

The surface was cloudy at first. As the patterns began to emerge, I saw the cult. My child self was there in the scene, struggling against the men in the dark robes. The images came clearly: the women who had prepared me for the ritual, the men who had come for me. I was not a willing participant and made them pay for their affront in every way I could. Small but ferocious, I scratched, bit and kicked, resisting with all my being. A strong arm around my waist with a hand over my mouth ended the uneven battle and I went with them, an occasional kick my only show of remaining resistance.

The water clouded over, and I took a deep breath. A resting point as I took in the impact of what I'd seen. As the water cleared, images formed again. I could see my child self, tied to the ground with dancing, frenetic figures moving all around. The fire leapt into the air, showering sparks, while the candle my child self was forced to hold glowed brightly. Knives slashed down around the child.

I was chosen.

Again the water clouded over, then cleared once more. I could see knives, cutting, and an animal sacrifice. The blood was used to mark the child.

"This was a confirmation ceremony," Gabe's voice came to me from a distance. "The cutting was to symbolize your being cut off from society and offered to the Dark side."

He paused, watching. "Is there anything else you need to know?"

My ever-present worry presented itself. "Did they get my soul? Did the ceremony work? Is my soul all right?"

"Ask the Elder."

She stood before me, strong and powerful. "Yes, your soul is all right," was the answer. "They didn't get your soul."

I heard the explanation within as she communicated it to me. "Your soul was strong. They thought they had it, but they did not. They were not able to take it."

Gabe's voice came urgently. "Carla, this is important. Look again. See how you were protected."

I looked once more at the water, seeing the scene as they tried to take my soul. There was something more. Gradually it became clear, as I saw a white light, surrounding the child that I was.

"The light is more like an egg shape," Gabe clarified as I watched. "It went underground, too, and was all around you. Your soul was strong *and* you were protected by the Light."

I watched and knew deep within that what he said was true. I was strong, and I had been protected. Relief flooded me, washing away my fears.

"They didn't repeat this ceremony. It was done and they thought they'd done a lot more than they had. They reached you symbolically and terrorized you, but didn't damage you on a soul level." He paused. "Do you need to know more?"

"No. That's enough for now."

The Elder reached to her side where she had a pouch, pulling out a different kind of herb, sprinkling it on the water. The images disappeared and the water returned to a bright clarity, again reflecting the sky above, white clouds drifting aimlessly by. Together we stepped away.

I found myself facing her, as she brought her smudge stick to my heart, around my body front and back, returning to my heart, clearing me of the experience and any residual evil.

Gabe's voice came to me again. "You're to thank her in the form of a silent prayer."

Facing her, I offered the deepest thanks for her assistance and for the healing of this time. I thanked the powers of the six directions, the spirits who had gathered here, and most particularly, this silent but powerful woman. Tears of gratitude washed down my face as I looked her in the eyes and we smiled. Together we turned and walked to the edge of the clearing, meeting Gabe there.

"I'm glad you're here," I told him, acknowledging his presence and help. He smiled, as we turned to walk back the path. I turned once more to say good-bye to the Medicine Woman.

She was gone.

"At the count of three, we'll be back at the gateway. All right?"

"OK."

"One. Two. Three. See the rocks?"

"Um hm."

The Guardian was there, allowing safe passage as we walked through the gateway.

"At three counts again, we'll be back in my office. "One. Two. Three."

I blinked, reorienting to Gabe's office, connecting with his lanky form in front of me, his black chair, and the faint smell of coffee cooling down. Gradually the rest of the office regained focus, including his desk with the computer, and the massage table in the far corner. With a huge sigh, I relaxed. I was wiped out.

Gabe quickly put his hands on my knees, running energy to revitalize me. I was exhausted, drained of strength.

"Come on, Carla, you need to get back into your body. Work at it."

Slowly, I felt myself beginning to respond.

"That's it. Get back into your legs and arms, fingers and toes. That's good. How about your nose."

His humor cracked me up yet again, and I chuckled, looking up at him. Smiling, I straightened in my chair.

"Why am I *this* tired?"

"It takes a lot of energy, going through different dimensions. You're not used to it, so it takes even more. And any of this cult work is going to take energy. I was pumping the whole time, but it takes a lot."

"I believe you. I really do."

"Ah, finally."

"Yeah, well, take it while you can get it." Again, I grinned weakly at him. He kept pumping energy, until eventually I felt more normal. With a smile, he pushed his chair back. We took a bathroom break and walked around a bit. It was kind of like getting land legs back after being out at sea.

"Getting the wobbles out," I told him.

Fresh coffee, some nuts and raisins and we were ready to process. Sitting once again, my right leg over my left, I found myself wiggling my foot thoughtfully.

"Tell me about this protection thing."

"A strong soul and soul protection go together. Where you find one, you find the other.

"Makes me wonder if I have messed with this sort of thing in other lives."

"Knowing you, Carla, anything is possible."

"You're bad."

"I know. But you like me." Again, we bantered, relieving the tension further.

Then back to serious. I had more questions. "You know, I keep wondering about the whole karma thing. I remember your Elders said we choose our families, but I really don't get this. It's a tad extreme, I would say."

"We don't have the full reason yet, though I imagine that we'll get it eventually. So far, we can guess that if we do choose the families we are born into, then you chose this family knowing about the cult and knowing that you had a strong soul and sufficient protection to get through it. We'll have to wait on the rest of the answer."

We continued to process, talking quietly of the thoughts that came to me, winding down from the experience. "I feel like they have ruined really special things for me, like the moon and ritual and ceremony."

"They can't ruin them. And do remember that we've been using these things as part of your healing. Their goodness and sacred purpose is stronger than the evil use they were put to. Anything can be used for good or evil, but we are using their tools for good to overcome the evil. Like the Sacred Fire. That has been protection and healing. The same is true of any other symbol they use."

"Like the stars and moon?"

"Sure. Remember how we've used Moon Mother and Star Maiden in their appropriate and sacred way. Their real power is far greater than what was used by those people. The moon is a mirror. It reflects the sun's light and reflects darkness. Evil people believe they are worshipping the moon. They are really worshipping the dark reflection of themselves. It's a reflection of their darkness. But the power of Moon Mother supersedes their power."

Another thought. "Gabe, tell me more about this Confirmation Ceremony that we saw."

"Well, my understanding is that Christian confirmation is to confirm that one is now a member of the Christian faith. A cult confirmation would be to confirm the child to the cult and Darkness, away from society and the Light. Remember that a lot of cult rituals are to reverse the Christian intent which would be to bring one to the Light."

I thought of my research and nodded. "But they didn't get my soul."

He was patient, knowing I needed reassurance on that. "No, Carla. You're OK. But it still was traumatic for you, and will take some time as you recover now from the trauma."

"Thanks. I do know that. And I'll work on integrating it. With the positive things we learned, like strong soul and soul protection."

"Good for you. Don't forget support while you do it."

I made a face at him, letting go of seriousness and maturity in favor of comic relief. Then we finished our session as he handed me some more peanuts to help me get grounded. We headed for the door, his eyes twinkling.

"I know, you could comment but you won't." What a challenge. It was too good to miss.

"Nuts from a nut," I cracked, backing up. Then, adding, grinning back, "and to a nut."

"Out of here, woman." I was gone with a wave.

"Drive carefully, Carla." That followed me down the hall.

The next morning I woke up restless. The session was still with me as I alternated from sadness to rage. Finally, knowing sleep was gone, I slid carefully out of bed, careful not to wake Jack. In the dark, I found my shorts, shirt and tennis shoes, tiptoeing downstairs. It had always been a game of mine, to see how well I could manage in the pitch dark. Now it came in handy.

Out on the sidewalk in the early morning light, the sky was slate gray, thick and heavy with the promise of rain. Watching my steps, I ran slowly the first few blocks, then picked up speed on the level street. Saturday morning made for light traffic, and the run was relaxing, working the tension out of my body. A mile and a half later, I was heading for home, coming back up the side street with the huge trees and kid's toys in the front lawns. Dogs were barking now as the suburb came to life for the weekend.

A quick shower, clean clothes, and I was back in the kitchen. Jack was at breakfast with the paper. "Where'd you go?"

"I couldn't sleep. Restless from my trip, I guess. How are you?"

"Doing OK. I have a lot to do this weekend," he added looking up as he pushed his cereal back, reaching for the coffee. The table was spread with the usual morning combination of cereal, toast, jam and juice, along with whatever was left there from the night before. Householder chores, we called it. The household thing. Also, a good distraction from the past.

I got my favorite cereal and sat down. "Why so busy?"

"They are sending me to London on Monday. I expect I'll be gone most of the week. They want me to work on the new program they're putting together at the office, trying to coordinate it with the London office."

"When do you think you'll be back?"

"I'll probably be back by Thursday. I sure hope so."

Nate's voice entered the fray. "Hi, Dad. Hi, Mom. Where you going, Dad?" Nate's energy was back at full speed.

"London."

"Can I come?" The cheerful and only morning person among us sat down. His mischievous grin made up for the messy hair and tattered shirt over holey jeans.

"You wish. When you're rich and famous," Jack teased back. Then he looked at me. "Jennie eating?"

"Not if she can help it on Saturdays. She'll skip breakfast if she can get away with it." I pushed my chair back, heading upstairs. "See you guys later." Time to get after the Saturday jobs.

That night I slipped into bed early, still tired from the trip to Gabe and my hectic day. Drifting off to sleep, I noticed the light of the moon shining in through the blinds, making patterns across the bed and floors. With moonlight patterns in varied strips, I finally fell asleep.

Several hours later, I woke suddenly, up on my left elbow, breathing heavily. The nightmare hung on the edges of my consciousness, lingering like a thick fog. Sweat rolled across me as I struggled to retain the images, then dread as I remembered.

I saw myself, right hand extended, the large man on my right in his dark robe and hood. His hand was wrapped around my tiny one, holding mine tight, directing it. Together the hands rose, his on mine, swinging in as big an arc as my little arm could manage, striking swiftly down, towards . . .

Towards what? There the images stopped, falling off into a chasm of nothing. A void of despair. Shaking, I got out of bed and went downstairs, determined to walk the terror off.

Finally I calmed, turned on a light and wrote in my journal. It often happened this way. This was the next piece for Gabe. If past experience was an indicator, I wouldn't hear from this dream again. It was a warning, giving advance notice of work to be done. For now, I had to put it away, and live my life for a month until I could take it to Gabe. I knew I wouldn't forget.

That week and following, I reminded myself repeatedly of the concepts of protection and my strong soul. This work was harder than I could have imagined, and was pulling on my reserves. I felt myself slipping, almost pulled towards a dark pit of despair behind me. Tentacles of grief reaching for me, calling to me in the night. Consciously, I pulled myself forward, using my awareness of my soul's strength to pull myself out of reach of those grasping tentacles of darkness.

The next morning I headed for the dojo and day class, hoping for a good workout. Maybe it would get the tension out. Quickly I changed, then moved to the upper deck to warm up. Brown belts Peter and John were there, over in the corner warming up. The green belt Big Jim was missing.

"We think he's on an undercover case," Old Joe told me, as we stretched together, referring to Big Jim's cop job.

"Hey, bro, how're you doing?" Darlene came in, bowing while waving at Old Joe. He grinned in response, shaking his head.

"Here she is. I'd better get ready." Darlene, tall, muscular, out-going and black, loved a fight, especially if she could hit hard. I stayed out of her way, letting them tease, then relaxed as she threw me a grin. We enjoyed the teasing as we got ready for class. The familiarity was part of "the dojo family," as Sensei called us.

Minutes later Sensei had us doing basic forms to warm up even further, then separated us into pairs to practice some basic sparring moves. I was with Darlene.

"Jab then block," he directed, moving towards Peter in demonstration, then fading back. "Then jab again to the face." He moved in abruptly with a quick jab. "Three parts to this one."

I was being careful as I sure didn't want to make Darlene mad. She hit too hard. Hesitantly at first, then more smoothly, we practiced the moves.

Suddenly it happened. Her second jab just touched the end of my nose. My vision went blood red while all rational thought instantly fled. Whatever I was experiencing had nothing to do with Darlene in front of me. I only knew that I'd been hit and "it wasn't fair."

Enraged, I pushed her with both hands on her shoulders, then moved in to push again, harder. In such a rage I could hardly see or hear, I still did take in Sensei's biting voice.

"Yami!" He jumped between us, flames still rushing from my eyes while I drew back to strike.

"No pushing." He glared at me, then stepped back. It was like cold water dumping on me. What was that? I saw Darlene once again in focus, looking alternately mystified and amused. Her look expressed her amazement. The little wimp had just tried to start a dojo fight. She couldn't believe it.

"Start again," Sensei commanded. Carefully, we bowed then resumed the practice moves. Jab, block, jab. First you, then me. Nothing was said. Then.

After class, all hell broke loose. We stood up from meditation, class over, and Sensei looked at me in amazement as Darlene strode over.

"Carla. What was that? She tried to hurt me, Sensei!" she mockingly whined to Sensei, her arm around my shoulders, giving me a hug. I laughed, shaken. I had totally lost it. Sensei moved over, shaking his head.

"I can't believe you did that." He didn't have to say "What were you thinking?" He knew I'd slipped a gear. It happened sometimes at a dojo, when someone went off, experiencing an old adversary rather than the person in front of them.

"I just never thought it would be you," Old Joe laughed, while Peter shook his head. Darlene grabbed me again in a bear hug, and we all headed for the showers.

Later, driving home, I was appalled. The black belt from night class had been right. Being nice was not a good defense. For one thing, it leaves too much rage stored inside, ready to blow. Depression and grieving weren't the only things I was feeling. I'd best work to get in touch with that rage, and the feeling of "it's not fair" before I got in real trouble. I shook my head again, laughing. Darlene, of all people, that I would go off on. What was I, crazy?

That evening I laid on the living room floor, flames flickering before me in the first fire of the season. How I hated to see summer leave. But fall was coming quickly. And I did love fires in the fireplace. Kanji laid with me, quiet for once, while I let my mind drift.

"Hey, mom!" Nate called from upstairs. "Want to hear this neat song?"

I couldn't move. I was glued to the floor. But I did want to hear his song. Losing ways to connect with him when he was fourteen, I had chosen to take an interest in his music. Perhaps through that door I could follow this teenager. I was losing any other way to talk with him.

"Sure, honey," I called back. Impatient by nature, he always called from other rooms. "But I can't move."

"No problem." He bounded down the stairs with his boom box. "Listen to this! Isn't it great!"

The noise ricocheted around the room. "Maybe I could hear it better if it were a tad softer?" He grinned and turned it down, as we lay in front of the fire listening. The last chords drifted to a close as I turned to him.

"I like it. You like it a lot, don't you?"

"Yep. It's terrific. Well, bye. I'm going out with my friends. See you later." The story of our lives. Jack at work and Jennie in her room, we lived solo lives in this fast-moving culture. At least we'd touched down for a second.

"When are you coming home?" My question was answered by the slamming door. Great. Sometime.

Quiet once more, I let my mind drift to more serious things. So many feelings, so many questions. What was going on here? I had to take some time out and think about this.

I had been approaching my therapy work as if this were a brief interlude of work that I didn't want to do. I knew I'd been minimizing its importance, which is another reason I didn't want to deal with a therapist here in town. I was probably scaring Gabe to death. A therapist once a month who lived five hours away wasn't exactly substantial support. But I was stubborn. The family stories were clear that I had always been one to do it my way. Even as a three year old, disappearing to cross busy highways alone. And here I was again. But was I right this time?

I reviewed what I knew. We were dealing with a cult. I had hoped that the cult activities had been brief, and my association tangential. It didn't look like it. A Confirmation Ceremony sounded serious to me. And I wasn't seeing any end in sight.

What did it mean to me? How long did it go on? Were any of these people still alive? Active? How would I find out?

And perhaps more importantly, how much was this going to upend my sense of who I was, my personal integrity, my spirituality, my psychological balance? We were working slowly, but it was becoming increasingly clear that this was very significant work.

Yet part of my mind debated. Were there really such things as cults? No wonder people didn't want to believe in it. I didn't want to. There was very little published material at that point on cults, and what there was mostly debated their existence. Not relevant to me, or helpful. My experience rang too true, and my therapy on cult issues resolved psychological and physical distress. This was not a fantasy.

Back to what I knew. I'd been in a cult. I had to do the therapy work. But how long would this take? Would my rage come out again, or would today's wake-up call help me be more aware? Would the depression get too deep to handle? Would I make it though this? And what about karma? Why had I been born into a family in a cult?

Questions pestered me like gnats, swirling around, buzzing and giving me no rest. Finally I stretched and stood up. I had a big task ahead of me, and it was time to acknowledge it. "The game's afoot," as my friend would say. The cult was real. My therapy with Gabe was necessary. There was no turning back.

OF SLEDS,
CROWS AND A
THREE-LEGGED CAT

Warrior Crow

The drive felt endless, the fall landscape adding to my malaise. Dreariness simmered everywhere, compounded by the browns, tans and grey of the landscape with stark tree branches reaching into banks of greyness above. A constant drizzle kept the windshield wipers sweeping sluggishly, trying to clear away the despair in my soul. Something was deeply wrong, but I couldn't place it.

Driving to Gabe, my psyche was now allowing the nightmare fragments to arise out of the depths to haunt my waking moments. Fragments of the dream floated in and out, like disjointed pieces of a horror film. The large hand gripping my small one, the knife, it's downward arc, reflections cast by firelight. What did it all mean?

Right now I didn't think I wanted to know, as I pushed the images aside and concentrated on those endless white dotted lines in front of me. Searching for relief, I pushed the book on tape into the cassette player, sighing as the introductory music began to lead into the story. An action thriller, busy enough to distract for several more hours of driving.

The next morning Gabe's waiting room was empty. A relief, once again. No sounds in the office hinted at his solitary presence. As he opened the door and looked at me, I stared back. I didn't want to do this. Reluctance kept me in my seat, accompanied by the tinny classical music from the small radio next to me.

He moved aside, providing room for me to walk through the door to the back portion of the office. Soundlessly, I got up, walked past him and to his office. Delay tactics were no help at all.

I settled in my chair, keeping my jacket on as if it would keep my soul warm. Looking around, it seemed as if nothing had changed. A few more stones on the table between his client chairs, and a good-sized black feather. The usual array of papers on his desk in the corner, though the computer was off this time. The massage table sat quietly in the right hand corner. Did I expect it to take off? Everything felt spooky today.

He came in quietly, matching my mood as he carried his coffee to the bar stool, and sat down in his roller chair. Eyeing me silently, he waited.

"I don't like it," I finally commented, fidgeting and feeing cranky. Hiding those scared feelings.

"Obviously." He'd noticed. What a surprise.

"How are you?"

"I'm OK. Better than you are today, I'm sure."

I nodded in agreement.

"You know, Gabe, I think I've made a transition here. I'm taking this seriously in a different way."

"What do you mean?" He took another sip of hot coffee, putting it down before he spilled it. Time to let it cool a bit.

"I've been thinking a lot about this. Up til now, I've been taking this one step at a time, one piece at a time. As if, after this one piece, voila, we'll be magically out of the dark forest of despair."

"And?" His eyebrows raised.

"I don't think that's about to happen. Much as I don't like it, I think I was in a real cult, that did real damage to people, including me, and that it went on for some time."

"Um hm," Gabe nodded, sipping coffee once more, blowing into his cup. "Unfortunately, I think you're really right, Carla. I think this is very much for real. So where does this leave you?"

"Well, I've been thinking about it. And it sort of reminds me of sledding when I was a kid."

"Sledding?" His eyes widened in surprise, dark curls framing the intense brown eyes, reflecting that this was probably the last thing he expected to hear.

"Sledding. I had one of those old wooden sleds with a guide bar in front. Very wonderful at the time. A hand-me-down, you know?" Gabe was still looking confused, so I forged ahead.

"I always wanted to sled with the big kids, so I'd drag my big sled, big in comparison to me, up the back of that long hill. It was a real trek. Then at the top, I'd stop to consider it again. The top of the hill was always full of bigger kids, sleds and their dogs, everyone in bright jackets of red, yellow and blue, wool hats, pushing and shoving. The big kids liked to take their dogs down the hill, too." Gabe was still waiting for the point. My eyes faraway, I ignored him for the moment, into the memory banks of time.

"I'd get on my sled, scared to death and inch my way to the edge. I knew I wanted to do it, yet was terrified. But finally the point would come, usually as I was digging my boots in at the back and holding on for dear life, when there was no turning back. Momentum would carry me forward on its own wild course, or I could get balanced, steer and let 'er rip. One would end up in a crash at the bottom or along the way, all mixed up with other sleds, dogs and mostly boys, or the other would end up with a long fast ride and a glide at the end into the woods. The wrong turn ended in the lake," I added with a certain nod.

"OK, Carla. So help me out with the translation here." It was becoming obvious that this New York city kid hadn't sledded.

"Well, I've reached that point. We've come up the back of the hill, and recently I've been holding on with my boots, trying to not go over and scare the crap out of myself. But I have made peace now with the need to take the ride, and it's time to get positioned and go. I'm accepting this as cult abuse in my early years, and I'm ready to ride it out to the end."

He leaned back, considering, sipping cooling coffee, nodding thoughtfully. A moment and a sigh later, he replied. "I think you're right, Carla. We're into it now. And I don't think there's any turning back. I think we're going to have to finish this journey. And our task is to keep the sled on track."

"I know. I'll do my best, even though I am scared to death." We both paused, considering the acknowledgement of the dilemma. Typing next door created an accompaniment to our thinking together, while the smells of an early breakfast drifted in. Warm sticky buns, if my nose were accurate. I returned to my train of thought. The cult abuse was real. I had to do it. I couldn't stay perched on the pinnacle of denial forever. Time to move on.

"All right. So, ready to go? What do you have for today? And let's keep on track of that sled of yours."

I sighed deeply as I leaned forward, elbows on my knees, turning my attention inward to the images. I didn't want to go forward. There was nowhere else to go.

"You know how, when I get back, I often get a nightmare in the first few nights that leads to our next piece?" He nodded, silent.

"Well, it happened again. And this one scares the shit out of me. I wish we could renegotiate the whole idea of doing this work."

"Remember, you've already experienced the actual trauma. All we're doing is healing it," he reminded me, as he reached over to his coffee. "Want anything?"

"No. Maybe some water later." Finally I struggled out of my jacket, dropping it on the floor on my right. Might as well face the music.

"OK. So now, tell me what you got."

"Scattered images."

He waited, while I sighed deeply again, reluctant to feel the terror of that moment.

"There was a large man in robe and hood on my right, his hand tightly wrapped around mine. There was a knife in my hand. He pulled my hand up and was swinging it down towards something. That's when I woke up. I couldn't breath." I could hardly breath now.

"Expand the images, Carla."

"What do you mean?"

"Go back to whatever happened just before that. See if you can get a fix on that."

I thought about it, then took a deep breath, shifted my arms and legs so that I wasn't crossing anything, relaxed my back and shoulders and let my breath out. Slowly I let myself slide into a light trance state.

"I can go just before that. I see the little girl, Carla. Two men are dragging her forward, into the center of the circle. She's fighting them, kicking."

"I see that. Keep going." He was with me. I could look some more.

"They don't like her fighting them. One of the men grabs her tighter and pulls her so her back is against his leg under the robe. He has a knife which he holds to her throat. She stops struggling. She's still really angry at them. And frightened."

"You're doing great. What else do you see."

Panic rose inside. A wave in my body. A blank screen in front of my eyes. "I can't go any further, Gabe. I'm too afraid. I just can't do it."

"It's all right, Carla. It's OK. We'll do this another way." He got up and crossed to the corner as I brought myself out of trance. Reaching under the small built-in desk, he grabbed a jug of water. Getting a loose mug from the desktop, he came over.

"Here, have some water, and get settled again," as he poured the spring water from the jug. "You'll be all right. We'll just have to do it with more distance and protection."

I looked at the dark green mug with its inscription "Save Mother Earth" superimposed on a picture of the planet. Distracting myself, I drank all the water, and he poured me another to have on hand. Setting my mug on the table at my left, I relaxed back into the chair as much as I could.

"Like how?"

Gabe rolled his chair up so that he was right in front of me. Reaching over to the table, he took the black feather. I straightened up to look closer.

"This is a crow feather. I want you to hold it. We are going to travel with Crow again. I want you to close your eyes."

Taking the feather, I felt its softness. Then I put it in my right hand, letting my eyes close, as I relaxed again into the softness of the chair. Gabe held my left hand in his right, giving me the connection to the office and his support.

"Now call on the help of Brother Crow. He is one of my power animals and he will help us."

I thought to myself, "Please, Crow, help us in this work," as outside I heard a crow call once. Then it was still. Other sounds could be heard, the distant traffic below, people in other offices now, a computer and printer, someone coughing. But no more crows calling. Just the one announcement of presence.

"We're going to fly again, but this time we'll each be on the back of a crow. This will help us have more perspective on what happened. Are you all right so far?"

I nodded, smiling as I shifted to the sense of a child-like excitement.

"Here's your crow."

I could feel the great presence, a black energy beside me. With childish curiosity, I reached out and felt the feathers of the giant bird, feeling pleasure at the softness as I stroked its wing feathers.

"We're getting on."

I felt myself again, with the spirit of adventure, climbing up onto the back of Crow. Then, with my arms around its neck, it carefully lifted up. Smiling with the pure pleasure of sensation and adventure, I called to Gabe, "I'm on."

I could hear the smile in his voice. "Good, Carla. Now get used to it. Fly a bit with your crow."

It was just too much fun. Crow was gentle and careful at first, and as I relaxed I was able to loosen my death grip on its neck.

Sitting upright, I found I could ride Crow as I used to ride horses, with the ease of practiced balance. Crow dipped to the right as I adjusted my weight, flowing with the movement. Then he dipped to the left, and I adjusted again.

"OK, you two. Enough play," Gabe's laugh sounded through the night air separating us. "Time to go a-hunting."

The soft feathers beneath me, the breeze in my face and the returning balance of my accomplished riding skill rose to a joy in me of pleasures remembered. I was hooked on the adventure, momentarily forgetting my fears.

Together we rode into the darkness. "We are riding through the Gateways in Time, back to that time and place that you have been dreaming. Just set your intention, Carla, and that will carry us there."

I concentrated on the memories from the nightmare, feeling the shifts as we crossed the Gateways into a deeper darkness and an eerie stillness. In the distance, I saw dim lights.

"There, Gabe."

"I see it. Stay high and we'll keep moving in."

Soon we were overhead, circling lower to get a better view.

"What do you see?"

"We're there. It's a large bonfire, a circle of candles and people sitting outside of it."

"What else?"

"Dark-robed people. I think they are men. They have torches and are making a pattern." Together we lifted higher to watch and learn the pattern and the directions of the torch-bearers.

"What else is happening?"

"I'm having trouble staying with it. I can't see very well."

"Crow is going to go down again, closer, so that you can look. He'll tip a bit so you can get a good view. Your balance should keep you on with no problem."

Crow dipped down, and my remembered equestrian balance served me well. Comfortable on Crow's back, I could watch.

"Look for the child, Carla."

"There she is, with the women."

"What's happening?"

"They are getting her ready for something. Taking off her clothes and putting a little robe on her. She is afraid and doesn't like it. She's hitting one of the women."

"Stay with it."

"I see the men. Two of them are handing their torches to someone else and are moving towards her."

"How old is she?"

"About three, it looks like."

"Good. You're doing great. Keep going."

"The little girl's mother and two other women bring her forward, inside the ring of candles. One of them is her aunt. The two other women are with the mother to make sure she does it right." I took a breath and let it out. The tension was making my muscles hurt. Then I watched some more. I needed to finish this.

"The men come for the child and drag her to the center. That's the part we saw before, where they have to get the knife to force her to behave."

"That's good. What's next? What's in the center?"

"It's an altar kind of thing. I've never seen anything like it. It's got colors, too." In the mindset of observer, I could describe it to Gabe, as he took in the symbols, colors and meanings.

"What happens next, Carla."

As I got the next image, my breath caught. "Oh, Gabe."

"Come on, Carla. It's already happened. We need to know."

"There's a baby. They've brought a baby and placed her on the altar. I'm afraid."

"Fly a bit higher and get more perspective. Remember, this is in the past. It's over now. We are just collecting the information."

"The man has the child me in a really tight hold. I try to wiggle away, but he's holding me really tight. When I try again to wiggle, he puts the knife to my throat and pulls on it a bit. My throat is bleeding."

"Keep going, Carla."

"I can see my child self giving up, as he's putting the knife in my hand and wrapping his around mine. He's pulling my arm up. Oh, Gabe, he's stabbed the baby."

"We can't stop it, Carla, but we'll see what we can do later on. Tell me what else happens."

"But that means that I stabbed the baby. The knife was in my hand."

"Remember, Carla, there was no choice. You were three years old, and forced." His voice was firm. "Now tell me what else happens."

Crow's feathers were a comfort now, the excitement and challenge gone. My voice duller, I described what I saw. "They've offered the heart up. A man in a red robe is holding it up in the air, offering the spirit and soul of the baby to the Dark side."

"What about your child self, Carla."

I watched from the safety of Crow. "They are leading her back to the women. The women don't do anything. I think they are all drugged. They just sit there, numb and doing nothing. The two men shove the child down to the ground among the women, turn and walk off."

I was stunned into silence by the events. The nightmare had come full force in all it's complexity. How I wish this weren't true. I didn't notice the silence from Gabe. Then he broke it.

"Carla, there's something we need to do."

A small spark of hope lit my internal darkness. Was there anything we could do about this? About the baby?

"This is for the baby. We need to help the baby. Does the little girl want to come along with us?"

I sensed into the psyche of the little girl. Of course she wanted to, sitting stunned among the women, horrified, she wanted desperately to do something about this horror.

"Want to? Are you crazy? Of course she wants to. She wants to help the baby. This was just too much. She wants to do anything she can."

"Then a crow will come to carry the little girl. Tell her not to be afraid and help her to get on." In my mind's eye, I let myself slip down near the child, telling her of Crow. She looked at me in wonder, then seeing my crow and another, she nodded. Crow came and landed next to her, unnoticed by the drugged women nearby.

"She's not afraid. She loves the crow and the feeling of the feathers. She's putting her arms around its neck. There, I've got her on it."

"Good. We're going to fly together. What do you see?"

I looked around, surprised. Crows were coming in by the dozens. "A lot of crows."

"That's right. We're going to fly together in a group of crows. We'll be protected by the flock. None can find us in here, amongst the others. Now, fly higher. We're going above the ritual."

Together the child and I lifted up higher, going above the ritual where we could see it all, spread out below us, the figures in shadowy relief with the lights from the fire and torches. The candles barely showed the women around the circle.

"Remember how the high priest was holding up the heart of the baby for consecration to the Dark side?"

"Yes."

"One of these crows here is a Warrior Crow. He's going to swoop down, just as the priest holds the heart up for consecration and pluck it out of his outstretched hands. Remember, there is no time. We can go back and interrupt this ritual."

"Why is Warrior Crow taking the heart just then?"

"He's taking it before the priest has a chance to consecrate the heart and soul to the Dark side."

Relief filled me. We could save the baby's soul, if all went well with Warrior Crow. We were flying high, surrounded by the protection of the flock. Once again I saw the scene move forward, the forced stabbing, the heart in the priest's hands as he lifted it arrogantly towards the dark heavens, pride in his offering sharpening his stance.

A shriek split the air as a dark form hurtled from above towards the priest. Startled, he jerked, ducking his head, heart still held aloft, as Warrior Crow swooped, ear-splitting shrieks from all the crows. Warrior Crow snatched the heart from the outstretched hands, bolting skyward back into the cloud of crows cawing, casting a cacophony of sound back and forth across the heavens.

"He has it!" Gabe confirmed what we saw.

The priest and cultists froze in place, paralyzed by the unexpected and unacceptable. Chaos broke forth as they began shouting, cursing, waving fists and knives, falling over each other in their rage, each trying to stop Warrior Crow as he fled into the night.

Above, the flock closed in around us. "Here's Warrior Crow." That, as the crow flew higher and into the flock for protection. "Quickly."

My heart caught with the fear of pursuit. Abruptly the flock banked and flew off into the night, speeding for the crack in time and space where the cult members, even with their occult powers, could not follow. I felt the change as we crossed the Gateways. Slowly, I began to relax. The flock spread out across the sky, those at the edges separating off and disappearing into the grey light.

In this new place, dawn was just rising, the grey of the clouds lighting up softly with gentle hues of pink, rose and violet. Slowly the clouds colored, areas deepening while others stayed light, creating a mosaic of soft curls of color. We flew on into the dawn for a short time.

"Look down, Carla. See the forest and clearing?"

I took my reluctant attention from the beauty, and looked down, noting the forest with the clearing just showing at the far edge. "Yes, I see it."

"We're going down in the clearing. The three of us will land together, Warrior Crow nearby. The rest will be over at the side."

Together the flock descended, down through the softly fading sunrise colors, into the tall grasses. I helped the child climb down from her crow after I got off. Travel legs were wobbly at first, another reminder of my riding days. Gabe was on our right.

Gracefully, our three crows flew over to the side, while the rest of the flock whirled above us, and flew off into the sunrise. Only Warrior Crow was left aloft, gently hovering above. The grasses were soft, waving gently in the warm breeze, as a small stream gurgled off to our left, bouncing through the few scattered trees and rocks there, singing it's song of sunrise.

"Warrior Crow will put down the heart that it stole, Carla. The heart is surrounded by a shimmering glow. Do you see the glow?"

"Yes. It's actually quite beautiful."

"It's the spirit of the baby. I want you to pull the spirit from the physical heart and gather it together so that you can hold it in your hands. Your little girl self can help."

"She likes that," I told Gabe, as the child and I began to pull the shimmering light from the physical heart. Like pulling glowing strands of silk and gathering them gently together, we worked as a team, her little hands helping to gather the glowing strands together while I pulled them free, the glowing beauty distracting us from the physical nature of our task. Attention focused on glowing strands, we worked together.

"I think we have it."

"Yes, you've got it all."

In awe we looked at the glowing orb in my hands, vibrant and full of life and energy.

"We're going to set it free, to go back to the Light. Before we do, is there anything you'd like to say to the baby's spirit?"

I thought about it, considering. This was the time for anything I had to say. I spoke directly to the spirit of the baby, the essence glowing vibrantly in my hands.

"I love you," I told the essence softly. And then, hesitatingly, "I'm sorry. So sorry for what happened to you. And for my part in it. For what I did. I hope you'll forgive me." I thought a moment more. "I want you to be free. To be with the Light."

Tears coursed down my face.

"Is there anything else you want to say?"

I thought about it. No, there was nothing else. That seemed to say it all.

"Then it's time to let it go free. Hold it up above you. That's it," as I raised the golden orb.

"Now release the spirit and send it towards the sun. The Spirits will take care of it from there."

I did as he taught me, holding the orb carefully between my hands, then gently opening my hands and releasing it to Source, watching as it flowed out, ever outward, until it moved towards the sun. Slowly, with my child self at my side, I turned back to Gabe.

He smiled quietly, then looked at both of us. "I've dug a hole at the edge of the clearing. Over there, by that large tree." He pointed off to his right where a massive oak rose into the sky, it's branches dominating the edge of the clearing. "The heart needs to be buried."

"The little girl and I will bury it." I listened to my inner voice and nodded. "She wants to wrap it in a big leaf first."

"All right. Take her and find the leaf, then let her put it in and cover it up."

We found a leaf. I didn't know they came that big, but the little girl loved it. Gently she wrapped the heart, placing it in the hole that Gabe had dug.

"She's very careful."

"I see that," he replied, watching her tenderness. "You're returning the heart to Mother Earth for care. Mother Earth will bless the heart and bring healing. Remember, as we are healed, so is Mother Earth."

We watched as she covered it over, scooping the dirt with her hands until it was flat. A curious childish gesture, she patted it carefully on top, then laid both hands on it in a child blessing. Rising, she brushed her hands off, then placed her right one in mine as we walked back to Gabe.

He smiled at us as we came, kneeling down to her. "You did a very nice job." Her response was a silent strangling hug, her little arms wrapped tightly around his neck.

"It's time for us to go, Carla. Tell the little girl that she is going to ride on Brother Crow to a safe and healing place. He will take her there. It's the place of the other children."

I explained to the child, realizing her silence now and her need for healing. She nodded her comprehension. Brother Crow was her friend. She wasn't afraid. Crow flew over, landing beside her and I helped her onto its back. She turned and waved, then Crow lifted off. Again she waved. I waved back as she disappeared into the clouds.

My mind's eye shifted to the meadow where the healing children lived, safe from terror and danger. There at the edge of the meadow, the leader stood in her blue jeans and grey sweatshirt, long blond hair blowing in the light breeze, her vigilant blue eyes scanning the skies, searching for the arriving child.

Gradually other children left their play and came to stand beside her, patiently waiting. A small one, about two, held a giant cookie. Another in a pretty little dress, had a small baby kitten for the child. I watched as Crow broke through the clouds, and the leader pointed. The child would be safe, cared for, and find healing in that place. Gabe and I sighed together, satisfied that the child was in good hands.

"Let's go, Carla." Our crows came over and we climbed aboard, lifting off together. The energy shifted as we flew through the Gateways, and returned to current time.

"He's bringing us to the office. When I count three, open your eyes and we'll be in the office. One. Two. Three." At the sound of three, I became aware of sounds from the present time once again: a computer keyboard clicking in another room, the Xerox nearby working at spitting out documents, a bell sounding the end of meditation.

And another sound, less expected, filled the air. The clear, vibrant sound of Crow, flying outside the window, cawing, three times. No more. No less. Welcome home.

My eyes flicked open, to find Gabe still sitting beside me, holding my left hand, watching my eyes. With a small squeeze, he let go and rolled his chair back. We both sat back further in our chairs.

"Did you hear Crow," I wondered.

He smiled. "Um hm. Three times."

"Pretty neat."

Then he rose. "Time for a break. Want some coffee or tea?"

I shook my head as I got up. We both wandered slowly to the restrooms. Returning, I slid down into my chair. Exhausted. Gabe walked in, closing the door behind him, coffee in his right hand while his left held an assortment of granola bars.

"Here. Eat this." It was an order. I was drained from our work, and weakly took the bar. My Earth Mother mug empty, he got more water and handed that to me, too. I hadn't moved towards opening the granola bar.

"Come on, Carla. My guides tell me that we need to drink fluids and eat. This is very exhausting work, and we need to replenish our energy." He reached for my granola bar, ripped it open, and handed it back. Reluctantly, I complied.

Slowly we snacked, each with our own thoughts about the experience. Raisins came next. By then, I realized how starved I was, and ate them without a fight. Finally I felt reoriented enough to talk about what had happened.

"I'm glad we freed the baby's spirit."

He nodded in agreement. "The guides told me that this one was mandatory. I asked and that was the answer. Sometimes when I ask, they say no. It's not our karma or our place. I have given up trying to understand why. It's not mine to understand."

"Why did they say yes this time?"

"The task was there, we had the ability to do it, and this one was ours to do. My guess is that it's because of your direct involvement in it."

"I hate that. Why was I made to do it? Why did I have to be involved like that? To hold the knife?"

Gabe listened to his guidance then nodded in comprehension, turning his attention back to me. "They needed what they call an unstained spirit to do it. You were a very young child and had never killed. The others had killed, rather, all those who were older. So you were the unstained spirit used in this ritual. They wrapped your hand around the knife as if you were the one doing it so they fulfilled the requirement."

"I wish it had been any other way."

"I know, Carla. I'm sure. But it was also an integral part of cult life. This committed children to the cult. The children couldn't leave once they thought they had killed someone. It put them outside the pale, separating them from the real world. From loving people and "normal" life. Now they, or you in this case, belonged to the cult. It's straight ahead mind control." I nodded reluctantly.

"How do you get someone to believe that they are an irreversible part of a group? This is a very powerful way. But of course, that purpose was really secondary, though potent. The real reason for your forced participation is that they did need an unstained spirit to hold the knife. They just never let an opportunity for mind control go by."

"What about forgiveness, Gabe? Can I ever be forgiven for doing something like that?"

"You're still caught in the mind control, Carla. You had absolutely no choice. Of course, you're forgiven. Have been. Any doubts are residuals of the mind control, so you have to remember that. Stay out of their mind control issues whenever that comes up. This is a pretty clear example of mind control."

I sighed, leaning back, relaxing a bit more. "All right. Thanks." I thought some more, scanning for unfinished concerns.

"Why this kind of sacrifice though?" My research hadn't gone into that.

Patiently, and with his characteristic kindness, he explained further. "They do ritual first with the infant to gather the life energy into the heart for offering to the Darkness. The heart is the central organ of the body for gathering the essence. That's why the heart is so important for this ritual."

My mind was skipping around, knowing that I would do the grief work later, needing this time for processing with Gabe. It was all so bizarre. I needed a time and place for discussing it. It's not like casual conversation anywhere else. We turned to cult dates, paying attention to dangerous times. I thought of my own family, my parents and sibs, and knew that I didn't have the energy for those questions now. Later, when more emotional fires were out.

Then Gabe asked about my home therapist, whom I'd fired. Oops. Gabe didn't like that one bit.

"I just want you to have more backup."

"My martial arts friends are actually pretty good backup. They aren't as intimidated by this as therapists seem to be. I think I'm OK for now."

"All right." Reluctantly.

I looked at the clock, aware that time was running out. "My throat is really sore and it wasn't before. Any connection?"

"It's from stress to the fifth chakra. Going through time dimensions while journeying can do that. It should be all right in a while."

Grinning sheepishly, he rose from his chair, walked back to his desk and reached under it, pulling out a medium-sized drum.

His guides had told him to bring it. He'd been embarrassed, walking into a professional building with it. Now he played, softly, the rest of the offices miraculously quiet, empty of clients. My question had been met with, "See what you feel."

Singing, he accompanied the beat, drumming an intricate pattern, full of power while he offered a blessing. Chanting as he drummed, he called on the power of the goddess. Then he asked the presence and power of the goddess to be with me, within and without, as I went forth from here, strengthening me. The chant was followed by the Beauty Blessing, and I let myself sink into the rhythm and the sound, flowing with the energy of the blessing. Gently at the end, he brought it to a halt. We both sat quietly in the aftermath of the blessings.

"What do you feel, Carla?"

"Kind of surrounded by goodness. By a sense of strength, too."

"Um hm. The chanting and drumming is to seal you. It's sealing you with sound, like putting a protective envelope around you. It's on the etheric level, the level of sound."

I could feel the difference. It felt like being in a wonderful bright, clear space full of light which had a crisp edge around it, containing the clear energy." Sensing further, I turned to Gabe, surprised.

"And my throat doesn't hurt any more."

"That's because the etheric level or the level of sound that we were just working on is also the fifth chakra or throat. Took care of that." He smiled as he packed his drum into it's case. Once again I felt the familiar gratitude, especially that he was willing to take risks. Like drumming in a professional shared office.

"I do feel all right, like I really can do the drive back home. And that's amazing given what we've been through."

"You'll do all right. Don't forget your medicinal coffee and hamburger."

"Yeah. Never thought I'd see the day." I chided him again, the vegetarian.

"**You** didn't. I was a vegetarian for 18 years. Then they told me that we both need to do this to get grounded after journeying. What a surprise it was to me."

I laughed at him. "I'll bet it was. How'd you explain it to your veggie friends?"

"I didn't even try."

At home, the sealing with sound seemed to hold. I was aware of the events and I continued processing them, yet they felt somewhat distant. Only very slowly did the impact creep up, encasing me in deep grief. Remembering my training with Gabe, I turned to my practices to support myself, spending time meditating, using candles and incense, talking with friends about neutral subjects, and researching Crow in native literature.

Crow. The Gateway to the Supernatural. The Keeper of Sacred Law, able to shapeshift through time, knowing that this wasn't the only reality. An excellent ally.

Meditating on our work, I considered my actions taken to right the wrongs. It helped. I didn't feel so helplessly lost in the process. Less a victim, there were things I could do.

Then there was my lack of knowledge of things esoteric. Again I searched the library and bookstore, developing my own personal library, this time of dreamwork, Native American lore and practices, as well as the psychic literature. I would learn and be prepared. Resolve walked with my grief, trading places frequently as I struggled to understand and integrate our work.

Surprisingly, my work continued to be strong, with an increased understanding and acceptance of clients with unexplained emotions. Sherri came to my office the following week. Slim, blond, 21, she rose in the waiting room with the grace born of wealth. Inside, in the safety of my consulting room, the facade crumbled as tears flowed down her face. She couldn't speak in her college classes, and didn't have any explanation. Gratefully, I knew I could help.

The following night I pulled into a close parking space outside the dojo, got out and carefully locked the doors. Beer cans blew past the car, bouncing off a trash barrel on the sidewalk. Loud music poured from the bar across the street. Karate was teaching me something. Perhaps most of all to use common sense. Quickly I walked to the wooden fence and the nearly invisible door. Flipping the latch, I was immediately inside, closing the door behind me, leaving the ordinary world behind.

The oriental bridge arched upwards, carrying me over the small pond and past the graceful dwarf red maple. Coming down the other side, I slid the glass door open, bowed as I entered, then closed it behind me. A strong workout would help loosen the tension that I was carrying, freeing tight muscles as I stretched, and releasing frustration as I practiced strikes, blocks, and the perfection of forms. A surprising support, it was serving me well.

Karma

Family life continued in spite of Jack's heavy work schedule, and my fears of irreparably harming the kids by action or inaction. We did manage to meet for an evening snack time, giving us a chance to check in.

The winter night was cold as Nate stomped in, kicking snow from his boots. I hated the cold. Together we gathered, as Jack announced his office wanting him to travel more. The kids were excited. I was worried. Could I manage? Would I be a good enough parent? Anxiety took my appetite as I tried to adjust to the impending changes.

A week later I was with Gabe in his office, my mind on my recovery. I would get through this, find the pathways to healing, come out strong and intact. Determination kept me going.

Once again we worked deliberately and precisely, recalling nightmare fragments, tracking thought forms and energy traces of traumas and clearing them. Months on end, we cleared my energy field of layer after layer of trauma, removing energy associated with cult events.

The tedious and necessary part of working in a steady manner, so that I wouldn't get overwhelmed. Pacing, Gabe reminded me once again. I had other words for it. Taking one piece at a time, clearing that out in a good way, and then carefully going on again. Very different from my impulsive, "damn the torpedoes" approach. That style would have left me dead long ago, I was sure. This strategy kept the boat steady in rough seas.

"Remember," Gabe told me. "Going too fast is a common mistake with survivors. When they do that, they get into overwhelm, which is just what happened in the original trauma. So they are then recreating the trauma state. This is not what we want."

"Sort of like doing to ourselves what was done to us?"

"Exactly."

Hmm. No, I didn't need that, so I would actually practice patience and tolerate the slow pace. At least I didn't crash this way.

Our morning energy work done, we settled back into our chairs, moving into quiet thoughtfulness, while we considered the work of the day. Gabe turned to me, perching with a new black mug in his lap, long legs crossed with the top foot moving slowly as he thought.

"Any questions, Carla? How are you doing?"

"Well, I have had something niggling around in the back of my mind."

"OK."

"I've been thinking about this karma thing for quite a while. I just wonder how I got into this mess and why. Things like being dedicated to a cult, or forced to stab a baby. What did I ever do to end up in this much of a mess?"

"That's the Judeo-Christian approach. That it's in punishment for your sins. Let me check in and see if there's more." He looked down towards the floor, concentrating as he focused on his guidance.

Looking startled, he raised his head quickly.

"What?"

"My Egyptian guide is here. That's really unusual. He doesn't show up much." I sat silently, waiting, as he looked away again, regaining concentration and listening. Finally he turned back to me.

"He's trying to put it into a framework that we can understand. It's like trying to take a very large teaching and translate it into a simpler language without losing the nuances." He listened some more.

"This is hard, but I'll do the best I can with this. Karma, he tells me, is not the concept that we have of 'what you sow is what you reap.' It's about patterns. The significant question to look at, for example, is what kind of pattern was set up with the murder of the baby. For you, it's a question of over-responsibility for the lives of others. You know, like the way you worry about some of your clients, especially the children. Right?"

"Uh huh. That part I can see," I agreed, noting the reference to my more recent client concerns.

"It happens when you're a therapist as well as in our personal lives. For example, your counter-transference, how you feel about your clients. Like the teen you're working with who is pregnant. You're aware of feeling over-involved in her distress?"

"Yeah. Her situation really has worried me a lot. And I know that my concern is out of balance. I'm more involved emotionally than I should be."

"Right. So it's a pattern of over-responsibility that originated at that time in the cult. It's more like a compulsion to rescue and/ or take care of others. The point is to change it from a compulsion to a choice. We want to be involved and feel responsible because we sincerely want to, not because we feel compelled to."

I sat quietly and thought. It all fit quite well. There were often times when I felt overly involved or overly concerned. I watched my actions so that I didn't step over any lines, but I knew in my heart that this part was driving me. One could burn out this way. It didn't feel choiceful.

"You know, Carla, I have some unresolved feelings about this too. I'm carrying a lot of anger and rage from that sacrifice of the baby."

I was surprised. Gabe rarely shared his feelings about our work together. Yet I was again relieved to know. It certainly was appropriate to the tragedy, and appropriate for him to have feelings about it.

"Is there no justice?" he questioned the guide. "What about the real perpetrators, who willfully killed an innocent baby?"

The answer was quite clear, and carefully Gabe relayed it to me, as he got it. We both needed to know and understand this.

"The abusers have turned their own direction around and set a pattern in motion for themselves. That direction is likely to lead them further into the darkness. My guide calls them 'renegade priests.' Sort of like turncoats. I think that relates to this guide's Egyptian priest background." He sighed, looking into the depths of his mug.

"They will create their own justice from the path they are now walking, and it's not a justice you or I would want to live out. Just think what it will take to turn that pattern around."

I nodded. "And focusing on the idea of patterns really helps. I think I like that. Besides that, it makes absolute sense to me. Patterns for them, and patterns for me. I can see it." I thought some more.

"I'm thinking of one of your Elders that you've told me about."

"Yes."

"The one who talked about our choosing our families."

Gabe looked back in time to our earlier conversations about his Elders and training, remembering as we talked. "Yes, he also said that it wasn't necessarily about paying back karmic debt. There were lots of reasons we might choose a family. And sometimes it was to continue to work out and correct a pattern. Patterns that were dysfunctional."

I was getting more clarity about it. "Like, for example, abandonment or control. The teachings do fit together. At least for me. Not such a punitive approach."

Gabe relaxed again. "I think we've had enough of the punitive approaches. I think karma is about growth and resolving negative patterns somehow. I'm sure we'll learn more as we go."

I nodded, my mind already switching it's fast track to another slot. "So I have one other question."

"What's that, Carla?"

I got really still and serious, then looked directly at him. "Do you think that I'm a multiple personality?"

"No. Why?"

"Someone told me that I had to be since I had experienced cult abuse."

"Well, you're not. I've thought of that, and checked for it, and you're just not."

"How do you know?"

He explained the differences carefully until I got it. "You have many ways of being and experiencing. You have the ability to compartmentalize your life when necessary. But you also have a continuity of memory. You know what's happening in each area of your life. That rules out multiplicity. It's a reasonable fear, but just not true for you. Someone's being dogmatic with you. Stick up for yourself. Don't just assume that they're right, and you're a bad person."

I smiled. Sticking up for myself was difficult these days, but I'd work on it. We closed the session then, leaving me with plenty to think about. The work was hard, yet challenging as I was really forced to look at the world I had known in a different way. Why were we the way we were? What was the soul's journey? The questions would keep me busy on my drive home.

The months went by, as Gabe and I worked slowly and carefully, mending my energy field and continuing our processing. Even with the slow pacing of the work, I was stressed, struggling to keep it together. My birthday arrived in the usual way, and it didn't cheer me at all. Working at the office all day, Jack out of town, I dragged my self home exhausted. Surprise lit my eyes as I turned off Front St and onto Woods, my street. There were Christmas lights in front of my house. In March?

Laughing I pulled into the drive, getting out to take a closer look. Who's mischief was this, wanting to grace my birthday with a total surprise? It took a week to solve the mystery, as I broke the wall of silence at the dojo, gales of laughter accompanying the admission.

"Your brothers and sisters," Sensei reminded me. "You were getting too serious." This kind of family was a good thing.

I had begun training with Judith, Gabe's teacher. Two weekend trainings had whetted my appetite for more. Deep in the evening I arrived at the retreat site, an old Civil War mansion high in the West Virginia mountains, shrouded in lengthening shadows. A romantic's dream, I thought, as I drove up the tree-lined gravel drive. The stone building, with several sprawling white wood additions in disrepair, was graced with two-story white columns greeting newcomers to the giant porch, azaleas to each side replaced further along with mounds of ivy. Oaks, maples and pines dominated the entry landscape, the gravel circular drive curving among them.

Inside I was shown to the ball room where we would meet, gracious in its high ceiling, shining wood floors and long stone fireplace at the end. On the other side, a white wood porch casually overlooked the immediate valley, ending in distant mountains turning deep shades of lavender and blue in the setting sun. I was in love with the place.

That evening after the first teaching, the group met in the wood paneled dining room, wooden chairs and tables accenting the deep wood beams. In the candlelight, everything shone with a rich vibrancy, flickering shadows falling on students milling around the snack table.

"Carla!" I turned in surprise at hearing my name as Sharon, a participant from another training, shoved her way through the crowd, past the snacks, and to my side. "I have some people I want you to meet. Come on!"

Reluctantly, I followed. What did Sharon want from me? I had previously mentioned, in a weak moment, that I was a cult survivor. Could I stay in hiding here? I'd have to talk to her about it. Quickly she led me to a small group of women, standing uneasily next to a deep oak pillar.

"This is Carla," she announced to them. "And," turning to me, "this is Sandra, a massage therapist."

I took in Sandra with her dark hair, stocky build and jeans, loose shirt and ankle bracelet. A long necklace hung from her neck with small earrings complimenting it. Sharon moved on.

"This is Angie. She's an accountant." Angie looked notably different, I realized, with her more professional slacks and sweater. Tall, blond and willowy, she was quite attractive.

"And this is Paula. She's a bookkeeper." Short brunette, inexpensive slacks and shirt, she looked shy, uncertain. As we all felt. Sharon looked exceptionally pleased with herself. What was going on? She turned to take in the four of us.

"And you are all cult survivors. I thought you might like to meet each other." Busted. I stood stunned. Why had it never occurred to me that I ever would meet any others?

Finding a quiet table in the rear by the huge windows, we shared our stories until well into the night. Different stories, same substance, fears, depressions. One was from the Ku Klux Klan, another abused in a kindergarten setting on regular field trips. The third, a large city cult. One story stayed in my mind, bringing healing almost instantly as the woman talked of being forced at the age of three to murder a baby, her small hand held by a powerful man as the knife swept down. A common cult ritual, she told me.

The dining room was empty when we stopped, snacks gone, tea water empty. Exhausted, we moved towards the stairs and hallway to our rooms for a brief night. This had been revealing for each of us. Interestingly, we didn't talk again. Of course, we wanted the support of the others, but not the fear and the stories. But the knowledge of them and their stories sustained me in the long months ahead. Hopefully it was true for each of us.

The next morning dawned gloriously and Judith resumed teaching with all eighty of us in assorted positions in the ball room. I chose a seat in the back, where I could exit if I felt the need.

Besides, the chairs were uncomfortable and Judith didn't take breaks. I could stand up if my toush got too sore.

I watched her carefully as she taught. Dark wavy hair framed her medium build, long black eyelashes accenting her dark eyes, surveying us as she spoke, watching us for reactions. Her black slacks and red and yellow top didn't look so extraordinary, though I was aware that she certainly was. Large gold earrings dangled and moved as she spoke, occasionally interfering with the microphone. Carefully she spoke, supporting her ideas with research. Why had I been surprised when she did that, I wondered? Was I still expecting fluff? The stereotype? Well, she wasn't. I continued to enjoy watching her teach the group, as well as take in the teachings. She was using the energy, and I wanted to learn how.

Three days later, the bomb dropped. A question about karma, and I jumped, immediately wary of blame. Judith said something about choosing our families and calling certain situations to ourselves. My two favorite non-cult students at the retreat turned and looked right at me. True, they did know that I was a cult survivor, but I had told them because I had trusted them. Their looks, though, felt pointed as if they carried a message. "See, it's your fault."

The self that could live in disguise sat there frozen, ignoring them, watching Judith as she went on with her teaching. I didn't move a muscle, but I saw Judith's eyes flick. She caught what had happened. I felt energetically hit from each side.

Inside I was shaking with terror, humiliation and rage. Schooling myself to stay in hiding, look normal, I got through the rest of the teaching session. But soon it was lunch time, and students all around me were getting up for lunch. Nodding at my friends, I moved to the side to wait. The disguise was in place. I looked cool.

The last student finished the conversation, and Judith flipped her hair back, dark eyes now inviting me forward. Several other women and one of the men were to my left along the wall. I didn't want them to hear as I moved closer to her.

And then to my horror, it happened.

My disguise slipped. Tears began to cascade down my face. Alarm filled hers. "Carla, what is it?"

"Your talk," I stammered. "And my friends . . ." That's all I could get out.

"Yes. I saw." Her voice was hard, the attitude of a mama bear protecting her young, a la me. "What's going on?"

With that she waved me over to the couch in the back of the room, seating herself on the old, beige-pattern stuffed cushions, indicating that I was to do the same. Sinking down beside her, I forced my hands to stop shaking, while she searched for a kleenex. Successful in the depths of her purse, she handed me one, and after a good blow, I was ready to talk.

"Your talk about karma." Hesitating, I finally got it out. "I was born into a cult."

I paused. I still really hated telling anyone that, especially when I liked them as much as I liked Judith. It gave her a perfect opportunity to turn me off. But I had to know. I couldn't leave it like this. I paused, but couldn't see a negative reaction flaring, so plunged ahead.

"It sounded like you said that it was our fault somehow for choosing the families we did. That it was payback. I don't want to take that understanding with me if it's not what you meant. And then when you said it, both my friends looked at me, and I felt hit energetically, like they were saying 'see, it is you.'"

"Yes. I saw that. So let me explain, Carla. I believe that we do choose our parents." Her eyes softened, as if she were looking elsewhere. "And you chose yours. You knew them from before. In a previous life. Do you remember them?"

I shook my head negatively, surprised into silence. That had never occurred to me. At the same time, an image came to my mind's eye of a village in a primitive area, packed dirt, people dressed with heavy coats as they moved around. A man and a woman who felt familiar. Yet different. The man felt kinder. I had to be making it up. What did it mean, anyway?

"They were good people when you knew them, and you loved them deeply. You saw them sliding into the darkness and knew they were in serious danger, so you decided to come in and help them. You thought that as a Being of Light, you could save them."

I thought of my rescue energy. I could understand that.

"There's just one thing you didn't consider, Carla."

"What's that?"

"The power of the group. It wasn't just the darkness your parents had gathered. You also had to deal with the darkness of the group as a whole. That was a *much* bigger deal."

"Oops." My tears had dried from within as I took in her words, sorting them in my mind, understanding how they fit my personality. At the same time, I saw and felt the cult energy as a group. No one could balance that.

"Yes, I'd say. Oops. Actually, I talk about it as a sort of spiritual arrogance. We look down and we think 'oh, I can handle that. I can bring my light to it and help them. Or save them.' We forget in that state how difficult it is here in the physical realm. We overstate our abilities and understate the difficulties here. It's spiritual arrogance. My light is enough to take care of this situation."

I smiled ruefully at her. "I get it. The problem is that right now, I'd probably do the same thing again, if I saw someone I knew and loved and thought I could help."

"I know. But what you hadn't counted on when you came in was the darkness that surrounded your parents. It was just too much. It's something to consider. We aren't all powerful."

That I got. I felt like a prisoner of war. I had gone in to help, and gotten captured. And my condition was the consequence. I wondered if the others had done that.

She continued, psychically reading my parents. "They chose you, too. They really thought that your light could match the darkness, and/or help them become free of it. It was a serious under-estimation of the darkness of that cult."

I relaxed and leaned back into the cushions. It made much more sense, adding another layer of understanding without the blame I instinctively shielded myself from. Judith was still engaged in our conversation. Another thought occurred to her, as she leaned towards me.

"What did your father do for a living?"

"He worked for a major oil company. He was assistant to the vice president, and was in line for a vice president position. He had to wait until someone died. It was just that he died first."

When I said major oil company, she sat up abruptly.

"Which one?"

I told her, and she smiled broadly. "That's really quite amazing."

"Why?"

"You won't believe this. The major contributor for this work of mine is an executive of that oil company. It feels like a wonderful kind of balance. Both men executives of the same company. Light balancing the Dark." We sat together for a few more moments in silence, relishing the irony and the balance. Then she smiled and rose.

Together we walked towards the dining room, just in time to join the line as it reached the food. "Good timing," I smiled at her. She smiled back, then turned to answer another question. I wondered how she did it, all the questions and demands. I gave up and filled my plate. The food was very good, and I didn't want to miss out.

I continued to record my dreams, knowing them as information from the unconscious. If I could decode them, they would help me be more conscious about my recovery.

A recent dream was of travel with two heavy suitcases. I couldn't find the way, and was asking others who weren't very helpful. Finally I just sat down and waited. I was very tired, and no one could or would help me.

In my daily life, I was aware of a growing fatigue, like a cloud following me, coming closer and getting darker. My steps seemed to be getting heavier, and working out was more of an effort.

It's those heavy suitcases, I thought to myself, ruefully aware of the burdens that I carried. But I can do this, and I willfully pushed ahead.

Again, my calendar announced my lunch with Pia. What a relief. The Double Dragon was a welcome sight as I turned a sharp left and slid into the parking space just ahead of on-coming traffic.

Pia was waiting at our table, a bit subdued while she sipped her tea. Seeing me, she bounced up for our welcome hug.

"I'm glad we do this," I reminded her.

"Me, too," she smiled, reseating herself. "It makes my day."

Our soup arrived without our orders, and we smiled and dove in. From the corner of my eye, I watched her. Yes, she was definitely subdued.

"So, what's going on?" I questioned as she finished the small bowl and put it aside.

"Oh, it's Shara. She can be a real pain at times. She's eight now, and mad because I won't let her wear short skirts."

I laughed with her, thinking of the hassles of parenting.

"And to think how things could have been for her if her uncle had sold her into prostitution!"

My nose wrinkled with the thought, black hair falling into my face as I absently pushed it back and returned an escaping earring. "Why would your uncle have done that, Pia? I don't understand."

"Shara's mother, my sister, didn't really want her. She couldn't care for her. So my uncle was raising her. That's what they do with unwanted girls. Sell them into prostitution."

"Wow." The world was a strange place.

"And now she's totally tragic that she can't wear a mini-skirt! I can't believe it!"

Again Pia's outrage, partly shammed, broke me up. Then we settled down and talked more, always sharing our concerns, large and small. Everyone has problems, I reminded myself. And sharing them with special folks does make a difference.

"You look tired, Carla," she noted as we finished paying our bills.

"I am. It's just a lot, with my travel to Chicago to see Gabe, and the family and job and all that. Just a lot."

"Hm. I don't know. Keep an eye on it." Her long black hair slid back on her slender neck as she tilted her head back. Then she looked directly at me. "Want to come to my yoga class?"

Together we walked out, arms about the others' waist, laughing and basking in our friendship. I was grateful for her in my life, and she appeared the same. At the cars, we made our next date, making sure it wasn't too long, then waving as we drove off.

It was Tuesday night at the dojo, and I couldn't concentrate. Couldn't speak out. Twice I needed to talk to Sensei, both times shifting in my place and having to move closer so he could hear me. Class ended and we lined up for closing announcements and meditation.

"We have a tournament coming up," he clipped off the words, looking sternly at the group. "Peter, I want you to go to help you get ready for your black belt test. Jeff, for your sparring. Carla, I want you to go, also."

Shock registered. My eyes got huge, staring at him.

"It will help you with your nervousness. You need to get out there." He spun around to face the kamiza, kneeling for meditation. We automatically following his unspoken command and knelt, my thoughts and feelings spinning with him. I thought about my emotional withdrawal. He wasn't going to let me do that. But a tournament? Yikes!

My dreams were of finding and developing courage. Finding it in the physical, in karate. Practicing it there, taking it to the rest of my life.

More dreams of danger: flash floods sweeping me away, a pet wolf cub let loose in the snow and coming to me for help. Danger coming from my right.

"You've already beat the cult, you know," Sensei told me a week later, as we relaxed after class. I looked at him in surprise.

"You're very functional, have your education, a good job, a healthy family. I'm sure they didn't want that." I nodded as he stood before me, skin glistening with sweat from the workout, tattered belt draped around his neck.

"Your job is to keep going. Fight for it, Carla. You can do this." He turned on his heel and left, sturdy form moving into the locker room. Quietly, I changed and left.

I'd begun reading about shamanism and loved it. Spiritual practices that were meaningful to me. Mysteries, too, helped me. They gave me something specific to fear, rather than my unknown terrors. I understood it. But this mystery book disturbed me deeply. Picking up a shamanism book, I read about a ritual, same theme, burying a shaman alive with just his head sticking out as part of an initiation. I shook as I read it. Why? That night my dreams were restless, sweat shimmering on my skin again as a I tossed and thrashed. Jack shook me, and I settled back into a restless dreamless state. Gratefully, I would see Gabe soon. What was wrong?

Buried

"Hey!" I greeted Gabe. I was still excited about the retreat, and wanted to talk with Gabe about it. We settled into our seats, while the sun streamed in the window on my left, over the table which now had a beaded feather added to his growing collection. Late April, and spring had finally arrived. I was hoping my dismal moods would lift with it.

Watching him, I realized that he was different, sluggish, eyes red, grumpy looking. "What's wrong?" I questioned.

"Allergies," he barked, knowing not to try to hide it. I cocked my head quizzically and he responded, shaking his negatively.

"We don't know what's causing them. Maybe something in the building."

"That's not good."

"Tell me about it," he grumbled, then shook himself. "But I'm good enough to give you a hard time, so let's get to work."

Briefly we shared about my retreat with Judith and her comments to me about karma and my family. Soon enough, he realized that I was jumpy.

"So, what's bothering you?" I filled him in about my dreams, a mystery book I had started and put down, and recent shamanic reading.

"This is why my kids monitor my reading and movies. Things set me off." I felt embarrassed, ducking my head to one side.

His feet hit the floor as he shifted to put elbows on knees, leaning forward. "With some reason, things set you off, I might add." That, with sternness. Not to get embarrassed by a normal trauma reaction. With a sigh, I settled back in my stuffed chair, letting go of the sound of people talking just beyond the door.

Gabe looked as if he were listening to guidance again, then looked directly at me. "We need a safe place to check out your reaction about the buried part of the book, and see if it's related to you and your abuse. We'll fly on Crow again today. All right?"

"Sure. That always feels like a safe way to find things out." Riding with Crow was definitely better than being with the cult.

He walked back to his desk behind him, and got some different sage. Quietly he lit it, smudging the room.

"What's that?" It had a different smell, and I liked it a lot.

"This is called white sage, and is somewhat different from the traditional sage that we've been using. This is more ceremonial and more for sacred uses."

"I like it."

"Um hum. Me too." He continued smudging the room, and then both of us. I breathed in the smell, relaxing.

The sacred scent filled me and surrounded me. I did love that smell. Relaxing again into my chair, I watched him replace the matches and sage with his rattle.

Then he sat in front of me again, gently swirling the rattle until it was making a delicate rhythmic sound. It created a trance state that was full, rather than the empty state of many meditations where one empties the mind. This state felt full of the sacred, with the scent of the sage and the familiar swishing of the rattle. A trance state with a sacred presence. I let myself relax into it as I allowed my eyes to gently close.

He began singing, softly at first, then building in timbre and resonance, filling the space even more with the energy of the sound. The Beauty Chant filled us with the essence of beauty as we focused in the different directions with the chant. I was aware of feeling a soft web of light surrounding and filling me, full of beauty, protection and spiritual presence. We were ready. I could hear him putting the rattle down, as I let out another breath, sinking into the chair even further.

"Here's Crow, Carla." His voice was soft and already felt at some distance. "Time to get on."

I could see Crow, as I reached up to pet his feathers and greet him. He looked at me with his intense black eyes, then shifted so that I could get on his back. Beside me, Gabe was mounted. Silently, we lifted up and into the darkness, through the Gateway to another dimension.

Flying side by side, I could feel Gabe and his Crow next to me in the darkness. Concentrating, I put my attention ahead, asking for Spirit to take me to the place where the question would be resolved. Was there anything to my fear of being buried? Or was there a simple answer? Or perhaps not even connected with the cult . . . what a wonderful idea.

Lights were ahead and I recognized them. "There they are, Gabe." So much for the "not connected to the cult" idea. Though I had liked it while it lasted.

"I see it, Carla. Remember we are hidden from them while we are on Crow. The crows blend with the dark of the night."

Soon we were coming within range, able to see the fire and candles, the dark figures moving around in their robes and hoods. "I see men in the center, moving very slowly this time, in a sort of a dance pattern."

Gabe watched too. It was an unusual sight for this cult. The men were dancing slowly in a strangely muted rhythm around the fire. The women appeared seated outside the candles again, in their usual position.

"Strange dance, Gabe."

"I know. I'm trying to figure it out." Then abruptly and more urgently, "Carla, I don't see any of the children."

"Uh oh." I looked around hurriedly, my stomach dropping in despair. "I don't either. I can't find them. They should be here."

"Let's go up higher, Carla. We should get a better view, and maybe we'll find them," as he rose higher, searching for the missing children.

"I don't see them."

"I don't either. Let's circle wider. They have to be somewhere."

Suddenly, his leaned forward. "There, Carla. Over there. Look beyond the fire and that small field. There's a woods. Do you see it?"

"I see the woods. I don't see the children, though." I realized that part of me was anxiously searching, and part of me was filled with dread and reluctance, clouding my vision.

"Look in the clearing, Carla. I see some figures. But I don't understand what's there. It's like doors, going down into something. Do you see them?"

Reluctantly, I looked, seeing the doors. Behind them were scant traces of the ruins of a building which had once been attached, old fallen timbers covered in the undergrowth, with foundation stones barely showing. "I see them."

"But what are those doors? I've never seen anything like them?"

I chuckled, partly with the relief of being an objective viewer once again, using my mind to solve a riddle. "Of course, Gabe. Those are common in the midwest. They are the doors that are left to a storm cellar. It used to be attached to the building that was there. They are primarily for shelter from tornadoes."

"But the doors aren't metal."

"No, they usually aren't. And the house is certainly long gone," I noted, looking again at the woods crowding close around, trees raising their branches in search of the sky, and vines choking what looked like the path away from the house.

"Looks as if they have rebuilt the storm shelter for some use. It could be fairly big inside there, though they usually aren't very big."

"Hm. Something new every day. All right. Look around, Carla, and see what else is there."

His getting me interested in describing the place had helped restore my curiosity and objectivity, but I felt myself sink as I noted the rest of the scene. "There are hooded adults there, men I think, and there are the children, standing around waiting. The kids are all naked, Gabe."

"Yeah, I see." I had been excited to find them, and lost it immediately when I realized they were all naked. What did it mean?

"Look for your child self."

It wasn't hard. I found her, huddled by the door to the cellar, shivering in the cool night air with the others. Her blond hair and slightly larger size than the grouping made her stand out.

"The doors are opening, Carla. Look inside. Let's see what this place is." We landed the crows and dismounted. They moved off to the side to wait, sheltered by the deepening darkness of the encroaching woods. Gabe and I moved closer, slipping quietly through the underbrush.

"It's hard to see," I said quietly. "Dark in there, and a lot of it is in shadow."

"I know. It's OK. Keep trying."

I was beginning to sort out the images. "It is much larger than the usual storm cellar. They've dug this out or else it was a natural cave. I can see it going back some ways." I paused while I looked some more.

"I can see black candles, pillar style, around the room. And some torches set into something in the center. That's their total light supply. There's also like a ditch there near the front. I don't get that. It's fairly deep. And some stuff piled up. Some people in robes moving around, setting the rest of it up."

"Um hm." Gabe was watching too as I described it to him.

"Gabe, I really don't like this place. I have never been near a place that has had such a totally evil feeling to it. It's a really evil place. And my feeling is that it has been used often and for a very long time. I hate this place."

Gabe, in his intense interest, had started crawling for the door, almost as if he was going to go in. My voice called him back to me.

"Wow, Carla. That place has a really powerful pull. I almost forgot myself. Crow is my power animal and he can't go in there. Which means that I can't go in there." He took a deep breath, sliding back to me in the underbrush, branches catching on his clothes and scratching exposed skin, as he thought about it, oblivious to the distractions of nature.

"You know, I thought that my curiosity was taking me in closer and closer. Now that I'm out of range of the pull, I realize that the place itself has a tremendous pull, almost like a suction. We're going to have to be careful with this one."

I found myself drawn slowly forward, seeking, searching . . .

"Carla. Get back here. I mean it. That place is dangerous."

His voice broke the spell, and I, too, moved back. Together we lay in the underbrush, watching again and trying to get a plan. What to do? I snuggled closer to the rich brown earth, remembering my earth spirit friends and feeling comforted, while leaves formed a canopy of shelter over us.

The adults in the shelter stepped outside, motioning to the other adults in the clearing. Together they joined forces, beginning to herd the children inside. My anxiety and tension rose with each passing second. "Gabe, what are we going to do?"

"Come on. We need more distance so that we can safely see. Get on your Crow, and let's lift off. We'll go up and watch from above."

Mounted, we rose, the flock nearby with assorted members flying in to camouflage us.

"Good. Let Crow circle higher. Great." That, as we flew in a larger circle, high above the cellar doors, candles and torches throwing eerie shadows outside the doors in the deepening darkness. "Now go a bit lower so that you can see."

I thought lower, and Crow began to descend, circling again slowly so that I could get a better look. Inside, light reflected against the sides of the cellar, torches blinding my view.

"I can't see well enough. I'm going a little lower."

"Be careful."

Suddenly I realized that I was descending more quickly, moving in closer than I had intended.

"Up, Carla," Gabe called to me. "You have to go back up. You're getting too close."

I set my intent and Crow flew higher. Then I headed in for another try. I had to see what was in there. I had to see what was going on. To see if we could do anything for my child self. It happened again. Surprised, I felt myself in the grip of a pull downwards. "It's so strong," I thought to myself. "I just don't understand."

"Up, Carla. Come on back up. Why are you going in like that? It's too close. That's why we are up here."

"I don't understand why I'm so pulled down there." Shaking my head, as if to clear it, I rejoined Gabe higher up.

"I think it's the pull to the little girl. You want so much to help her. You can go look again, but you have to be more careful. Don't put yourself into any danger."

"Yeah, I know. OK. Here I go again. I'll be careful." I knew that it was up to me to look, so that Gabe could see with me. And I desperately wanted to see what was going on. Yet, I also knew that Gabe's explanation didn't resonate with me. It didn't feel true. It didn't feel like the real reason I was being drawn in. Oh well, I'd worry about that later. Down we went, circling slowly as the men in the robes were herding in the last of the children.

Moving lower, I watched the children being placed around the interior, while the candles danced and flickered and the torches flared. The place still felt overwhelmingly dark and evil. There it was, the pull again. But I had to see. I went just a bit lower.

Suddenly I felt a suction feeling. As if I were gripped in the force of something far larger than I could manage. Slowly my mind began going numb, feeling like dense fog was filling in all the assorted cracks between neurons. Paralyzed by the power of the pull, Crow and I went lower and closer. Fear gripped my heart, squeezing and holding me in a vise. Breath stopped and my eyes started to cloud.

"Carla, Carla, pull up." Gabe's voice was urgent, far away.

My mind was deadened, barely registering a power reaching out, inexorably pulling me in. A deep, deep darkness full of evil, holding me, pulling slowly and surely. I couldn't get free. This was not about my feelings for my child self. I was held captive, slowly losing consciousness as we drifted lower.

"Carla!" A note of panic filled his voice. It felt as if it were from across the world. My imprisoned resources couldn't respond.

Suddenly, it was broken. The pull was missing.

"Pull up!"

Automatically responding, my body followed the instruction, urging Crow upwards. Instantly we swept out of range of the power, my mind clearing as we rose. What had happened?

"Carla, higher. I sent another, larger Crow to fly under you to break whatever was happening. Get higher yet."

Slowly we arched higher, discouragement filling my every pore. We couldn't get in there. I knew it now. From the safety of height, I watched as the last robed adult entered the fire-lit room, closing the great doors behind him. Now we couldn't even see inside.

"You can't go that close, Carla. You were pulling all of us in."

"I know. It's too late, anyway. Look."

He turned his Crow and looked back at the clearing with the closed doors. Sighing, he turned to me. "We have to land and wait. We just couldn't get any closer."

Resigned, I landed Crow, Gabe nearby. Together we sat down to wait. "What was going on, Carla? That was really dangerous. Why did you keep going in too close?"

"There's a pull there, almost like a magnetic power. Once I got in it's grip, there was nothing I could do. Your sending the larger crow broke its hold so we could get out. Otherwise, I think I would have been sucked clear into it. And you know, Gabe, I'm not sure I would have ever come out. It feels like a pull that goes on and on and on. Clear to the heart of the darkest place ever." I sighed, putting my head on my knees. "We couldn't get her."

"No, but we'll wait here until they come out. And then we'll see what we can do." Together we settled in for the wait.

Much later, my body cold and stiff from the night air and dew, I was aware of the darkness just slightly ebbing. The great doors opened, only a few candles still burning. Gabe nudged me. Cultists began to emerge.

"What do you see, Carla?"

"They're all coming out, slowly, as if in a daze. The trance state, I suppose. And they are carrying the little girl."

"Is she conscious?"

"No." It surprised me.

"Is she alive?"

"Yes." With relief, I let my breath out once more.

"What do they do to her?"

"They just sort of dump her there on the ground. And now they are all walking away. What are they doing? Why are they leaving her?" Now I was getting mad.

It was getting slightly lighter. The long, dark night was over. "They are walking to the parking lot, Carla. The ceremony, whatever it was, is over. The others that we saw at first were holding the energy with their slow dance while these did the ceremony itself. And now they are going home. Looks as if just a few are hanging around, talking. Probably waiting for the child to regain consciousness. But they are in the parking lot. I guess they think it will be a while."

"What can we do?"

"I'm signaling for another crow. Here he comes. See him?"

I looked up in the beginning dawn, just as the crow landed. "Yes. Right here."

"He's going to gather the child up and we'll take her to a safe place. Are you ready?"

"You'd better believe it. Time we were able to do something." Yet, as I watched the child, the feeling that something was not right filled me. I shook my head, trying to shake it off, but it wouldn't go away.

Crow came to the child, gathering her up gently and lifting off.

"Quickly, Carla, we have to get out of here before they come back to get her. Get on your crow. Let's go."

We all lifted together, my heart heavy. Something wasn't right.

"It's all right, Carla. We'll watch her carefully." Then we were up in the air, pivoting sharply and rising higher, the flock pouring in to surround us. Quickly we flew for the Gateways, bursting out into another dimension. I let my breath out. At least we did that much.

As we flew, the darkness faded and sunrise lit the sky around us, turning it orange, tangerine and rose. Daylight had come. We flew on, the flock pulling away to the sides and disappearing into the sunrise. Moments later, Gabe turned to me. "I know a special place that we are going to. You've not been there. We'll be there soon."

I watched as the third crow gently carried the unconscious child. I was worried, more than ever before, but couldn't pinpoint the cause.

"There, Carla. Look down. Do you see the woods, and the clearing? There's a small stream running off to the one side, with a bridge over it."

"I see it."

"We're landing there. Guide your crow in. The one with the child will follow us." We all landed, the third crow gently placing the child on the earth beside us.

"She's still unconscious, Carla. We'll sit here with her, until she wakes up." The three crows settled once again off to the side, near the trees. I watched the child, covered with something white, smudged and dirty, blond hair tangled as she lay there. Moving closer, I gently placed her hand in mine, holding the small fingers and stroking them, waiting.

"Feel this place," Gabe told me.

With my senses, I reached out. It was a good place. Getting beyond my concerns, I could feel peace here, and love. There was a fresh sparkle in the air, and a gentle breeze brushing the tops of the soft grasses. A joy seemed to glimmer here in an almost visible shimmer in the air. I relaxed the tension in my body. Surely this was a healing place.

"Look at her eyes, Carla. She's starting to wake up." Her eyelids were beginning to tremble slightly, then she opened them tentatively. "She sees you sitting there beside her."

"Um hm." I watched her looking around, dazed, confused. "She doesn't see you yet, Gabe."

"When she sees me, she'll know me as an Indian in buckskins. There, she sees me now."

"She's really dirty. Like, really dirty."

"That she is." Then, addressing the child, Gabe spoke. "Little One, there are things that Carla needs to know. We will go to a place where all the bad things that were done to you will be taken away. Kind of like erasing a drawing. It will all be washed away in fresh sparkling water, and you will be all clean of the bad feelings. Will you come with us?"

She looked at him, still hesitating.

"I don't think she likes baths. This sounds like a bath when you talk about water."

"You can pick flowers along the way."

I chuckled, watching her perk up. Clearly this child loved to pick wildflowers. Nodding to Gabe, she took his hand and slowly got up.

"Carla, as we do this, she'll be cleared of all the evil from that place. You need to remember that."

Walking together, I watched her reach to the side and pick the flowers, white daisies, red paintbrush, and the blue and pink lupine. Gathering them together in her left hand, she turned shyly, handing them to us. We both smiled, nodding our thanks while she reached for more.

Soon we approached the beautiful, sparkling stream, water splashing and dancing across stones and around lichen-covered rocks and branches, grasses on the edge trailing in the pure flow.

On our right, off to the side, there was a glistening area where the water splashed down a brief waterfall, quieted again in a shallow pool, then swirled out the other end, carried away downstream past more grasses and stones. Together we knelt by the waterfall, Gabe directing us so that the child was between us. He turned to me, motioning.

"There is a dipper here," He took it down from it's hiding place. "I will dip water from the waterfall and pour it over the little one's hands and arms. The water will wash away the pain and the hurt, and it will flow away on down the stream."

I watched in wonder, noticing that the little one was glad and that she trusted him, putting her hands out to him. Gently he took the dipper, got water from the waterfall, and poured it over her hands.

"As the water pours over her hands and into the pool, a picture will form there. Tell me what you see, Carla."

Reluctantly, I looked into the water. "I see cellar doors open. It's dark inside. There are candles. Men in black robes. Children, naked." Beginning to get frightened again, I drew back.

"I will drop a pebble into the pool and the picture will dissolve into the ripples . . . there, it's gone." After a pause, "Ready for another picture?"

Quietly, the child told her story through pictures—a story of being tied and buried alive, of drugs that quieted her but left her conscious during the ordeal until the air ran out and she lost that consciousness, of a young girl who assisted the men—a girl thought to be her older sister. And in the times of too much difficulty, Gabe dropped the pebbles, allowing relief as the child shared through her pictures.

Finally it was over. The waters washed away the pain, hurt and terror. It turned to play as we cleaned her body, splashing each other to make it a game, until we were all three soaked, but she was finally clean of the dirt, smudges and marks. Sitting at the side in the sun, drying out, I turned to him. "Why, Gabe? Why did they do it?"

Quietly he turned inward, reflecting. "They were putting out the Light. They buried her in ashes in that hole to bury the Light, and then when she lost consciousness, their ritual decreed that they had put out the Light of purity. It was a gift to evil, to the Dark side."

I thought about it while we turned again to the child, all of us drier and more relaxed in the warm sun. Gabe smiled at her, plucking some nearby flowers and grasses, assembling them into a delicate bundle and presenting them to her playfully. She reached out shyly, delighted. Then he spoke softly to her once again.

"Little One, this is a special place. A deeply healing place. There are many Medicine Helpers here. Would you like to meet one?"

She nodded, making me smile. Her interest in her surroundings was coming back, and she looked around for the healer.

"Turn around, then, and he will come to us along the path, over the small bridge. He will come slowly so as not to frighten you."

Gabe turned to me. "He's an old man. In a brown robe."

"She doesn't like robes." Instinctively I knew. It didn't take a rocket scientist, I reflected. Gabe turned back to the child.

"This robe is different. There's no hood." The old man came into view. "See, he doesn't wear a hood."

The old man stood quietly, just this side of some large berry bushes beside the path. Kneeling down, he allowed the child to examine him. She went tentatively towards him, reaching out a small hand to touch the edge of the robe.

"It's scratchy." She rubbed the robe's edge again.

We all smiled as Gabe responded. "Yes, it's scratchy from the material. It's wool."

She stood up and stepped back a step, looking at him all over. "There's a light around him." We all smiled again, aware of her sensitivity.

"Yes, you're right. There is a light around him." Then Gabe turned to Carla. "He waited there for her so that she'd feel free to go to him and check him out, which she seemed to have no problem doing."

"Smart man." I felt Gabe's smile. He turned back to the child.

"Little One, this is a very special, healing place. There are many healers here. You may stay here if you like, or go with Carla, or go with the other children."

"Are there healers with the other children?" she asked, as she tentatively touched the old man's hand.

"No," I responded. "There are no big people. There are good and loving children, but no healers."

The little one had decided. She liked this man. "I want to stay here."

"You can stay here. We will come back to check on you the next time. Then if you want, you may go to be with the children. Or, stay here."

She smiled a shy smile to each of us, then turned to the old man, who stood up. Quietly, she put her small hand in the hand of the man with the scratchy robe who had a light around him. They turned and walked slowly back the path towards the bridge. Just as they reached it, they stopped as she turned and waved. The man smiled reassuringly to me, and then they were out of sight.

Gabe and I walked back to the clearing where the crows waited for us. "It makes me nervous to leave her here."

"It's all right, Carla. This is a good place. It's near a very special healing place that I know well. She'll be very wonderfully cared for, and you'll be surprised how she'll heal and how happy she'll be when we come back."

I was reluctant, but trusted Gabe. Back on Crow, we lifted off into the clear air and back into the timelessness of that other realm.

"Three." I felt the dimensions shift and opened my eyes. We were back in Gabe's office. I rolled my head to loosen my tight muscles. It had been quite a trip. No wonder I had been upset with the story of someone being buried alive. Life makes more sense than I would prefer at times.

Little time was left in the session. We'd been journeying for a long time. Quickly we processed the work we had done, both of us weary and a bit overwhelmed. At one point, Gabe looked at me quizzically.

"What?"

"I just remembered. When you saw your little girl self, she had blond hair."

"Um hm," I confirmed.

"But your hair is dark now. What happened?" His head was cocked to one side, studying my hair and eyes.

"You know, I think that's another unfair thing about life. When I was small, I had blond hair and blue eyes. There are some family photos of me then. But when I was four or five, it all began to change. My hair darkened, and my eyes changed too. I think it's really unfair. The blond hair was cool." I gazed back at him ruefully.

He grinned at me. "Surprises, surprises. You're always full of them, Carla."

I grinned quietly back. "I know." Then I glanced at his clock, and began to get up, realizing my legs felt like rubber.

"Don't forget the hamburger and coffee, Carla. Get really grounded." I gave him a hug and let myself out, still wondering at all we'd seen and done. I'd have to ask him another time, who was that old man in the scratchy brown robe with the light around him?

Carefully letting myself out of his parking lot, I entered the flow of traffic, eager to get to the interstate where I could drive more on automatic, giving me time to consider our session. McDonald's was an hour away. Just about time for me to get through my first review and then take a break.

The month between sessions with Gabe was more than long. It was interminable, a never-ending grayness filled with shifting shadows and a constant companion of sadness. Stealthily I sought out quiet time, sitting by the window in my healing room while the night sky deposited shadows of increasing depth and pattern around me.

Nights were hardest, flinging me back to the early days of this cult work where I wanted to steal a blanket and sleep under the bed, remnants of a childhood coping skill discarded when I realized they'd find me no matter what. The impulse pushed against my controls, warning me of an overload. Something was left unfinished.

Karate was my solace, a place where I could concentrate, focus, fight my demons in human form rather than their ethereal slender wisps of shadow. Constantly I battled my demons of fear.

The tournament had gone well, the day class students teasing me unmercifully. I was a nervous wreck, hiding in the corner until my event was announced, and Sensei came to get me. But he'd been right. It had forced me out of my own shell. Responding under attack, I had expressed the skills and techniques I had learned, earning myself two second places. Not bad for a new kid, my classmates teased. And a girl at that. Family. The ups and downs of it, I reminded myself as I let myself gratefully out the gym side door afterwards. But I was glad. It felt good to find a response to a challenge.

Yet in class, my heightened fear state continued to show. Working with Peter in day class, I struggled against his strength, trying uselessly to bring him down from the attack.

"Start over!" Sensei's voice whipped across the room as he spied my useless struggle against superior strength as Peter stood, the immovable object despite my grappling at his arm.

"Never pit your strength against your opponent. You're expected to be smaller, less skilled. Use energy and technique. Come on, Carla. Stop useless struggles."

Again I tried the move, as Peter attacked with a sharp strike to my neck, met by my moving into the blow, grasping his arm, shifting my weight and flipping him artfully into the air.

"Good. Do it again," Sensei commanded as Peter rose with grace, bouncing onto his feet and grinning at me.

Work and clients kept me busy the rest of the time, but the evenings gave me space to brood, as I deliberated, trying to find my way through this new darkness. Jack was busy or gone, Nate, now a senior, was with his friends. Jennie stuck to me like glue.

I really wanted the darkness and the time to ponder the depths. Try to figure it out. Sort the vague dreams of rituals, not for murder but for sacrifice of light and purity. Nightly they came. I wanted to think about them alone.

It was useless, and I was sinking like a stone. Jennie was right there, at my side, constantly. I got no peace. Even going to bed, turning off my night light, she was still sitting there, chattering away. The magpie in her heaven. Finally I would chase her off, demanding she close the door. Jack would come to bed later. The pattern became nightly as my frustration at lack of alone time grew.

Dreams followed my footsteps through the night. Dreams of lying alone and sick, something white covering me, systemic illness weakening me. Dreams of Jennie playing somewhere and not safe. Dreams of being in a waiting area of a building, sick and not knowing if I would live or not. Awakening, I paced, using my Sacred Path cards to find direction and strength.

I met Ben for lunch, his towering form waiting for me as he stood patiently outside Mickey's Bar and Grill, oblivious to the snow pummeling his overcoat while cars on the highway flew by. Solid Ben. Not much fazed him.

Inside we ordered hamburgers, fries and Cokes, while warming up to the sounds of water glasses and silverware and the smells of chargrilling from the kitchen. A fun lunch, I was always glad to see Ben. But I knew I wasn't up to par, and saw his worried look under the bushy white eyebrows as he masked it with chatter about his family. My own awareness matched his worry. But what was wrong? I didn't know.

Vortex

Early summer it might be, but it was **hot**. My Datsun's air conditioner barely kept up as I drove the interstate to Gabe's office. Of course, my Datsun was getting pretty old. But I loved it. And it was better than the Pinto I'd had in graduate school, I reminded myself. After the news came out about those, I was always afraid I was going to blow up. Hopefully, as I got out of graduate school debt, I'd get something better.

Stepping out into the scorching heat at Gabe's parking lot, I gasped. It wasn't any cooler up north. North was supposed to be cooler. So much for that theory. In about three seconds flat, my shirt and shorts were sticking to me while damp black curls sheltered my face. Escaping into the building, I sighed.

Generic office building air conditioning felt good. Walking down the hall to his office, I was aware of the day's odors, the antiseptic from the doctor's office and a cigar smell oozing out from under the lawyer's door. Stale cigarettes in the hall container added to the mix as I stepped into the cleaner air of Gabe's waiting room.

Deliberately setting my large Diet Coke on the square table by my chair, I grinned at Gabe. "Why'd you turn up the heat, Dude?" My chin high, it was a friendly challenge.

He shook his head, his expression conveying hopelessness.

"Trouble. You're always bringing me trouble. If you don't have it, you make it." Comrades in battle. Teasing continued it's importance.

"So how are you?"

"Not so good, actually."

"Why? What's going on?"

I told him about my fatigue, remnants of scary nightmares, a sense of overall depletion. I was getting discouraged. This was not what I had in mind for my life.

"And furthermore, Jennie is driving me nuts! Just nuts! Nuts! She won't leave me alone, Gabe. She's always just right there. Even on Saturdays now, she's up at breakfast, talking on and on. Far be it from me to be able to just veg out somewhere and think about all this. She's right there, chattering away about something. Or finding something for us to do. The girl can think up more things for us to do . . ." I was taking a breath, ready to rant on, when I looked more closely at Gabe, lost in thought. Oops.

Instead of some teasing reply, which I expected, he'd turned silent and thoughtful on me. Less than a minute later, he was looking directly at me.

"Carla, we've seen this behavior before."

"Uh oh."

"Remember when we hit some really difficult work with your incest recovery? You were having some pretty serious depression and could easily have gotten suicidal. It was a tough time. And she did the same thing. Remember?"

I did remember.

"I also remember that she's your canary in the mine. She's worried about you, Carla. She's not very self aware, but she's a very psychic girl, and she's acutely aware of how you feel. When she's doing this behavior, it's a warning sign to you. The canary is telling you something." He was seated in his chair now, coffee on his stool while he leaned forward, elbows on his knees, urgent. He wanted me to get this.

I thought about it. He was right, historically anyway. "She is pretty psychic."

"Yes, but not clear to herself that she's picking up on you psychically or on what she's got. She's just feeling it, and showing you with her actions. So, Carla, what's she picking up from you?"

I knew where he was heading, and I sure didn't like it. I didn't want to look at how I'd been feeling. Feeling it was enough. I sulked, scrunched back in my chair.

"How depressed are you, Carla?"

Quick evaluation, followed by, "Well, some."

"How much?"

"Well, a fair amount, I think." Defeated, I sat back up straight, leaning forward, matching his posture. "I just want to be alone. It's OK with my work. I can concentrate on that, and I'm still doing good work. But when I'm not there, I just want to be alone."

"Sleeping?"

"As much as I can."

"Eating?"

"I'm not hungry. Nothing looks good."

"Right. And what are you doing for fun?" He was checking the bases. The conclusion was obvious to both of us.

"All right. All right. I'm depressed. Anyone would be."

"Time to think about meds. Talk to Ben." He knew Ben did my meds when I needed them.

"All right. I will." I could be gracious in defeat if I had to. Trouble was, I knew he was right. Time to be cooperative. One did have to choose one's battles, after all.

"So, let's get you on the massage table and see what you need energetically." He stood up and stretched, reaching for the ceiling and then relaxing, pulling the table out from the corner. Coffee on his desk, he pulled the stool up to the table, while I arranged the sheet and got settled.

Carefully scanning me, he filled my energy system, noting leaks. We spent time patching energy ruptures and filling them until he found a particularly large one. He had me identify it: a knife with a large inverted black cross. I had taken the knife to protect a child in the cult. The guides said that I had to take it out. A confirmation that I was no longer choosing to hold the pain for another. A choice and an action that was mine alone.

Meticulously, Gabe taught me how to remove it, teaching me how it was on another Plane, another level of existence. Seeing with my inner eyes, he coached me through the process. A good skill to have, I thought to myself as I placed it on a table in that other realm. We finished our preliminary work and took our break. Still, I was dragging my feet, the depression pressing on me like an invisible weight that I couldn't describe adequately. The sense of foreboding came back, washing over me and giving me the shivers.

"So, what else?" he queried.

I reluctantly thought of my answer, and then put it all out there. "Lots of bad dream fragments that I don't remember. Restlessness. But you know, the thing that I keep going back to is the storm cellar. That was just such an evil-feeling place. The energy pull was like a vortex, dragging me in there. From beyond that even, as if the source of the vortex originated way back deep." I was thoughtful, turning my attention into my own experience and feelings, allowing my mind and feelings to travel through the threads of loose associations.

"That vortex pull seemed to emanate from deep within the earth and beyond, almost from forever, if such a thing is possible. Coming from some deep unknowable place, through the depths of that storm cellar and reaching out to whatever it could pull in."

He sat on the bar stool beside me, listening quietly, nodding, encouraging me to go on.

"The vortex was profoundly evil. It was such a dark place, as if it and the work associated with it, had gone on for centuries and centuries. It was deep. Palpable. Like a thick, sinuous inky fog snaking out in search of prey.

Gabe waited patiently while my mind sifted the images and feelings.

"And you know, I can't help it, but I've thought so much about the little girl. Something just wasn't right. There was something else wrong with her. When they brought her out. She just didn't look right. A feeling I had. I know she was dirty and covered with the ashes, but there was something else wrong. It's as if her spirit glow was gone."

I was done. That was it. Gabe sat quietly, listening to guidance. I waited patiently for him, having learned. His head was turned slightly to the left, deep eyes serious, the dark hair framing concern in his expression. Quietly, he rose. From his desk, he got the white sage, silently smudging me again and then the room.

"Grandmothers, Grandfathers, Powers of the Four Directions," he began. His prayers were quiet, powerful, gathering energy until it was tangible. A thick substance that I could feel with my senses. The space was now sanctified, pure, and full of spirit. He stood on my right, giving me some sage to let it continue burning. I held it over my heart, while he put his right hand on my hip and his left on my shoulder. Quietly but forcefully, he sang the Beauty Blessing, the energy vibrating through me and through the room. He stood back.

"We can't go into that evil vortex, Carla. It is much too powerful. Neither can our guides."

I was surprised. Not even the guides? I thought they could go anywhere. Do anything. They were so powerful. This must be quite a place. I didn't want to think about that. Fear wasn't what I needed right now. Warrior time. Focus.

"Instead, we are going to go to the Sacred Fire. At the count of three, we will be there."

I settled in to prepare myself for the energy jump.

"One. Two. Three."

I was aware that we were standing together in the meadow.

"Look around. What do you see?"

I looked. "A circle of Native Americans. They look like Elders, similar to the ones who guarded the pathway before."

"Yes. These are the Grandmothers and the Grandfathers. They are here to help us. There's another. Do you hear him?" I could hear the smile in Gabe's voice, as I listened in that other plane.

I smiled too. "Yes. I hear him. White Wind is whinnying." I saw him race up towards us, white head high with his spirit, tail arching, flaring back behind him, as he reared, spun and raced for the distance, to guard from afar. His own blessing and presence for our work.

The Sacred Fire roared before us, even higher than before. The heat from the flames warmed my face, making it hot as a rush of small embers were carried up by a searing draft, flung into the air to be following by more, dancing in the wind. The smoke curled around us, filling me with the comforting smell of woodsmoke. Blazing, the flames reached ever higher.

"Feel the Presence and Power of the Sacred Fire." It was an immense presence, filling and surrounding us with Power.

His voice came again as he stood beside me on that other Plane. "Feel the pull of it, the rush of sound as it reaches clear to the heavens."

It seemed to have grown even larger and did, indeed, reach for the heavens. It was as if an enormous source of energy filled me and poured through me, yet the force of energy within me was only the smallest particle of the power in front of me, as the Sacred Fire grew in heat, intensity, and energy.

"For something like the vortex you described, we need an equal and opposite force to counter it. The Sacred Fire will be that equal and opposite force. I want you to visualize the vortex now."

Reluctantly, I turned my attention inward, to be able to see and feel the vortex. "There it is. I do see it. And it's whirling. Man, I hate that thing. Do you see it spinning, Gabe?"

"Um hm. I see it."

"It's pulling anything it can into it's depths, and it's as if those things disappear completely from all light and life."

"Now watch the Fire, Carla."

I watched. Mesmerized. The Sacred Fire rose from it's base, slowly moving even higher, developing a force and direction all it's own. Slowly, then more quickly it whirled, increasing in force and power, lifting up further into the sky.

"Gabe, it's moving towards the vortex!"

"I know. Watch it, Carla."

My heart pounding, my mouth grew dry as I watched the Fire move across the heavens. Holding my breath, I watched in suspense as the Fire whirled in ever increasing ferocity, a clockwise spin growing tighter and more powerful with each passing second. Approaching its pinnacle, it turned towards the earth and the vortex, waiting below.

I looked again at the vortex, realizing it was spinning counterclockwise, deep, black and furious. Evil and hate reached out from its core, pulling, pulling, reaching for light and life, to pull it in and feed the ever-hungry nucleus. Slowly the Fire approached, as the vortex reached out to suck it in. The ultimate triumph, to feed off that sacredness.

Slowly, ever so slowly, the two forces met, each revolving in it's own chosen direction of Light and Dark. Gabe and I both held our breaths, waiting for the outcome between these two primal forces.

Time stood still.

Like ultimate-stakes arm wrestling, the two powers held their own. One force blazing clockwise, the other vibrating with darkness, steadily and powerfully sucking counterclockwise. Lifetimes seemed to pass, while we held our breaths, watching the matching forces fighting for the ultimate victory. Light and Dark, paired.

Then slowly, there appeared a subtle shift. Something was different. Like two heavily-muscled arm wrestlers, the shift was there, yet there was nothing obvious to tell us the outcome. We waited yet again.

Another shift, then another, and another.

"Gabe." Urgent. Was it true?

"I know." He sounded just as breathless.

The power had shifted, and slowly the direction of the vortex was changing, turning ever so tentatively. Gradually. Clockwise. Reversing its powerful, destructive direction.

We both let our breaths out. I felt a release of energy around me as the Grandmothers and Grandfathers relaxed ever so slightly. The outcome had not been foretold.

"Watch, Carla. Watch what is happening."

The vortex sluggishly continued reversing its spin. With a tediousness it released its power, giving in to the force of the Sacred Fire. Gradually, reluctantly, it settled into its new pattern. The Fire separated, moving back into the heavens on its return path to its source. I watched with split attention, aware of the Fire returning while I carefully watched the vortex. Then I saw it.

"Gabe!"

"What do you see?"

"Things are coming out of the vortex. It's as if it's releasing things that have been pulled in there over time. I can't believe it! Look!" My voice was rising higher in my excitement. I could hear him chuckling, relieved at the outcome and at what we were seeing.

"What's coming out, Carla?"

I settled to watch, while I sensed inward. "Everything that's been pulled in. Everything, Gabe. All of it." Excitement gave me a chill up my spine in spite of the heat.

"Be specific. Tell me what you are seeing. What's coming out?"

"Oh, man. Souls, Gabe. Souls and lights, weapons, belongings, more souls." I knew in my heart that's what they were. I could see them, the luminous lights belonging to others, those souls taken in evil ceremonies. Sacred objects. Weapons used in sacrilege. Candles used in black worship. Medallions used for protection by the innocent. A complete mix of things used against those of the light, their souls and their sacred tools. Breath let out slowly, stunned by the immensity of it.

The return of the sacred filled me completely. I didn't know whether to cry from joy, or jump up and down from all the excitement. I think I did both.

"Watch, Carla, and see what comes out for you."

In all the excitement, I hadn't thought of that. His comment stopped me dead in my tracks. Astonished, I refocused, leaving my celebrating to cautiously return to the continuing flow of souls and objects washing out from the center of the vortex.

Watching, searching the growing stream of souls and possessions, I stayed soul-still. Would there by anything for me? What might it be? Suddenly I knew. Seeing it, I knew it for what it was.

"A shimmering light, Gabe. It's a soul. It's a part of mine."

"Give it to one of the Grandmothers. She will keep it safely."

I agreed, watching it as it floated to a waiting Grandmother's outstretched hands, where she held the globe of light in her cupped palms, cradling it safely and reverently. Satisfied, I turned back to Gabe.

"What else is there for you?"

I watched the continuing stream from the vortex, like precious objects cascading in the current of a great river. Deeply relieved and satisfied at the freedom emerging, I watched the emptying stream, another object swirling from the core of the earth and out into the night. Surrounded by the other lights and radiant objects, this one glowed in a special way. I knew it belonged to me.

"It's a knife."

"Is there anything else for you?"

I watched again, but the objects emerging had no special psychic pull or recognizable light. The cascade was slowing down and soon there was very little emerging. Then, nothing more.

"No. Nothing else." With a joint sigh, we returned our attention to the work at hand.

"Bring the knife here to the Fire." Gabe had turned to the Sacred Fire, back in its place, roaring majestically before us.

With the will of my mind, the knife came to me as I stood by the Fire.

"Now give it to one of the Grandfathers."

I turned, facing the Grandfather who stood straight and calm behind me, handing him the knife carefully, hilt first as I'd been taught in my martial arts.

"Now tell the Grandfather what it was used for."

I looked at the wise old man, the white hair tumbling down his back, weather-beaten wrinkles lining his strong face. His buckskin jacket was held in place with a belt, beading decorating his clothes. Standing before him, empowered by his strength, I knew the answer.

"It was used to ceremonially cut out my soul." Grandfather nodded as I uttered the words, affirming the truth of my statement.

Gabe also nodded as I turned to him. "Yes, it was an offering. They gave your soul as a ceremonial tribute. A gift to the Darkness." He looked at the knife once more, then back at me.

"Can this knife be used for good?"

"Yes." The answer had come to me with a surety.

"Then accept it from Grandfather, and place it in the Fire. You won't be burned. Watch what happens."

Bowing slightly to Grandfather, another habit from my martial arts and the only way I knew to convey my respect, I accepted the knife from him. Carefully, I placed it in the Fire, giving a small shove as I let go.

I watched as the flames accepted the knife, flowing rapidly up and down the blade and over the handle, dancing with hungry tongues of fire. As the knife heated, it turned from black to red. Then to orange. Quickly the flames swept up and down, heating it to gold, and finally to white. Watching spellbound, I described what I saw to Gabe.

"It's purified. Now take it out and give it as a gift to Grandfather. You won't be burned."

I reached tentatively in, then remembered the times we had stood in the Fire, unharmed. Trusting, I grasped the knife, pulling it from the flames. Turning to Grandfather, I again handed it to him, hilt first.

"This knife was not created for evil purposes. Some are, but this one was not. This knife was created to be used simply as a tool. Tell Grandfather to take it and use it for its proper purpose. It is a gift."

A gift I was glad to give. It was so good to be returning something to the Old Ones who had stood watch with us. "Grandfather, this is for you. Please use it in light as it was meant to be used."

He smiled to me, acknowledging me as he held the knife. Then he stepped silently back one step, his part in our work completed.

"It is done. We are finished here. Thank Grandfather for the care of your knife." I did as Gabe instructed.

"Now thank Grandmother for the care of your soul." Things were moving quickly. I had nearly forgotten that she was holding it so tenderly. I stepped before Grandmother, marveling at the light shimmering around her and around the globe of light in her hands.

"Thank you, Grandmother, for your reverent care of my soul. I am grateful for your help." Her grey hair rippled around her as her kind eyes looked lovingly at me. She nodded her appreciation of my thanks.

"Grandmother will give it to those who know how to return it to you. It will be done for you." Again, I looked at Grandmother, nodding my thanks. Her smile lit her face, and I knew she would know what to do.

"Now thank all the Old Ones for helping us. Their circle has assisted us in this work." Together Gabe and I thanked them. I turned to each, my right arm upraised in salute and thanks. They nodded in return. I knew they'd been quite willing to help.

"It's time to go, Carla. Anything unfinished for you?"

I thought about it, still overwhelmed by the work. "No, not that I can think of. I think we covered all the bases."

"Good. At three, we will be in my office. Ready?"

"Yes."

"One. Two. Three." I felt the shift as we crossed dimensions, and slowly opened my eyes, letting the energy flow up my legs, stretching a bit to loosen up the tense muscles. Looking at Gabe, I was surprised. He was clearly stunned and shaken at the work.

"Gabe?"

He shook his head, as if to release some of the feelings.

"Let's put the table away, then we'll talk."

The office back in order, the table in its place in the corner, we sat in our respective chairs. Office sounds came to my awareness with a phone ringing, and people talking in the hallway to the business office. The smell of popcorn drifted in as someone prepared their snack. I watched him as he took a deep breath and settled in. I leaned forward slightly, my body asking the question again.

"Carla, I would never deliberately go for this. And I would never on my own know how to do it. I was given a lot of direction. This was **big**!"

I sat back, thinking of the power of the work and the implications. This wasn't just about us. Indeed, it was huge. I watched him while he sorted his own emotions and thoughts.

"This has released everything that has ever been taken in by this cult, over the generations that it has existed. That site has been used repeatedly because it was naturally a vortex for the energy that was gathered there. Kind of like ley lines that you hear about, yet it worked in reverse with a natural pull. The cult must have discovered it long ago, and then used it for their own worship of evil."

"What happens to all the other things that came out?"

He thought and listened to his guidance. "It all went up into the atmosphere, to be returned by spirit to the proper owners. The goodness went to the victims, to assist them in their healing journeys. The evil has been returned to the senders." He paused. "What was awry has been set right, for many people over a very long time."

Together we sat, still in awe of the magnitude of the work. This had affected countless lives, the impact reverberating throughout the world and across time. It was a sobering thought. I began to get a bit nervous about the consequences, always fearful when I considered payback. Such a common part of cult life. Gabe sensed it.

"We did not do this. It was done through us. This was Spirit." I understood that. We had no power to do this. We were, truly, the instruments.

He looked at me again. "It's like we were the gateway for the forces of Good to achieve this shift. Very amazing. It still shakes me a bit."

I smiled at him. "Me, too."

Gabe continued. "You know, I think I've learned through difficult experiences in other lifetimes that we don't take credit for the power. It's not our power. That's how some people get into trouble and begin to think *they* have the power. It's never theirs. It only flows through them."

We were both exhausted, consumed by our thoughts and reflections of what had happened. It was good for us to have a chance to reflect on it together. I had another consideration.

"You know, Gabe. It comes to mind how different this is from hypnosis. This was happening with and to us, and was on another plane of existence. I couldn't possibly have made it up, like a visualization, if I'd tried. It just unveiled itself as we went along. Quite a different process."

"You're right. Been thinking about that for a while, haven't you." His eyes crinkled in the small grin, slowly recovering some of his own energy. "There is a really big difference, but hard to describe until one experiences it."

I continued. "The other thing that comes to mind is that some of my exhaustion has been from the soul loss from their ceremony. It seems to me that when we do our healing work, we reopen the energy of the experience. Either to be cleared or healed. Or sometimes not. In this instance, it reopened a pull on my system and was draining me energetically. As well as emotionally and physically."

"I think that's true. That's why we continue to clear you energetically, and keep filling you. To keep you in shape to do this kind of work. It takes a lot of energy to do the processing and healing work you're doing. And our work is indeed reopening the events. They've been sealed to a degree, although you seem to leak a certain amount of energy in order to keep them sealed. Then we open them, and we've seen both the positive results and the risks.

I looked at the clock beside me on the small table. "Time for me to go, kid. And for you to get some lunch and recharged."

"Yeah, I know. By the way, Carla," he added as an afterthought while standing up and stretching, hands towards the ceiling. "Have you talked to your brother or sister about this recently?"

"Are you kidding?" It was sarcastically spoken. "They were never abused, remember. My brother was raised in the perfect family. 'Leave It To Beaver,' and all that."

"What about your sister?"

"Oh, she knows she was abused, but not this. She had a psychic tell her that she wasn't abused like this, so she's sorry that I was, but nothing additional. Amazing, isn't it."

"Yep. We get the memories if and when we are ready. Not before."

"Actually, that's probably good for them. I find them really pretty fragile, too. But it still makes me mad."

He grinned at me as we walked to the door. "Yeah? Gee, what a surprise."

Opening the door, he was serious again. "We did a lot of work today. Be sure you take good care of yourself. You might want to pick up some peanuts in the shop downstairs to keep you til you stop."

"Sounds like a good idea to me. Probably some chocolate, too." I grinned mischievously at him, pleased for an excuse for chocolate. A brief good-bye hug, and I was walking out his office doors, leaving Gabe to his own reflections. Downstairs, I fortified myself from the long rows of nuts and chocolate in the first floor pharmacy. Good nourishment for traveling, I reminded myself.

The drive home was another done on auto pilot, my drifting thoughts consumed by the work we'd done, the images that I had seen, and the healing accomplished. Green fields, new plants, and animals in the fields passed unseen, as my thoughts stayed on our session. The vision of the vortex and the Sacred Fire coming together would stay with me for a long time.

That vision, and the feeling that we were actually able to do something to make a difference, kept me on a pseudo-high for several days. But the inevitable crash came. I actually noticed because Jennie was immediately at my side. Remembering what Gabe had said, and my reluctant agreement, I called Ben.

"Hey, kid," I started slowly.

"Hey. What's up?" He sounded relaxed, and I imagined him in his easy chair at home with a drink and the TV. I'd called in the evening so I wouldn't bother him at work.

"How about a cup of tea?" The question was tentative. I hated to admit that I needed help. I twisted the phone chord in my hand, creating even more tangles than before.

"Frisches in fifteen?" came his question.

"It's raining."

"Rain never stops docs. See you." The phone line went dead. We had a long-standing agreement. If either of us called for a cup of tea, there was a serious problem. We'd be there. He meant it. Part of me had been thinking maybe tomorrow. Or, next week. Dragging my feet, I rummaged in the top shelf of the overfull closet for an umbrella.

Fifteen minutes later, we were at Frisches, seated in a booth by the window, rain pummeling the glass beside us so that we nearly had to shout. Ben was in rare form, probably relieved that I had finally cried "uncle." Finally, he could do something concrete to help. The dream of a physician.

Our tea was refilled several times while he entertained me with stories of his family. Finally I started wiggling in my booth. Depression was making it hard to concentrate, even with Ben. He sighed, pulling out his script pad for my antidepressants.

"Don't forget the side effects, Carla. We've done this before, so they should be familiar."

"I know. I know." Grumbling.

"Hey. Better living through chemistry." It was the office motto. I remembered the times we had said it when I worked there, and smiled ruefully. I hated to acknowledge that he was right, but it was really time. Dang.

With a motion, he called the waitress and took care of our bill. I dreaded the thought of the rain still smashing into the windows, envisioning myself soaked to the skin. It never bothered Ben. He figured you got wet. Then you dried. Nothing emotional about it. Wish I could do that.

Standing and struggling into raincoats, I thanked him again.

"That's what friends are for," he grinned, giving me a hug around my shoulders. He walked unhurried into the rain, water pouring from his white thatch of hair and over his tan raincoat. Turning with an impish grin, he waved before disappearing into the black night and driving rain.

Friends, I thought to myself, putting up my umbrella. They're a pain in the behind. And what would I do without them. That night I started the meds.

The next day I had a brain. More than two synapses to rub together. Relief flooded my body. While I still felt the crushing weight of fatigue, my depression had lifted. From the last time on the meds, I recognized the change in my thinking and knew the emotional relief would follow. Thank God for small favors. I would wait with some patience for the emotional side to lift. Jennie found a life and disappeared. My own life returned to a more normal routine of work, business and fun lunches and family routine.

One morning I awoke to a dream of being in a place that seemed like a university, although I knew that I was sick. A group setting, the people were wonderful, caring for me with a love and compassion that I had rarely experienced. Different individuals, all in white robes, were coming in to check on me at various times, and I knew it to be a group effort. An odd place, everything seemed to be differing shades of white, suspended in a rarified atmosphere of light and love. I loved waking from that dream, feeling cherished and refreshed. The fatigue still followed my steps, but the dream gave me hope.

Years later, I had a session with a local astrologer, Terry, who worked in the back office of his bookstore. Short, rumpled brown hair and bookish glasses, his round table was filled with charts, random Xeroxed papers, a large globe and mounds of books. The back window emptied onto an alley letting in sounds of sirens rushing their precious cargo to the local hospitals. In the midst of seeming chaos, he consulted his charts. At the end, I had a final question.

"What about a period about five years ago. Anything about my health then?" An afterthought to the session.

He peered at my chart, consulted two books and some files, then looked over at me.

"Well, that time was an interesting one, according to your chart. It seems you would have been afflicted with some kind of debilitating disease which would cause a lot of lethargy. It would be a difficult time, and also a dangerous one for you in some ways."

He looked some more, aware of my stillness and intense interest in his answer.

"It looks as if this was quite a struggle. Could have been a severe illness. Yet it was necessary as a way to slow you down so that you could absorb the psychic and emotional hits that you were taking then. Your tendency would be to think you could just take it and go on, but your system needed space, time to integrate and reconfigure itself. You had to be slowed down significantly in order for your body and energy field to have the time it needed to heal. You couldn't go at your usual pace and take those blows."

He looked up, brown eyes asking if the information fit. It certainly did. Too bad I hadn't had that perspective then.

East Meets West

My dream practice was continuing to develop, the positive mixed in with the scary. Dreams of successfully confronting danger, followed by dreams of spiritual wisdom and encouragement. Waking at peace, and with curiosity, I would reach for the paper I had scratched on in the middle of the night. A sense of spiritual presence comforted me deep into the nights and on into the daylight hours.

One morning I awoke to find a note about the obvious: TThe *great* importance of *waiting* while healing goes on." What a bummer. I could have waited a long time without wanting that one. And yet, I was learning patience. In spite of myself. Maybe in a couple more lifetimes, I'd have a handle on it. With great luck.

Yet even with the support of my dream practice, I could tell that I was continuing to slide. My energy was increasingly depleted, my spirit was shaky, and emotionally I stayed in a funk. I had real working tools, and they were helping. God knows, they were probably keeping me from a full out crash. But it was a tough time. I remembered the lesson from karate and Sensei. Don't run away from my fear. Faith is a verb. I tried to practice it as a real thing each day. It was tough.

A week later, and I was glad to get to Gabe. Life at home was a bit overwhelming. I walked in, dragging my behind. He looked at me, and grinned lopsidedly.

"Yes?" as he settled in his chair, rocking back a tad.

"I feel trashed."

"Why?"

"My energy swings, it's hard to keep up in karate, people telling me what to do when they don't know the whole story, telling me what their guides are telling me to do. Zeesh. This gets very confusing. Who do you listen to?" I swung a sandal in one hand and my Diet Coke in the other.

"So, seriously, what do you think?" he asked me right back. "Do you know?"

"Actually, I'm finding it confusing. Some of the things that people are saying are really bewildering. Like they all have different ways to get my health back, and different reasons for why I'm sick. And the things that their guides are saying, too. When most of them don't know what's going on with the rest of this."

He frowned. "You know about their personal opinions, Carla. Just acknowledge them, and do what you know to be best."

"That part I can do, and have been. It's when they evoke their spiritual wisdom or their guides that I move into doubting myself."

He sighed, looking within, then back at me. "Spiritual guidance can be a tricky thing. You can't take whatever you get from the spirit realm and consider it 'spiritual truth.'" That was a good reminder. "You have to consider it as you do any other information. You consider it and test it out, as you would anything else.

"It's especially true when someone is channeling. The channeling is only as good as the channel. It's sort of like pouring pure water through a pipe. Sometimes the pipe is clear, and the water comes through in its purity. But if the pipe is rusty, the water comes through murky and clouded. It's true with channeled messages, too. If the person doing the channeling is clear, the message will come through well. But sometimes they are not, which leads to distortions. After you listen well, you can begin to hear more clearly what is the channel or person, and what is the spirit guide."

"That makes sense. I get that." I put my sandal down and relaxed, sipping the Diet Coke.

"The other thing you need to remember is that you are at the center of this process, and so you need to decide what is truth for you. Truth as an abstract concept doesn't work here. What's true for someone else may not be true for you, for example on what will help you to become healthy. This is your journey and you're in charge."

I sat up straighter, responding to his talk. In a way, I knew all that. Yet, I had needed the reminder. Everyone I knew had been telling me how to get well, and were mad if I didn't follow their advice. This was more empowering, and put me back in the center of my healing journey.

"Thanks, kid." I smiled at him. "You know, I really am glad you're my therapist." It was deeply true. We were well matched.

He grinned again, going for that coffee addiction placed on his stool.

We had a good session, working with his Australian aborigine guide to help us get out negative thought forms implanted in insects by the cult. The guide had us "smoke them out" by using extra amounts of sage. We'd had the window open. No problem.

As I was leaving, I noticed the first glimmer of an actual problem. The key in the elevator control panel as I stepped into the elevator. At the end of my sluggish ride down to the first floor, the creaky slow doors opened on a bank of firemen, complete with yellow suits and axes. Second clue.

Now, standing across the street accompanied by chasing children and the smell of McDonald's fries mixed with sticky buns from the mall food court, I could see the ladders going to the top of the building, searching for the source of the alarms.

What to do? Nothing. You can't exactly tell the firemen that we were smoking out thought forms on instruction of an invisible aborigine shaman. Give me a break.

Only later did we learn of silent smoke alarms and wind drafts that could suck the smoke back into the ducts. Indigenous healing and modern society were not a perfect fit. Gabe had to remind his guide that we worked in office buildings, not the Australian outback.

At home, I awoke restless, the dream haunting me, sweat covering my body under the covers. Confusion filled my mind, as I remembered the room of the dream with people milling around. Chaotic energy. Trying to gain understanding, I sometimes used the screen technique, pretending to watch the scene on a huge TV screen far away. I tried it, but this show was too scary. I didn't want to watch. Bad things were being done to people, and I didn't want to know.

In the back of my mind, a question formed: "Do you know what they did to your sister?"

Fear rippled through me, and the cold sweat returned. I tried to see it on the TV screen, but it faded to gray and disappeared. What happened to my sister? I reached for the comfort of Jack's body. He was gone. I'd forgotten about his trip. Restless, I got up to pace the house before returning to an anxious sleep. I would take the dream to Gabe.

I felt like Alice and I'd just fallen through the hole. Disoriented, life not making any sense, I had no energy at all. Wearily I dragged myself from task to task. Jack returned home with tales of adventure. Jennie and Nate were holding their own. I went to work and slept. I knew that I needed help. What was the problem?

I called Gabe for an emergency session. He reminded me of Summer Solstice. Of course. How could I forget the seasonal anniversary reactions. We processed that, yet my health slide continued. I waited, tried patience, worked on my health and emotions, yet nothing got better.

The time came when I even had to quit karate. This was getting way too serious, I thought dejectedly, sitting on the upper deck watching my friends move in the synchronized rhythm of kata. Longing to be there, knowing I couldn't possibly keep up.

My karate family was more than sweet about it, sitting with me after class in the bar/kitchen, talking about comebacks, encouraging me, giving me hugs as I got up to leave. This was so important. What would I do without it, I wondered to myself.

"Practice in your mind," Sensei spoke sternly, wanting me to stay strong emotionally. "You'll be back. Don't give in to this." Warrior to the end. And I would be back. I hoped.

I actually went to my regular physician, a sign of desperation if ever there was one. He ran tests which all came up negative. Well, I felt as if I had done the appropriate thing. Somehow, I had known they would come up that way.

Next, I called friends from the healing community, searching along the alternative care trail. This ultimately led to a homeopath in a nearby city. He was reputed to be more than good, and I needed help.

I arrived in the late afternoon. And was not reassured. It was the end house on the street, and something about it made me nervous. Perhaps the lack of a professional air. I had never seen anyone who worked out of their home. Not to mention that I and many of my friends would practice just that way short years later. But then, I didn't need a reason to be nervous. It was just there, as usual those days.

The gravel driveway ended next to the small white frame house which needed repair. Gutters were clearly clogged, gravel and dirt allowed small snippets of grass to pretend to be a lawn. Further back, grass grew wild with a few small gangly trees. The early fall leaves were beginning to create dappled patterns on the ground, the colors reconnecting me to a perception of beauty as I tuned in to my earth spirit friends, sensing their presence. It helped me steel myself against my misgivings. Something was making me really edgy. The reminder of beauty helped me keep going, to see this new person. I needed help. A small label by the door simply noted: Richard Owen, Ph.D. Nothing fancy here.

Opening the door, I found myself in a small reception area. Seated behind the shiny wooden desk directly before me was a thin woman topped with blond, frizzy hair, weird earrings and a very high voice.

"You're here for Dr. Owen?" she queried near the top of the voice range.

"Yes, I am."

"Fine. Take a seat in the next room," as she turned back to the stack of papers on her desk. Nervously I followed her directions, walking through the door on my right, and seating myself on a long couch flanked by two stuffed chairs. Before me was the largest big screen TV I had ever seen. The wall on my right was lined with bookcases. I leaned over, checking the titles. Celtic and travel, for the most part. Interesting.

Hearing a rustling, I turned my head left quickly to the window, just in time to see a three legged white cat dart out of sight behind the floor length drapes. The leaves of the nearby plant wiggled with the tug from behind the curtain. I sat on the edge of the couch, wondering what I had gotten myself into. This place felt strange.

The door on my left opened, as an overweight man walked into the room, stopping in front of me, evaluating. I felt naked, feeling that he could see right through me. I had too many secrets, and wasn't sure I wanted him to know them. I just wanted him to fix me. I glared at his appraisal.

"Hm. All right, then. Come this way," he smiled pleasantly, which for some reason made me even more cantankerous. Through the doorway, we turned right in a tiny hall, then down two steps to his consultation room dominated by a large wooden desk.

He sat ponderously behind the desk which I found covered with a machine, some loose bottles, and assorted crystals. Papers were piled everywhere, with stacks threatening to slide off the desk and merge with the mounds on the floor. This was worse than Gabe's office, by far.

I sat down in the straight chair indicated, with a short couch behind me against the wall. Again, he stared at me, tilting his head this way and that.

"What?" My sulky voice.

"Just checking." Then he seemed to come back to himself. "I will need to take a polaroid picture. Is that all right?"

"OK."

He did, returning to his chair as it creaked under his weight. He placed the picture in the machine.

"What's that?"

"It's called a radionics machine. It will help us a great deal. These are used extensively in western Europe, though not in the United States, unfortunately. Seems the FDA doesn't like them. But, as I said, they are used widely in western Europe and are very helpful. Now, I'll also need just a small clip of your hair. Is that all right?"

I'd never heard of such a thing. But I had passed desperate. "All right. If it will help."

"Humph." He cut a piece off, putting it in the machine too. An hour later his initial evaluation was completed.

"Humph." Again. "Well, yes."

"What?" I wanted answers. He looked at his results.

"The rarest of the rare, you are." He shifted in his chair. I didn't want to ask what he meant, though later I always wondered. "All right now. For your diagnosis. For starters, you are running at about 40% of your physical capacity. Does that feel about right to you?"

I was surprised. It felt quite accurate. I only nodded, as if fearful I would give something away. Why, I don't know. He was here to help me.

"This is a particular period of time. It's a seven month period in which you have been working a decision. The decision has been whether to live or die. It appears that you have made the decision to live. Does that feel accurate?"

Actually, it did. I was exhausted, but determined to get to the bottom of the problem with my health and to fix it. I had a life to live and I wanted to do it.

"Um hm. Well, we have work to do. By the way, did you know that you have a female spirit guide?"

"Yes. I'm aware of that."

"She's a mature woman. A family member from a long time ago."

That I didn't know. But it was reassuring that he could perceive my guide. Perhaps he would be all right, after all. A small spark of hope lit up in me, deep within. Yet I would retain my suspicion throughout our work, always fighting him to a degree, never reaching the easy trust I had with Gabe. He reminded me of an old-time wizard, and I just couldn't bring myself to trust him.

"I'll be starting you on a strict diet along with some homeopathic remedies and some vitamins." He listed them, giving the remedies to me. I'd never heard of half the vitamins, yet I would learn of them in the years to come, many of them supported in later research and becoming well known as beneficial. A man well ahead of his time, he knew his stuff.

"Come back in two weeks, and I'll have the more detailed evaluation completed. I'll also have your diet prepared." I didn't bother telling him I hated diets. And I detested and feared people being able to read me. Too many secrets. Practiced in blending in, hiding, it was not my idea of a good time to have someone see me accurately. But I needed him, and kept my feelings on a thin leash.

Two weeks later I was back in the disaster of an office. The three legged white cat had again appeared from behind the drapes, following us to his office where she jumped on the barely surviving small tree. More leaves scattered to the ground as she rustled among them.

Richard had followed me into the consultation room, smiling pleasantly, motioning to my chair. I wanted to hit him. Something about him still frightened me. I think it was the wizard feeling. Fear brought out my aggression with him, rather than retreat. What a pleasure I must have been to treat. Settling in, he turned to his papers by the machine.

"Well, I did the full evaluation with the radionics machine here. Let's see. It appears that you have both mono and epstein barr at the same time."

"My physician tested for mono but it didn't show up."

"I'm not surprised. But it did show up here. That's quite a combination, by the way." Richard went on to detail all the other things wrong with my system, including the heavy metal toxin levels, allergies, and more than I wanted to remember. Then he handed me a batch of papers.

"This is your diet."

"All this?"

"Yes. No meats, condiments, coffee . . ." He went on to describe all the things I couldn't eat, then started to discuss the things he did recommend. I was overwhelmed, sputtering.

"I can't do this."

"It's all right, Carla. All I'm really asking is that you eat real food."

"Huh?"

"Just real food. You know, nothing artificial."

I thought about it. Candy, snack crackers, McDonald's.

"I don't think I eat real food." This made me really grumpy. Tired, and no addict food? What was he thinking?

He smiled, folding his hands over his stomach and leaning back. "You can do it. I know you can." He didn't even have the grace to look worried. Real food wasn't in my vocabulary.

Much later, I asked him how he'd put up with my attitude. "It's just your warrior spirit. I can deal with that." Deal with it we did, achieving an uneasy truce, good enough to let me work with Richard and find my healing over time.

"So, Richard, why aren't I clairvoyant? Other people who have been abused are clairvoyant." The question had been bugging me again. I was back in his totally cluttered office while he ran more readings for my remedies. I couldn't believe anyone could work that way. Giant and small crystals were piled here and there, scattered around the machine and on it. Papers were in tilting stacks, threatening with each breath to fall to a scattered mess. Leaves from the tree cluttered the floor to his left, and shelves on the right held books, random papers sticking out, and piles of bottles. Not to mention the phone, a few extra diagnostic instruments piled here and there, and the abandoned juice mug. And he knew where everything was. Incredible.

We had come to a semblance of peace in our relationship, to the point where I now talked openly with him. While he did remedies, I figured I could perch on my chair, peering over the stack of papers, crystals and the radionics machine, and talk away. He was used to it.

"Why do you want to be clairvoyant?" He looked up briefly, that half-hidden smile that he seemed to have with my questions present as usual.

"Well, I want all of it, of course. I want to be able to see, and to hear."

"Why?"

"You know, I watch Gabe work, and it really helps him. Think how much it could help me in my work. And you are, too. What do you mean, why? It would be a big help."

He let out another sigh, leaned back in the creaky chair and gave me his full attention, or rather, this conversation his full attention, giving up the remedy readings for the moment.

"I think you chose not to be, on some level, Carla. If you could see, you would see things that you are not ready to see. Like rituals that would be too much for you."

"When I've gotten through this, will I be able to see?"

"Oh, yes, I think so. For now, you have translated that skill into your enhanced intuitive powers. You really are remarkably intuitive, you know."

I had to think about it, but I did know, back there in the recesses of my mind, rather than with any particular clarity. But his mentioning it put the issue in focus. I did recognize that I was particularly intuitive. And this did make sense.

"Besides, Carla, there are some risks with being clairvoyant that people have to be careful about."

"What do you mean?"

"Some people use it as a sort of power. Watch the people you know who are clairvoyant or clairaudient. It's an easy thing to misuse, you know. There are not a few people who use it as a way of being 'better than' their peers. Notice some of the people and see if you find that."

"Do you think I'd do that?"

"No, I think you have better clarity and awareness of the dangers. But it is an interesting thing to observe. Fairly subtle, but there."

A white streak flashed in the periphery on my right, while the fichus plant swayed dangerously, startling me. I jumped, while Richard made annoyed noises.

"That cat. Spook! I'll put her in the other room. What a pest. Too bad I can't put her outside, but she'd never make it, you know."

"Because of the missing leg?"

"For sure," as he got up to remove the offending surprise. Then back to the business of trying to get my health back.

Times got tough again, and I had to remember the ritual calendar. Every time I got symptomatic and had an increase in nightmares, Gabe or Richard and I referred to the calendar. Sure enough, ritual dates causing problems. The time of year could trigger me, or a smell, the sound of the insects changing, a casual scene with the fall grass turning colors. Anything could be a trigger. It was tough sledding, as I thought again of my sledding analogy with Gabe.

My sessions with Gabe continued to consist of energy work, taking implants etc. out, and increased processing. One day we seemed to finish a bit early, and I knew it was a time to ask the question that had been in the back of my mind for months. I led up to it slowly.

"Gabe, do we have time for one more question?" He looked at his watch, cocked his head to one side and then nodded at me.

"Let's give it a go."

I told him about my nightmare about my sister. Remembering it, I shivered. I had been putting this off, and couldn't hold it at bay much longer.

"What did happen to your sister, Carla?" he asked quietly.

I ducked my head. I just didn't want to deal with that. She and I hadn't been on good terms for years. Yet there was something there, pulling at me like a child pulls a mother's arm to take her somewhere. "I don't know."

"You know, you always avoid the topic of your sister."

I still wouldn't look at him. "She's so hard for me to be with. I do know that she abused me so much. Remember, we dealt with that in my incest work. Her locking me in the closet and setting me up for sexual abuse. I just don't want to deal with her."

Now I looked back up at him defiantly, having gotten cold feet. Easier to go after Gabe. "You have a problem with that?"

He smiled, knowing that I was back, out of the victim and scared stance.

"Not me." The challenge. "You can stay that way if you want. It's your life, you know."

There were days I could punch him. I crossed my left leg over the right, and folded my arms in front of my chest, none of it consciously. "All right, what do we do about it."

"Well, we could go back to the nightmare."

"You're a lot of fun today."

Gently, quietly with his rattle swirling and my fading into a trance state, we did go back. I saw what they did to my sister, able to describe it graphically. The way they tortured and abused her while blaming her for a petty transgression. I understood the suffering she had endured. Sorrowfully, I gave her light and energy in that time to assist her, and together Gabe and I returned to the present.

My relationship with her was never the same. Her mistreatment from the cult had been extreme. How could I hold any resentment towards someone who had been so badly treated. And in the process,

I gave up being her baby sister and victim, becoming her peer instead.

I knew she wasn't ready or able to remember. All I could do is pray for her. Didn't mean I would give up my caution, because I would not. I would always be careful around her, as much of her behavior was unconsciously motivated. But the relationship did shift that day, never to be the same.

A month later, I drove the long miles to Chicago once more. Oh, that Gabe worked closer to where I lived. But fall was in the air, and the drive was beautiful. Leaving my car in the outdoor lot, I walked like a kid to the building door, kicking the falling leaves and enjoying the smell they always carried. The brisk air was energizing, making it hard to return to office canned air. Reluctantly, I let the large doors close behind me, taking the slow elevators to his floor.

Once in his office, I noticed a new picture on his wall above the massage table. "What's that?" It looked like a hand painted watercolor to my inexperienced eye, and was of a man standing with different symbols around him.

"One of my guides," he answered, looking pensively at the painting. "He helps in my work. I knew him in another life."

"How does he help in your work?" The man was in a white robe, and in a pastoral setting.

"He helps with the children who have been abused." It was a rather simple answer, but his body language told me that was all I would get out of him today on those questions. Sighing, I turned back to business as he relaxed in his chair.

"So how are you, Carla?"

"Well, I've had good days and bad days. I mean, I get all hopeful when we work, and think maybe *this* is it. And I do feel better for a while. And then I feel all wiped out again."

"I expect that. How's it going with Richard?"

"That's fine. He's really a big help, even if we do argue a lot. He said that I've had something like four active viruses, and one of the heavy metal poisonings is lead. I think he has his work cut out for him."

"I think we all do," Gabe laughed at me. Then he turned more serious. "Really, Carla, it's important to keep in mind at all times that this is going to take time. You've been really sick. The work that each of us is doing will help, and hopefully over time, the low spots won't be as low and won't come as often. The work we're doing is slowly clearing your system and helping your healing. This is just not a quick fix."

I sighed heavily, leaning back and crossing my legs. "I know that's true. It's just that patience didn't come in my package."

"That's true! Now why don't we get you up on the table and see what there is to clear today." Together we moved the massage table out and covered it, while Gabe got the stool. Lying on my back, I was ready for him, looking at his picture again on my side. Then I settled back while he scanned.

"So what have you been noticing emotionally?" he asked after the first time over my system, working now to more carefully discern the energy around my solar plexus.

"That I'm really pretty nervous. More than the usual range. That's been pretty uncomfortable."

"Um hm. So I have the first part of the problem here," he responded, sitting back for a moment on his stool. "This is an etheric cocoon that is starting to activate."

"What do you mean?"

"Well, some of these things stay dormant until we do your clearing work. Some are preprogrammed to start to get active, or activate, if we get near certain material or memories. Others are implants that will start to activate if you start getting healthy. It's to make sure you don't get healthy and talk about what happened."

"Humph. They're not going to stop me or my healing." Now my back was up, as my family would say. That put me in the warrior mode. He smiled, knowing it would do just that.

It was a good session, and I was more aware of a pattern. I'd been having nightmares about a small boy who'd been murdered.

Sure enough, I'd taken charge of his soul, trying in my small way to protect him. With Gabe, we found the boy child as well as my young self, and we took both children to the man in the picture. The man was seen there as Three Wolves. The boy was delighted.

"By the way, Carla," Gabe reminded me. "There is another little girl here with Three Wolves that we know, too."

Suddenly I remembered the child we had brought to the healing place after she's been buried. She had been so little and so fragile then.

"I want to know how she is."

Gabe listened.

"She's what you would call a 'camp counselor', Three Wolves tells me. She has healed well and now she has a group of girls that she is helping. When it's her time, she will also come back to the earth. But she is safe and happy here."

I smiled to myself, grateful for her healing. Together Gabe and I left, walking the small trail in the woods while the girl child this time merged her footsteps with mine, blending into my essence.

"She's willing to come back with you, Carla, and be with you and help you be strong." Gabe was watching the two of us. I was relieved. Help, any way I can get it.

"Carla!" It was Pia's voice on the phone and a delight to hear from her. I hadn't talked to her in weeks. She was bubbling as usual, and I could imagine her long black hair swinging as she emphatically talked about how her life was going.

"So how are you, Carla?"

"I'm OK, Pia. Just working away."

"Clients and your therapy?"

"Yep. And I don't like the therapy work. I get tired of it, I want a different life, and none of that's going to change. So, I just keep plugging along." I smiled thinking of her. Thank God for people like Pia in my life.

"So," she paused, thinking, "let's watch a movie!" In my mind's eye, I could see her eyes glittering with mischief.

"All right. Good idea. Your place or mine?" I knew my family wouldn't mind. They loved her and my time with her. Good pieces in my life.

A week later I woke in the morning, shaking from the unusual dreams. I'd been having several of this variety, and it always left me rattled. One was about the foundations of Jack's and my apartment being bulldozed. It didn't seem to matter that we didn't live in an apartment. The other was about the seashore with breakers where people were standing. A huge wave suddenly washed in, scattering the people to the depths. An ongoing sense of foundations being destroyed, yet in each dream I was clear that I was all right.

I still felt shaken, with the dreams doing nothing positive for my confidence in my life or my day. Grumpily, I gathered myself together for the work day and headed out to the office. The early morning sun glittered on the trees and homes as I turned left out onto Front Street. Traffic was light, and I breezed through green lights and past the shopping center, soon turning left again into my office parking lot. My day had begun.

At the end of the morning, the fourteen year old boy dressed in black shirt with tattered black pants and big chains marched out of my office. My hope was that the anti-depressants would help. He was a good kid and I liked him, and was trying my best to reach him. The phone was ringing as he shoved the door closed behind him. I turned back into the consultation room, reaching across the desk for it.

"Dr. Sorensen."

"Carla, how about lunch?" Ben's warm voice reached across space, accompanied by the clatter of the medical practice behind him.

"Sure, Ben," I replied warmly. I could use a boost from the gang. Their constant ragging on each other and pranks would perk me up. Friends continued to be a welcome addition.

Night of Shadows

Days came and went, and the months followed the weeks. Inch by inch, another round of seasons rolled by. I was working on all areas of my recovery, especially the physical. Little piece of recovery by little piece. Energetic, physical, memories—we worked them, one by one. My biggest enemy was my impatience, but I'm not sure there would ever be another way to do the work. Systematically, carefully, methodically, we were working our way along the path. No real emergencies or disasters. Just my impatience, low energy level and recovery.

This time I was headed for Richard, and was incredibly restless. There was nothing in my current life that I could connect to it, which made me even more anxious. I fought it with paying attention to the beautiful fall colors of the leaves. We lived in a great area for that, with a multitude of different kinds of trees which changed varying colors, making a virtual artist's palette of colors as I drove south. The evergreens sprinkled in created a soothing counterpoint to the reds, oranges and yellows of fall. Focusing on beauty, I managed the drive in spite of my anxiety.

It was with considerable relief that I pulled into Richard's gravel driveway, after listening to my tapes in the car for the hour and a half drive. At least it wasn't as far as Gabe's. Parking under the small tree, I got out and stretched my stiff muscles. I walked around a bit before going in. Even driving was taxing with my low energy. Wandering the small yard, I wondered about my pervasive restlessness. There was always something, and the last few weeks, the restlessness had been driving me crazy. Made me wish I was still training in karate. Then I could just hit someone and feel better. With a sigh, I turned for the two steps up to the concrete porch, and let myself in.

Stepping into the waiting area, I took a seat on the stuffed couch, and glanced again at his books on the large coffee table. Celts, Ireland, and the general selection of office magazines. Patiently, more or less, I settled to wait.

Richard walked quietly through the door, nodding and I followed him through the crowded hallway, down the two steps and into his overcrowded office. Spook was there, bouncing around behind the curtains, chasing birds just outside the glass.

"Go on, Spook, scat," he fussed, waving his arm as he settled in his chair, eyeing me carefully over the massive desk. "Let's see. Hmm."

It still made me uneasy to have him checking me aurically the way he did. That naked feeling. But I was somewhat accustomed to it. I waited. "Well?"

"Hm. Yes. Well, we have some work to do. How are you feeling?"

I complained about my restlessness, my fatigue, and my general grumpiness of the work. I hated having to deal with any of it, but that was a broken record, so I left that part out. He knew about it. He listened, fiddling with his radionics machine, adjusting for homeopathic remedies.

"All right, let's do some energy work on you." He got up, and squeezed around the desk to head back up the stairs. Spook ran ahead of us, disappearing out into the waiting room and the heavy drapes. Richard and I turned right, and I lay down on his healing table.

It was the smallest room I could imagine. There was barely room for him to fit around the table. I liked his table, as it was piled in blankets and throws and felt really comfortable. On each side of me rose bookshelves, filled high with books, pillows, blankets and even more equipment. I had learned from him that he'd moved here from much larger quarters. I was sure he had not thrown out one thing.

Behind me was a large stereo system, which he ambled towards, putting on the usual Enya CD. I had grown to love it, as hearing it was associated with Richard working on me and bringing peace to my body and mind. Peace is no small thing. A very real outcome of energy work, and worth so much when one is dealing with such trauma.

"So tell me about your anxiety," he began as he adjusted the volume, pulled the curtain at my feet and came to stand beside me. His large form had become almost comforting, even though my perpetual watchfulness was always there. Furrowing his thick black eyebrows, he watched me carefully.

"I'm just really having trouble with my anxiety," I said again, seemingly for the hundredth time. Probably third. "It's more than it's been for some time."

Over time we had elicited different memories and glitches in my system, and he'd taken them out energetically. At other times, he just shook his head, pursed his lips and took them out without telling me.

"What are you taking out?" I'd ask, especially in the beginning.

"Black stuff." That's all he'd say. I had to assume that if it were a memory that I needed somehow, he'd let me know. And I wasn't hunting for more. I had my hands full of yucky stuff. He did tell me when it was something useful or necessary. What about today?

This time I lay quietly while he built my energy to the tune of Enya. I let my mind slowly drift, and found myself tensing as I lay there.

"What do you see, Carla?" he asked softly.

As he asked, the picture clarified. In my mind's eye, I saw an old stone wall.

"Where are you?" he asked quietly. I knew.

"I'm inside a very old building, that's been used in this way over a very long period of time, but only at certain times of the year."

"What's it look like?"

"I'm seeing an old stone wall in front of me. Large rectangular stones, roughly cut, placed together to form this wall. It's not well mortared, and there are lots of cracks. It's an inner wall. I'm like, between walls in a small passageway. I'm not to ever be here."

"And you're how old?"

"Four." It was very clear this time.

"Who is with you?"

"I'm with the big kids. I am the smallest one there. I think I bugged them by begging and begging to come along. We are all leaning up against this wall at different points. It forms a curve, as if the room itself is in a circular shape."

"What do you see?"

"Something is going on in there. I can see through the cracks, though I'm aware that it's really dirty here. This is not where people are supposed to be. The older children found this passageway.

There are candles, people, knives. It's a bad ceremony, but I'm not clear what's happening. I think they are killing someone. It's not really clear. I do know that only the 'big' people are there. Important people. But I don't know them all, and I should at least recognize them."

"What happens."

"I think the older kids get scared. I'm already so scared I want to wet my pants. The kids are pulling back, grabbing me by the arm. We are running away. They saw more than they wanted to see. We are splitting up and going to pretend to play so we aren't missed as a group."

"Another ceremony, Carla, one you weren't to see."

"Got that," I responded cryptically. He took more out of my energy field, and then we were done.

"OK, you can sit up now," he told me as he moved to the other side of the table, resting against his shelves that held blankets for the massage table. I tugged at my shoes as he handed them to me one by one, shaking out my hair in the process. With a sigh, he looked wearily at me. In my work with him, he was aware of the ugliness of the cult as much as I. I knew it affected him, although I also sensed his ability to deal with it. He knew his own dark side as well as his striving for the light, and he could cope with the darkness.

"This appears to be nearing a critical time in the life of your cult," he started. "Fall is usually intense anyway. What I am also getting is that there was a regional meeting where all the local cults came together. It was once a year, and their time for this gathering was November 19. I'm not surprised you've been anxious, since we're approaching it."

My anxiety peaked. "Richard, are those people still around?"

He checked in with his guidance. "No, my sense is that the last of the active members have all died. This seems to be one cult which actually died out."

"Well, there's that to be thankful for."

Quietly I waited to see if there was more work for us to do. I was feeling edgy again. *Enya* played on, usually soothing, now making me even more restless. He motioned for me to lie back down again. Quietly, I followed his instructions, waiting.

"Hm. What do you see, Carla?"

"I was aware of something off to my left."

"Um hm. Describe it to me."

"A clearing. I'm awfully small, I think."

Richard tuned in to the age, finding me at two, so small I was tethered to a tree to be sure I didn't wander off while the cultists worked.

Watching, I saw the men laughing, the young boy on a stand, sexual stimulation of the boy, and the hanging. Shocked, I drew back into the comfort of the blankets on the table.

"There is something still more important here for you to learn, Carla," Richard reminded me quietly of his presence, grounding me again in his work space.

"What?" I was resentful again of what they'd done.

"Watch and see what happens."

Watching, I did see. The men never let an opportunity pass by. Small as I was, they told me it was my fault. Looking with adult eyes, I recognized it as the sexual perversion and murder that it was, yet I knew that my child self totally believed them. It was my fault that the child had died. Everything was my fault. The programming had begun early.

"I hate it, Richard."

"I know, Carla. Me too. But you're recovering and that's what you need to look at now. I just think that last one was especially important for you. They started the programming very early with that cult. Nasty folks, they were."

His talk steadied me. They were nasty folks. I had to remember that. They used the child, and they used me also. This was not a good time, as my brother would say.

Listening to Richard's comments and tone, I knew that it was time to finish. Stretching, I slipped down off the table as he pulled the curtain to his healing room. His secretary walked by to his office, Spook darting under her feet. We were done for today, and both of us were tired. Giving him a hug and farewell, I was on my way.

Work kept me occupied much of the time, holding my cult worries at bay. Or that was my premise.

It was a Friday evening, and I was reading on the couch. Nate was out with his friends, with my hopes and prayers for his safety. Jennie was upstairs puttering in her room. I was worried about her. She seemed to be up there by herself more and more. I was sensing a general withdrawal in her lately, but couldn't find a cause. My mind slipped gears, wondering about her. Restless, I put my book aside, noted Jack working at the table, and wandered upstairs to see Jennie.

"How're you doing?" I asked the usual parental question, leaning on the side of her doorway.

"OK." The common adolescent response. At fourteen, what else should I expect, I wondered to myself. Especially from this one.

"Can I come in?"

"OK."

She was sitting on her full-size bed, surrounded by small girl treasures, sorting. Both the kids were sorters. It seemed a way of creating internal order, I suspected. I lay down on the end of the bed, the antique family quilt supporting a packrat's paradise.

"So how are things going for you?"

"OK."

This was going terrific. I rolled over and looked at her.

"You've seemed kind of quiet lately." She nodded. "School going all right."

"Yeah, it's all right." That part was quieter. There it was. The ripple in the pond.

"What's wrong with it?"

"It's so preppie." I understood that. The neighborhood school, yet this was an upscale suburb in many ways. Old families had lived here for generations. If you wanted to find the all American family, this was the place. And she was right. The kids were preppie. My kids weren't. It was a dilemma.

I'd need to keep an eye on her. Probably more parental worry than most. Jack didn't seem to know what to do, and that left me. I was the professional. I was supposed to know. But we so often don't in our own families. It's too close. And my worry skewed my perceptions. I was responsible for her. Could I keep her safe?

Another week and I was on the road to Gabe's. I had gotten a late start, and immediately regretted it. I could sense something different about this drive. Something intense was bothering me. My anxiety was escalating.

"**I'm tired of this,**" I ranted to the powers that be. The management, I remembered my brother's reference to God.

"**I hate it. When is this going to be over? Isn't it enough that I'm exhausted. Do you have to scare me half to death too?**"

I was feeling very cranky about all of it. How much could I endure? How strong was I? Never mind. Don't tempt the fates. I turned my attention deliberately to the scenery and the driving. My mind drifted anyway.

Thinking about it, I knew it was more than my chronic level of anxiety. Then I remembered Richard's comment. Today was November 20. Maybe that was part of it.

My attention back to the road, I found the light disappearing quickly. As it faded to darkness, I gripped the wheel more tightly, anxiety rising to fear. Fear of . . . ? I didn't know.

And then I did know. Fear of the road, of a call almost. In the darkness, I felt the pull. First the lure towards the bridge abutments. Gripping the wheel, I forced the car to stay on the road, breathing a sigh of relief as I passed the offending concrete which seemed to draw me in towards it, begging me to smash there, be one with it. As I passed, the intense allure dissipated. Breathing slightly more easily, I passed the fields laid to rest, old corn stalks standing sentinel under the heavy cloud cover and light rain beginning to fall. No stars. No moon. Just darkness and something pulling at me. A compulsion, almost.

Another bridge abutment, and the same thing happened. Then the interstate went up and over a country road, and I felt the draw again, this time to the empty gaping hole between the lanes of the overpass. How easy it would be to drive into that space, to see the car turning end over end. Slow motion as they showed it in the movies. Vividly it played in my mind, calling me to create the images. It would end the anxiety and bring relief. Again, white knuckled, I glared at the pavement, forcing the car to stay between those dotted white lines.

More relief as I got beyond the overpass, the interstate taking me past dark farmhouses with twinkling beacons of light, bringing me back to this reality, out of my daze. The miles slipped by as the rain quietly fell, soothing my nerves with the swish of the wipers.

Another overpass, and suddenly I realized the same thing was happening. I hadn't been actively suicidal for a long time, yet here it was, in full force. This time the pull was to the edge of the freeway, the black gaping empty vastness beside me, calling, urging me that way.

"So easy, so easy," whispered the wipers as they swished back and forth. "This way. Over here." My tense grip tightened until I was back on the flat surface again.

"I can't do five hours of this," I thought to myself in despair. "This is like wanting to just get out of my skin, I feel so anxious. And it's almost stronger than I am." That thought made me mad. I hadn't worked this hard, for this long, to lose the battle now. And this was definitely a battle. Didn't look like the ones in the old-time fiction, but here it was and it was real. Intense and powerful, something was gripping me on a regular basis, pulling me to destruction.

"I wonder how others do it? Other survivors. Those who aren't so strong. They sure have my respect. At least I know what's going on, and that I have to fight this." Again, I wondered what else I could do. I needed help. Time to call on the big guys.

"Grandmothers, Grandfathers, Powers of the Four Directions!" This was urgent. I began to pray, going on to state my difficulty, asking protection and help. I couldn't do this myself.

Done with my prayer, I continued driving, wondering what else I could do. Insight finally hit. The old lightening bolt. Driving with my left hand, I reached with my right behind the front seat, leaning back and stretching for what should be there. Sure enough, I felt the white plastic box, tugged on it, and pulled it to me. With a sigh, I opened it and pulled out the tape, popping it into the cassette player. Tapes of Judith's workshop, I settled in to focus on her voice, her essence, her words, her prayers, using her as a focus.

"Stay focused on Judith," I thought, listening to her teaching. It worked. The focus on her and her teachings drowned out the anxiety and the pull to death. Gradually my body relaxed to an easier state, as I continued the drive. Always alert to the danger, I still stayed focused on Judith, calling her to me. The hours flowed by, until I eventually drove into the familiar street of Jack's sister, porch light on to welcome me.

The next morning, I drove on up to Gabe's. The same anxiety was present, but more manageable in the morning light. The one hour drive rolled away under the wheels as I listened again to Judith's voice.

The elevator smelled of cigar smoke, I realized as I rode up, wincing with each creak. Not enough that I was incredibly anxious. I had to ride the oldest elevator in town. The lawyer must have gone up just before me, as I recognized the same smell sneaking under his door as I walked past his office. Music came out of the next waiting room, as a young boy entered. I turned right down the other hall to Gabe's.

Dropping into my chair in his office, I looked tensely at him. It didn't take a rocket scientist to know that I was having a hard time. He sat down quietly in his chair, putting his coffee to one side. No banter this morning.

"What's wrong?"

"I don't know. I'm just so anxious I can hardly stand it. I feel like I just want to get out of my skin. Out of my body. And I was absolutely actively suicidal coming up." I could see him settle more deeply, grounding his energy as I told him the story. Finally I finished. "It's like the biggest job of my life was to get safely to this chair and to you."

"Where in your body is the distress, Carla?"

I scanned, experienced now. Where did I feel it?

"In my solar plexus."

"So let's get to work." He rose to pull out the massage table and I joined him. Lying on my back on the table, I was ready. Grinning sheepishly, he pulled on my pants legs, smoothing the wrinkles. "All the better to see you with, my dear," he chuckled. I smiled back at him. At least we could lighten it up a bit. Then he got the white sage, lit it and began his prayer.

"Grandmothers, Grandfathers, Powers of the Four Directions," his voice rang out, full and resonant, asking for blessings for our work and the space in the office.

"Grandmother Moon, Grandfather Sun, protect us. Show us what we need to see. Help us to know what we need to know . . . to break this evil and send it back to it's source." With power in his voice and stance, he concluded his opening prayers, while I continued to struggle to control my trembling.

"Anything new come up with Richard?" I told him about our last work and the date of November 19. Seemed important. Then we were silent, focusing on the work at hand.

Gently he laid his hand on my solar plexus, after his typical smoothing of my shirt. I grinned weakly again. Quietly, he ran energy into the solar plexus, to heighten whatever was present. We found it: an astral entity, tortured, implanted by the cult, and connected to my third eye and throat chakra. Whenever I got close to knowing anything about this part of the cult and the regional gatherings, the torture of the entity would be released, and my feeling would be wanting to get out of my skin. Translated to experience, it meant suicidal without the emotional despair. Just wanting out, as the entity wanted out.

Together we worked, blessing and healing the entity, removing it and releasing it to go up it's own evolutionary ladder. Then I could talk about what I came to call the Night of Shadows. Quietly, without fear or agitation, I looked at Gabe. It was time now to look at the forbidden. To speak it out.

"Tell me what you see," he commanded. Uncharacteristically, he gave a small start, then looked at me again. "There's something here for you to learn."

I looked and sensed into the cult and that date. Images, blurry at first, came to mind, clearing as I waited. Yet my child's mind couldn't understand.

"It's very confusing." I paused. "There are lots of black robes. More than I've ever seen before. Richard had told me that this date was about a regional meeting, and I think this must be the culmination of several days of ritual working."

"And?" Gabe brought me back to the search for the unspeakable.

I watched, yet still had no coherent words for what I saw. I recognized the child confusion at the images. Finally, I settled on the closest approximation.

"Black swirling things. Like black scarves. I don't understand."

"Look carefully."

"The black things are above and sometimes separate from the black robed people. And sometimes they go into the people. They are swirling above and all around them."

"Who's controlling whom?"

Understanding flooded my awareness. There before me was an image that I was never to forget.

"The black things are controlling the people!"

I knew now. "The people think that they are controlling the black. They see it as power. They think they are in charge, but they aren't."

"That's right, Carla. This is possession. The evil spirits are possessing the people. The people in their ego, think they are gaining power from this ceremony. This was the primary purpose for all the cult activity. To gain, use and control increasing amounts of Power. In fact, they are the ones being used."

"The evil energy is coming into them, so it can control them more effectively, overcoming what might have been left of their light and/or good judgement."

The insight was very clear and stunning to me. This was about evil taking over the cult members, members who thought they were running the show.

"You got it," he responded grimly. "Now who do you see?"

"I can't see their faces. I taught myself long ago not to look at the faces."

"Look this time. Who do you see dancing?"

Looking, I startled in surprise, recognizing one form. I could see some faces and some were female. This was a surprise as most commonly in the rituals it had seemed to be men. One of the females was young, with light, long hair. It seemed to be my sister's essence. It was how I always recognized people. By their essence. This was my sister's essence, at a young age.

"And does a black thing go into her too?" Gabe's voice, seemingly at a distance while he stood beside me.

"Yes, it does." I let out a sigh.

"Um hm." He already knew.

"OK, Carla. You've seen all we need for now. Come back to me." Slowly, groggily, I turned my attention to him. "Come on and sit up. We'll take a break and then talk about it." Still slowly, I slid down from the table, and joined him in moving into the hall towards the rest rooms and getting a drink. This was a lot to absorb.

Back from break, we settled in our chairs. I was still stunned at the powerful image of darkness taking the cultists. It was impressive, to say the least. Together we processed the work.

"This ritual was extended over many days, Carla," he told me, as he thoughtfully listened to his guidance, "and there were many aspects to it, including tortures and sacrifices. But the culmination was what they considered to be a gathering of power. We know now what it really was."

"Very impressive. And to think that they thought they were gathering power. And it was really possession. I think this will take some time to consider."

He grinned. "No kidding."

We went on to other conversation, interrupted by Gabe noticing one other problem in my energy field. A suicide entity, he took it out with the large bronze singing bowl from his table.

"The message that you were to get very clearly was that it would be better to be dead than to remember the Night of Shadows. 'Accidental suicide' was a considerable risk as you got closer to remembering. Now that's gone. The implant is removed, and the risk is gone, too. You should feel better."

I checked with myself, noticing that my breathing had relaxed, and the tension settled in my body. "It's important for me to notice that I do feel better, or I might keep the message going," I noted to him. He nodded. It was a relief to not feel driven to my own death.

"There's one final piece here, Carla. A test. What's the spirit standing behind me look like?"

I was startled. I knew I wasn't clairvoyant. He pressed, teaching me how to use my inner vision. I was to look in the direction of his guide, and yet search for the image that came within my own mind. The focus was internal, making my eyes soft rather than straining. Finally I described the spirit, hesitantly.

"It's a black man, large, with loose colorful robes falling around his frame. He has some cloth wrapped around the top of his head so that I can't see his hair. But he seems really old."

"That's right," he grinned. "It takes more energy than you usually have, but you can do it."

Another image came to mind. And I understood.

"I can see myself, standing at the edge of that ritual, watching the black things. I could see, and I knew how dangerous that was. There's a part of me that knew that if they knew I had psychic skills, they would use me and the black things would come into me, too. I can see myself shutting down psychically, closing off my third eye, trying to close off my light, so they wouldn't know and use me. It was my way of hiding."

Gabe nodded; made sense to him.

"You know, my sister had some psychic skills, and they were grooming her for more training," I added with increased clarity from the work we had done.

Gabe listened to his guidance. "Yes. This cult was in tiers. The lower levels were drones sort of, used to create energy for the upper levels. Your dad was on about the third level up. Your sister was being groomed for that level, and you hid out."

"My father was there with his rage and his sadism, but he didn't have much in the way of psychic skills."

"Um hm. I think that's right. Your sister had enough psychic skills that they used her."

We processed the ritual further, Gabe having me look at the figures, especially the hands and feet to clarify details. My clarity continued to increase. Looking at my sister, I saw a bracelet on her wrist. It had particular silver charms on it. A church, an ice skater and a diploma, among others. Later I would ask her about it, if she'd ever had one.

"Oh yes," was her response. "I loved that bracelet and wore it for years and years." She went on to tell me of each charm and its significance. I knew them. I had seen them. It made me sad for her in many ways.

The long drive home was relaxing and a good time to process our work. The air was cold, but the blue sky lent a crispness to the scene as I pondered what I had learned. The gaping holes on the freeway overpasses were now only that, spaces between lanes, rather than terrifying monsters calling to me. The hours flew by.

Life was busy at home, the kids gone most of the time. Band took up their energy, with both of them at practices and exhibitions. Saxophones, trumpets, clarinets, music, and travel instructions all filled our lives. Trophies, awards and friends made it worthwhile for both Nate and Jennie.

Yet I worried about Nate. I'd been hearing the rumors. The principal chasing him through the school parking lot, the police with dogs chasing the whole group of boys, the illicit t-shirt worn in the school. Nate was full of it, and I found it so incredibly difficult to reign him in.

This Saturday he was getting up late, and I was cranky about it. What was it about teens that they thought sleeping til noon was normal? I didn't get it, and it irritated me to the extreme. Later I would understand: welcome to parenting teens. I just hadn't done enough of it then. And I'd been holding my frustration, increasing my anxiety. Finally, I'd had it. Anxiety pulsing my every nerve, I went up, knocking on the door.

"Nate?"

"Yeah, Mom?" He opened it, dressed and ready to go. So much for my frustration. I opened my mouth, ready to have a go at it anyway, when a second picture superimposed itself in front of Nate. I saw the young boy hanging. The one that I had experienced at Richard's. And I got it. I also saw my fear.

"Nothing much. I just wondered when you were getting up."

"Oh, I'm heading out now," he added, passing me as he walked out the door, giving me a hug. He was a loving boy. Wild, but loving.

Turning, watching him go, I understood. I never could discipline him as much as I should have, and now I knew why. Programming. A boy child, if I disciplined him, I was unconsciously terrified that he'd hang himself. Somehow, they had wrapped that message around the event. I would be responsible. I had to be remarkably careful, or terrible things would happen to this boy child. Mind control is an awesome thing. And parenting was a terror to the programmed mind.

The Weaver

The work with Gabe continued, session by session, with persistent progression. We discovered more cult atrocities and slowly chipped away at my healing. We found cult members dragging me in my little robes unwillingly into rituals and sacrifices, forcing my participation and observation. We worked with implants and souls, and found three-year-old Carla keeping the soul of yet another small child, trying to protect him from his terror. Again we released the soul to the spirit guides to restore to the owner, and again Gabe returned the evil to the senders as the spells were broken. I continued to fight to stay on top of the work as well as my health. The battle was on.

The presence of Gabe's teacher, Judith, in my life was a real blessing. I focused on her teachings and those of the spirits who came through her. Together they taught me of the Sacred Wound.

The teaching had come on a blustery wintry night, as we formed our student group in front of the fireplace, Judith seated in the large rose-colored stuffed chair. The side lamps cast their muted glow as we talked and listened to the teachings, punctuated by the wind gusts pounding the window panes, rattling the old glass and peeling wood.

Gabe had taught me the native belief about choosing our birth families and the family's agreement that we come to them as their children. Judith continued the teaching.

"We choose our life lessons before we incarnate," she told us, as I wiggled in my place on the patterned Oriental rug, wondering about my family. "To work on that lesson, we choose a family which will create the dilemma that we are working on.

"With the difficulty created by our family, our task is to do our healing and our growth as a soul so that we are more whole and full of light." The fire glowed and flickered softly as her words reflected in the light.

"We aren't meant to live our lives as victims of whatever happened, rather to learn the lesson presented. The one that we incarnated to learn. That's why it's called the Sacred Wound. The wound is to be transformed, for that is the task of this lifetime. Otherwise, we would have chosen another beginning, creating a different dilemma for another learning. Our task is to heal the Sacred Wound."

I listened, captivated. It was a concept which compelled my attention, gave meaning to my struggle. Yes, I'd been victimized, and still suffered from the result. What would I do with that? How would I transform it? What growth on my soul's journey would come? The questions gave me another focus for my work, one that gave me more balance and hope.

Jack was gone. It would be for three weeks. Maybe more, but probably not, he'd told me. The research should be done by then.

My respect grew by leaps and bounds for single parents. You don't get how much the partner does to help, even to maintain a presence, until they're not here, I thought to myself. I was very aware of the restrictions single parenting placed on my time, travel and availability. And teen-agers were a world unto themselves.

We did well, reforming our tight unit where plans were made, schedules checked, and meals conquered. The real challenge was nighttime. I suspected Nate of taking serious advantage.

"When did you get in last night?" I inquired at breakfast on a bright Saturday morning.

"Eleven," was the cereal muffled reply, as he looked up, eyes twinkling.

"Are you sure?"

"Yeah, Mom. I even came in and told you like you asked me to. You asked me if I'd had a good time, and I told you yes, and you said fine and went back to sleep."

"Nuh uh," I insisted, putting my spoon down. "That's not possible. I don't remember any of that."

Jennie giggled. "He really did come in at eleven. I heard him."

"And what were you doing? You were supposed to be in bed." Jack was the night owl and had kept that shift. I was the morning bird, and knew the early stirrings. The night shift felt missing.

"I was in bed. Reading. He really did come in then."

I was outnumbered, and it felt hopeless. They both giggled. Nate looked at me mischievously. "I love those antidepressants, Mom. You say the funniest things when you're mostly asleep. And you do sleep soundly." He grinned again, as he pushed his chair back, leaving for the day.

The scene was to be repeated over and over, with multiple variations. Often Nate or Jennie came in during the night and told me outrageous stories, getting me to agree, then telling me about it in the morning. The trouble was, it sounded like me, and I would have vague remembrances of it. This was the part of antidepressants that no one had told me about, and I didn't remember from previously. Maybe because the kids hadn't been old enough to enjoy it. Now sound sleeping was a blessing and a curse.

The balance of my life. Soul retrievals, energy implants and single parenting with teen-agers. Rituals and sacrifices balanced with Pia's sorrows. We all had troubles. We all had joys. Remembering the latter was usually the challenge.

The weeks flew, with another session with Gabe coming soon. My dreams were becoming more intense as the time approached.

The theme emerged of disaster about to strike, followed by the realization that I would be all right. Even with the reassurance from the dreams of a positive outcome, my fears were building. I couldn't seem to shake them. The days passed, and my anxiety grew, seemingly without my attention or cooperation, like storm clouds amassing just over the horizon. Dreaming about my desperation all night, I awoke in a cold sweat. Help had been so near in the dream, and then had evaporated.

Being forewarned was good. Being a nervous wreck was not. I thought back to my martial arts training, pulling it to me. There I had trained as a warrior and with warriors. I knew there were times of being afraid. I sought them out and remembered them. Remembered the night I had walked across the deck with Sensei, just before my green belt test. He had been very precise and unemotional, talking only of my focus and responses.

"Never focus on the fears," he later told me. "That's how you get hurt," following the warning with a story of a fighter getting broken up from focusing on his fears. "Always focus on what you're going to do; how you're going to do it." The lesson was applicable here, too.

With the frightening dreams, I remembered the time and the story, pulling back into myself the strength of the testing and the victory, as well as the lesson about dealing with fear. The remaining days until my session with Gabe, I spent practicing my strengths. The dreams seemed to fade.

It was bitterly cold as I packed for the journey. This would be a longer trip as Judith would be teaching for the weekend after I had my session with Gabe. Shivering, I loaded the car. "Nothing like winter in the midwest," I thought gloomily. Maybe it will snow a little. That makes the clouds tolerable."

A few flakes and the trip was easy. The next morning I was in Gabe's office once again.

"You look better, Carla," Gabe commented, finished with his stylistic first appraisal of my energy field. "Stronger, somehow."

"I've been working on building my energy field."

"Well, it's working. That's good. So tell me what's going on." He relaxed and leaned back in his chair, sipping the coffee as the steam rose. I was too nervous for anything.

Forcing myself to steadiness, I told him about the nightmares and the increasing nerves.

"What do you need for support?" he asked, when I was clearly getting anxious about the work ahead. What did I need to be able to muster the courage to go forward and stay in the work?

"I think I need to know that the people who were hurt will be all right, and that God's in charge. The evil seems so powerful sometimes, and I worry then."

"I remind myself," Gabe nodded thoughtfully, "that I know what my path is and I keep on that, and I have to let the others take care of their part. Like there are spirits that come to take the entities when I take them out. Their job is to take them elsewhere, for healing or whatever. And there are guides who are to escort evil spirits to another place, not in a bad way, but for healing."

"It's not for me to know how the universe runs, or what the Grand Plan is, or how this will come out. I'm to follow my path and do my part, and then trust in a greater wisdom than ours. We couldn't even understand the whole thing if we did know about it. We can't even get karma right." He ended on our shared puzzle, smiling ruefully.

I smiled back. "All right. I can do this. I'm ready to get to work."

"Well then, let's go, woman," as he stood and moved to pull the massage table out. Face up, I made my body relax as we settled into our work mode. He scanned me, both of us noticing that nothing was, as yet, standing out. For a moment, he leaned against his stool, chin in hand, thinking, then went to his desk for his rattle. Quietly, standing at my feet, he began to **Sing** me.

Lying there, I took the sound and the vibration in, relaxing in the tones. It was beautiful. As the power rose in his voice, I was aware of God's presence all around me. It even felt in me, with the vibration melting through my body. It was the first time I had been fully aware myself of Spirit in sound as it filled the room.

Gabe moved away from my feet and to my right side, striking my body up and down on that side with the rattle, then on my arm and leg.

"What are you doing?"

"I'm helping the thought form to stand out more."

He ran more energy. Left side, and then right. Still, we didn't have a solid sense of direction. Lying quietly, I stilled my fear with the force of my warrior training.

Abruptly, Gabe stopped, remaining totally still in full alertness. Aware of the change, I watched. "What's wrong?" Something was very different.

He stood beside me with all his senses extended. I moved into my intuition and psychic senses, trying to discern what was bothering him. A prickly sensation filled the air, as my anxiety escalated. Forcing myself to breathe slowly, I watched him.

"I have a feeling that there's a Presence here that is going to be very displeased when we undo this." He paused, listening, checking and feeling again. "We're going to stop here and get a fix on what that's about."

He waited and listened. I focused on my internal Warrior, keeping my anxiety from going over the top, putting myself in the stance that I had at tournaments and testing. Remembering Sensei. Waiting, I trusted Gabe's skill and knowledge. Waiting on Spirit. Praying. We had never had a specifically negative energy in the room before. I tried to breathe.

Relaxing slightly, he looked down at me as I lay on the table. He was smiling. "The Big Guys are out. This room is full of angelic power. They'll take care of it."

It occurred to me that faith was thanking God, not just begging for help. God in whatever way that was. I shifted to thanks for presence and protection. We each do our part, I thought, grateful for Gabe and his wisdom in waiting until we had the reinforcements we evidently needed.

He shook the tension out of his body, returning to my left side again, concentrating. With his hands on my joints, he again increased the energy.

"Found the entity."

"Tell me."

"It's like an octopus shape with one branch going down into your left leg, one going up into your chest on the left side, and one going up and then down you left arm. The core is on your left side in the lower abdomen."

I watched as he reached for it, putting his hands out to touch it, then startled as he jumped quickly back, reflexively putting his hand out to steady himself.

"What happened?"

"It tried to bite me." He seemed startled, but not all that concerned.

Putting his hands out once again, this time more cautiously, he addressed the entity, commanding it. "By the authority of Spiritual Law, you must tell us your function."

My eyebrows went up, looking at him questioningly. He had never done that. And how was the entity supposed to tell us it's function? The answer was in his movement, as he turned to me, expectantly. I got it, though a bit slow on the draw. The answer was to come through me. I focused internally, waiting to see what would come to me.

The answer was immediate, if not clear. "To keep me captive," I told him, my expression conveying my confusion.

"Why?"

Again I focused, and again the mystifying answer came, "To keep me in bondage. To the cult, I suppose." It was all I could get.

Again, he addressed the entity. "How were you put into her? Show her the process."

Reluctantly, I allowed the scenes to develop in front of me. Together we watched. Finally I put it into words. "It was through blood sacrifice."

"Yes." He quiet affirmation was more intense than any denial could have been. It had been hard for me to get it, then to allow myself to really take the knowledge in. My own dismay and reluctance were running high. First I got the red color of the sacrifice, then the words, then put them together. Gabe, watching with me, clarified, staying in the objective for the time being.

"They tortured the man, then collected his pain and put it together as an entity. They tortured him slowly. The purpose being to gather a lot of pain to put the entity together. Then they disemboweled him."

I was aware of feeling squeamish. Agitated, I wanted to get away from myself. Yet I could see and feel the reality. My warrior stance kept me steady.

"They put the man's blood and guts on me."

Gabe paused, watching again. "Yes. And it was done by a priestess. Do you recognize her?"

"No. She wasn't old. In her thirties and pretty. Brunette."

"Yes. She came and put his insides on you and formed an energy entity with the blood and guts on you, rubbing it into your skin. It was one full of pain."

He thought some more, and listened. "It was used to control you. How old were you when your family left the cult?"

"My best guess is that I was five. I know that we left those relatives abruptly, never to see them again. My sister has told me that happened when I was about five and a half."

"Um hum," he continued thoughtfully. "At about that age, kids get more independent. This was used primarily for her to practice her skills, and then also used to control you as a child." He paused. "I hadn't thought of it like that before. We practice our healing skills, and they practice their cult skills."

He returned to the topic of control. "It was done to other children too, as a means of control. They used everything that happened to help control the cult members, including the children." We were fighting to stay objective so we could continue with the work at hand. Feelings would come later.

We knew about the entity, and Gabe knew that he could take it out. He was deliberately slowing the process down.

"I'll take it out, Carla," he reminded and reassured me. "I'll fill it with angelic light. Actually, the angels who are here will do that. That's to calm its pain and suffering. It only tried to bite me because of the constant pain. Once it's calm, I'll reach in and pull it gently out, and it will be taken to a place of healing."

He still seemed to be stalling for time. Now he paused and I was sure of it. "What?"

"There's a problem here."

He paused again. My heart contracted, fear taking hold against my wishes.

"The woman who did it was a High Priestess and she'll feel the pull. She'll feel the entity leave you and go. It doesn't matter where she is or what plane she's on. She'll still feel it. And I don't want to be between her and you when she comes back to stop us or object or get even or whatever she wants to do."

"Why not?" I still didn't get it, at least not fully. Gabe had always been adequate to the task. But I was beginning to receive more clarity about the power of the force we were dealing with. This High Priestess was no small deal.

"We need a bigger Power than I am to stand between her and you, so when she follows the energy back to complain or fight back, she will end up contending with that power."

He paused again, letting me take in the gravity of our situation and to consider options. No wonder I had been fighting such big anxiety. This was big work.

"You certainly don't want to deal with her, and I don't either." Truer words were never spoken. "She's going to be very angry to have her work undone."

Again, I considered. This was different than just taking out an entity. This included taking on the High Priestess. The presence Gabe had felt in the beginning. The one that didn't want today's work to happen. The High Priestess might well fight back and neither of us needed to be her target. Gabe continued.

"I'm going to call on the Weaver, the one who weaves the patterns in the Universe, to come and pull the thread loose and unweave the pattern that the High Priestess wove to keep this entity in form. The Weaver will take apart that pattern, and will then be between the High Priestess and us.

Fighting my fears for our safety in all the different realms, I agreed. Quietly, we set about the work.

The prayers were full and powerful, Gabe's voice resonating clearly in the room. My silent prayers added even more energy to his.

"Star Maiden, Moon Mother," he began, "be with us. We pray to the Goddess, to the Weaver, that we might be your servants." Fully and deeply, he continued, asking the Weaver to come, to be with us, to pull the weaving loose. "So be it."

Another set of prayers were offered, to the God/Goddess of Form, asking for Their needs to be met, specifying the needs and the assistance requested. Clear and direct, the prayers were, to me, absolutely appropriate and necessary. Prayers that I would not have thought about, but as his voice carried them, I knew the Power was with us, assisting us. Gabe closed the prayers.

"We ask that when this High Priestess experiences the unraveling of what she had done, and throws her temper tantrum, that she will confront the Powers that she has betrayed, the Powers of Form and Pattern. We ask that in invoking her powers, she will accomplish her own undoing. So be it."

I shook as I lay on the table. I was beginning to understand the fuller power of our work this day. "We're undoing the High Priestess?"

"She'll undo herself."

I looked at him questioningly.

"It's getting more clear to me as we work. I understand now that she's at the developmental level of throwing a temper tantrum. She's going to come back with that level of rage. As she comes at the Powers of Form and Pattern with that rage, it will come back on her and be her own undoing."

Then he smiled mischievously. "Sort of like, you can't fool with Mother Nature. When she screams her rage back, her own energy will come back on her."

Quietly we worked, with me on the table, and Gabe working carefully with the entity. I was aware of wanting to get away from my own body again, of my strong feelings of revulsion. He cleaned me off on the etheric level, clearing the blood and guts. I was able to relax.

So very gently and carefully, he gathered the entity. We waited every few moments as the spirits filled it with light and calmed it. Quietly, he took it out, one segment at a time, gathering it together, and then gently gave it to a spirit.

"They'll take care of it," he answered the question in my eyes. "Time for us to take a break."

The work of removing the entity had gone remarkably smoothly. The interaction between the High Priestess and the Spirits was on another level. That was not ours to do. And with the kind of preparation we had done, their part went as planned. I had a brief glimpse of a beginning temper tantrum, then in a blink it was gone. Not our work.

After the break, we resumed our places with me on the table. "Sort of an intense day, what you think?" I asked him, trying to relieve some of the tension.

He smiled down at me as he checked my energy levels. "Not our average, even for us." His attention returned to my energy field as he began to fill me up again where we had been working. Drifting, pieces began to fall into place for me. Things like my distrust of women which had never made sense. Most of the perpetrators were men. Yet clearly not all. Other missing pieces settled into a pattern as I mused on the meanings, while Gabe worked on my field.

He spoke up again. "I'm told by my guides that you were protected during this last work we did just now with the High Priestess and the ritual. They protected you from being overwhelmed by your feelings."

I was aware that, while shocked, dismayed and repulsed, I had not been overwhelmed emotionally. I had been able to see the process as if from a distance. Now I understood that I had been assisted in the distancing. If my full feelings about what had happened had flowed through me, I would have been immobilized, retraumatized or worse. The thought also flashed through my mind of all the therapists who try to precipitate strong emotions so the client will heal or the therapist will know they have made progress. This was an example of a time when it wasn't appropriate.

"They are going to let some of your feelings flow now, so I just want you to be ready. It may come in sort of waves. If it does, we'll just ride it out."

Slowly, the spirits let the feelings return. We found numbness first, induced by the drugs I had been given. Revulsion over what had been done to the man. Fear when they dragged me to him. Pain and guilt when they blamed me. Gabe with me each moment, I cleared the feelings and clarified them, gaining a deeper understanding of the power of the mind control.

The cultists had covered my hands with blood, leaving me trembling with sorrow for the man, pain and guilt for my supposed responsibility. Together Gabe and I cleared my hands, purifying them forever, claiming the energy for healing. Light shimmered around my palms and fingers as I held them for the blessing, a tingling that would last three days and nights. Transformed, I left his office in awe of the work of the day.

At home, I went through my usual re-entry, this time my short night walks accompanied by squeaking snow against my boots protesting the deep cold. I didn't mind. My work with Gabe had given me an inner warmth that even dissipated the cold wind scattering snowflakes from the sweet-smelling pine trees as I passed. My hands tingled, reminding me that they were now healing hands, the tragic transformed. I knew the road ahead was still rough, but this hiatus gave me a sense of hope and strength, and I was grateful.

Pia called, sad and distraught, her voice reflecting her distress. We met at the Double Dragon for lunch, seated by the window as the low gray clouds reflected her inner landscape.

"Eric is always gone," she dolefully reported. "He's so passionate about loving me, but he's just never home." Her long sigh gently moved the straight luminous black hair, pieces now falling in front of her face. Quietly, I listened, supporting, pouring tea. My emotional well full for the moment, I wrapped her in my love as we talked.

Etheric Seal

I lay on Richard's massage table, pulling at my jeans so they didn't feel so tight, marveling again at the seeming chaos in his healing room. Blankets and pillows were piled high on the shelves on my right threatening to topple over me, remedies filled the counters on my left, and the stereo system softly gave us *Enya* from behind. I was enjoying *Enya* now, finding it comforting as I connected it with healing work.

Richard was squeezing around the table, ready to start. As usual, I fussed at the mess. Yet for all his clutter, I did recognize that he was extremely bright and focused.

I sighed, settling in for another healing session with him. Our work had been going well, taking out traumas bit by bit. Miraculously, after we worked, they didn't bother me any more. "That's the energy work," he always reminded me. "That's what really finally clears it out of the system." Thank God. Now I could sense his attention was somewhere else.

Quietly, *Enya* playing an accompaniment, we finished the energy work and moved back to his office where I relaxed in the chair, thinking about the work we'd done. Then I leaned over his desk to look at the remedies he was preparing. He glanced up, eyeing me over the top of his glasses.

"Yes?"

I think I could always fuss and debate with Richard because he had the gift and discipline of never taking it personally. Another reason to thank God. I had to get it out somewhere.

"It's just so hard, Richard. Sometimes I do get very tired of all this. I have a hard time understanding."

He leaned back in his chair, adjusting his position with the squeaks, and sipping on a homemade vegetable cocktail in a tall glass. It smelled faintly carroty. I was sure I wouldn't like it. He had tried to talk me into it. I was only willing to take healthy living so far.

"Remember the old card system that we used, when we first started doing the pre-computer work? The way we sorted data?"

Ruefully, I nodded. The machine had been huge, filling the side of a room, and I had fearfully loaded my college research cards into it to get the stats. Miraculously, I had gotten some. Computers were a whole new world, but I was kind of glad I had the comparison with the old ways of doing research.

"This is like those old card sorts. It's as if the only cards you have been seeing are the bad ones, the ones with the pain and suffering of the cult. You also need to see the others that are a part of who you are. The strengths and skills you have, as well as the tragedies and despair."

"Oh, come on, Richard. There isn't anything that can fill this in and make it better. This is who I am. It's all I can see." I wouldn't give in easily, and besides, it was all I could see then.

Yet the image stuck and from then on, we worked with that concept. Gradually he helped me fill in the card system. Some of it was with past lives.

"You know, your past lives have been a big help in this cult work, Carla." We got several past lives back that day, processing lives of beauty, power and psychic skills well used. He was right. They were a support. Integrating them helped me be strong.

"Hm. There's another past life surfacing here. You want to know about it?"

I hesitated. He hadn't asked about the others, just told me. Clearly this one was different. But I did need the whole picture.

Carefully he told me as he got the information. I saw a few of the images, cringing from them. A small boy, a page, Spain, the Inquisition, carrying messages, growing to a respected man who was expected to assist with the Inquisition tortures. A peripheral role. Always distasteful. Unsure, I went along. Until one day, I became crystal clear that this was wrong. I walked away. Deep regrets of power misused, dark nights of self-recriminations.

"Oh, Richard," I sighed, "I just don't want to have been a perpetrator. Maybe that's why I was born into this cult. Maybe it is payback. Maybe I am a bad person."

"Carla. Carla. You need to get the complete perspective. All of us who have power in this life have also abused power. We all have to learn both sides of the use of power. We will use it well and we will abuse it. I know the past lives when I have abused mine, and I am trying very hard to correct that now. It's just part of the human condition."

I thought about it, yet knew these questions would follow me. He felt my worry, eating away in my soul.

"Look at it this way," holding up his hand, fingers extended. "Each finger is a life. My thumb is not responsible for my index finger. Yes, it's all related, but all we can do this time is live this life with the highest degree of integrity possible. That's what we do each time, and in the process we will form the essence of our soul." With that, he pointed to the palm. It was an image I could accept.

Other past lives did help fill in the card system. One of my favorite ones was a preVictorian setting. I had been a female in a very elegant setting, wearing dresses with big skirts, and writing poetry. I could see the images clearly from that time, even the formal gardens, wondering if that's where my love of formal gardens originated. Sometimes I drifted, thinking of that time, gaining strength from the beauty and poetry which I could call back to me.

Over time, we would consciously fill in the cards in my card sort, both with current events and past lives, finding lives of ordinary times, of elegance, of poverty, lives as warrior and as healer, but always of growth progressing. It was part of carrying on.

I found my health slowly improving as winter turned into spring. I could walk short distances, like up the street and back. I still slept deep sleeps after lunch, but I had more energy for my work with clients. Fortunately, my case load continued to be stable. An income always helps. I've always considered it a good thing.

It was good to see Gabe again, resuming regular sessions after months of listlessness and my weakened state.

"What does Richard say about you now?" Gabe wondered, perched on his stool, balancing his new crutches. He'd fallen over his kid's toys. The usual martial artist's kind of accident.

"Well, he says that right now the current state of my health problems is 15-20% physical and the rest is emotional and in the etheric body. He's dealing with the physical, and I've been working on my own emotional state, finding reasons to keep on going, and dealing with the home front. But I don't know what to do with the etheric."

"We'll see what comes up. You do seem a lot better."

I nodded, thinking of my increased assertiveness and humor. To have humor reappear in my life again was a welcome change. Not everything was dismal anymore. Most of it, but not *all.* My spark of life was beginning to return.

"The bad news is that I'm really tense again. That comes and goes, you know, and now it's back. I'm having dreams of being overwhelmed, and I'm sleeping in tense positions. I scan my body when I'm sitting and walking, and the tension is always there. It's not been quite like this before."

He was watching my energy as I talked. "Remember how things have been surfacing for you in layers. As we get one layer taken care of, there's room for another to come up. It's long and tedious work, but we're getting there. And without you having a crash, which is no small thing."

I glanced up at him, an appreciative grin. "I especially do like the 'without a crash' part. We do good work."

"And now it's time for this tension level you've got, woman. So, let's go." He ran his hands over me, about an inch off the surface, looking for clues.

Stopping, he hobbled to the end of the table for his beginning prayers, calling in the Grandmothers and Grandfathers, and asking them to create a sacred space.

"They've told me to **Sing** you," he told me, referring to his guides. He began the song, again of power and sweetness combined. Then he moved into the Beauty Blessing song, surrounding us with beauty on all sides. I laid quietly, joining my prayers with his, feeling the space fill.

Moving to my right side, he checked me again. Finally he sat back down on his stool. "I just can't get anything, Carla. It feels like a lot of resistance. What are you feeling?"

I checked in with myself. "I'm feeling the resistance, too. But it doesn't feel like me. I mean, I know I don't like going back to the cult to do the work, but I will. I have before and will again, if that's what it takes. But this resistance feels like more than that."

Again we focused, trying to determine where the resistance was coming from. An odd image arose for me, one that I hadn't seen for quite some time. I remembered a vacation when I'd first seen it.

Lying under a giant oak tree, exhausted, I had fallen into a fitful sleep. Rousing only partially, I felt the presence of others, and looked up. I saw an image of myself as if I were on a pallet with a Warrior at each of the four corners. It's clear that I was desperately ill or wounded, and these four Warriors were my guards. I was lying on a mesa with the land dropping away before us, the guards facing the distance, watching and protecting me.

At some times when I was most sick, I had wakened in the night to find them there again, always standing silently, spear upright in the right hand, shield in the left, and armbands glimmering in an iridescent light. I would fall back asleep, assured of protection.

Now they were here again, the first time in a session, standing on all four sides of me, solid, focused, protective. Their very taught posture spoke of awareness, readiness for whatever might come, spears held upright and shields ready. The armbands glistened with a reflection from another light as they stood in silent readiness. They were holding back something. Protecting me. What was it?

Slowly I became aware of the pressure. It was as if the cult were pressing in on us. It felt like a circle of them, pressing against the sacred space with the Warriors holding them back at the edge. I caught my breath, both frightened at the intensity, and awed at the protection.

"Do you feel that, Gabe?"

He nodded, understanding. "The cult's here, too. They are forming the pressure." He paused, feeling, listening, watching. Nodding, he came to a decision.

"Oh well. We have our sacred space, so we might as well go ahead. I don't see any strong indications that we can't."

Running energy, he found an energy form, carefully removing it, and giving it to a spirit. Then he worked some more, trying to find the source of difficulty. Together we talked. It was as if we couldn't think bizarrely enough to perceive this one. What hadn't we covered in our months and years of cult work? Where would the clues be?

Again, finding an energy disturbance, we continued, working on thought forms and implants. Freeing me from a time of being tied down during a ritual. Still, the incomplete feeling followed each of us while the Warriors held the space.

"My guides tell me that we still haven't broken the circle," Gabe told me after a pause.

I checked my awareness, and yes, the pressure was still there, and the cultists. Pressing against the sacred space. How could that be?

"So how do we break it? It's not exactly a comfortable feeling, and I certainly can't leave this way." I was getting frustrated. What a surprise. My patience with the work was getting better, but there were limits to everything.

"They tell me to **Sing** you again." He hobbled and hopped to my feet.

"Be careful," I warned, that mother instinct emerging on its own.

He shook his head. "I'm getting better with these." At my feet, he **Sang** again, running energy through my feet while he sang. And again, it was the Beauty Blessing, yet it was so different. As he sang, the tones began to vibrate, resonating through me and vibrating in the air around us. There was a shimmering in the air, vibrating on the sound. The cult was just outside the sound, with the shimmering between us, making them look cloudy to me.

A rhythm developed to his singing, as his voice deepened and intensified. I found myself moving internally to the rhythm, becoming aware of the vibration increasing. Sound, vibrating, filling me, pulsating through me and flowing through all of me. The table that was holding me resonated to the sound, vibrating with the tones and the rhythm.

Slowly, as the singing built, I became aware of the cultists fading. My awareness shifted from the vibration to my astonishment at watching the figures shift behind the shimmering of the sound. Gradually I was aware, as Gabe continued to sing, of the Grandmothers and Grandfathers surrounding us. The cultists were fading out, being replaced by the Grandmothers and Grandfathers watching us, blessing us.

Gabe's voice began to slow, the vibration softening and flowing out of it, until the singing stilled. Yet the sound held in the air, quivering there in place, until that, too, was gone. We waited in the quiet, while the song slowly faded from the waiting air. Finally, I turned my questioning gaze to him.

"What happened?" The question was almost a whisper, a certain awe filling me.

"My understanding came through the singing. The ritual that they did was sealed at your etheric level by the chanting that they had done. That's how they kept it a part of you. My singing the Beauty Blessing replaced their chanting and the etheric sealing. It was like taking the one out and putting the other in it's place."

I considered, comparing my feelings and my experience to his explanation. They certainly fit.

"The Grandmothers and the Grandfathers came to replace the cultists in the etheric sealing. Now instead of being surrounded by cultists with an etheric seal, you are surrounded by the Grandmothers and Grandfathers with the Beauty Blessing as an etheric seal."

"It feels like I can breathe again."

"I'm sure there's a difference," he grinned. Then he chuckled. "I watched the cultists just sort of wander away as I **Sang** you. They became confused, their eyes became distant and unfocused, and they just wandered off with no real sense of direction."

"The High Priest stayed the longest. He looked quite confused. His eyes glazed over, he looked really dazed, and someone came up to him and led him away, with their arm over his shoulder. He was lost. And then they were all gone, and the Grandmothers and Grandfathers were there with the Beauty Blessing as I sang."

I tracked him as he talked, comparing it to my experience, grinning when he talked about the cultists and their confusion. I always liked that sort of thing. It was time for that.

Then I checked my internal experience. "It all fits. I no longer have that jangled feeling, rather it's a soothing feeling."

"Makes sense. Replacing that chaos of the rituals we found today that had all been sealed on the etheric plane, with the soothing of the Grandmothers and Grandfathers and the Beauty Blessing should make a real difference. No wonder Richard talked about the etheric, too. I expect this was it."

Another moment to rest, and then I swung off the table, while he hopped inexpertly on his crutches out of the way. Time to close shop and for me to hit the road. Lots to think about on the drive home.

I was restless in this session, the last clients in my day. Watching and listening to the couple in front of me, I recognized the pattern I'd seen so often before. Over and over they struggled, from topic to topic, each trying to prove their point. Repeatedly, I had tried to help them find the middle ground. Nothing was changing. Finally, the time nearly up, I took the chance.

"Let me ask each of you one question," I interrupted the current debate. They looked at me, waiting out the imposed truce. I turned to the husband, darkly good looking, confident in his opinions. Casual in his chinos and shirt, he wore the harried executive look. Impatient with the declared truce, his fingers drummed the edge of his planner on his lap.

I thought quietly to myself, then looked steadily at him.

"Would you rather be happy or right?"

"That's easy," he nodded, knowing the dilemma at once, his face indicating reluctance at the answer. "I'd rather be right."

I turned to his wife, her eyes cast to the floor. Then she looked straight at me. "I'd rather be right, too."

"So, I want you each to think this week about the problem this is causing for you, where that attitude might have come from, and how far you want to take it." We ended the session, each of them shaking hands with me, reminding me of the end of a round of combat.

When they were gone, I turned to the large manila envelope on my desk, pulling the papers out for another, more in-depth look. It was the *L.A. Task Force for Ritual Abuse* literature. I wasn't sure what I was looking for, only that I had found this resource listed, sent for it, and believed that the information I was searching for would be contained here.

Scanning, a section commanded my attention. This one discussed programming. It noted that the most intense programming was in the child's first six years. Well, I was in the cult for the first five years of my life, so I got that. Reading, I began to understand at a deeper level of my being. They systematically attended to programming opportunities for the children, depending on the child's age and developmental stage. It wasn't just a fluke, and it wasn't personal. Like, it wasn't that I was bad. It was about programming.

Reading further, another item caught my attention, referring to programming of spiritual beliefs. Beltane was coming soon. May 1. It was a time that cults celebrated in their twisted ways, and I was aware that those time brought me more stress. More issues had been coming up, and my spiritual beliefs were among them. The spirituality of my childhood just wasn't holding. Especially when I was away from Gabe.

I found what I was searching for. It was a discussion of the five spiritual beliefs that are programmed into cult members. Three of them dogged my footsteps, especially when I felt overwhelmed. I recognized them immediately, and their haunting "truth" to me. At times, I really did believe that Satan was stronger than God, that God didn't love me, and that God wanted to punish me. When depressed, tired or bewildered, these skeletons rose out of the closet, rattling their bones of futility, coming forth to haunt me once again.

It wasn't about me and it wasn't true. This was programming. And reading the material was like finding a weapon to fight my battle with, reminding me of the *Chronicles of Narnia*. My own silver sword of wisdom, able now to slash the cords that bound me spiritually to the cult. When those thoughts came now, I could cut them away, knowing their origins, rather than drift on despair. Tucking my silver sword in my belt, I cleared my desk, ready to head home for the day.

Weeks later, back in Gabe's office, I was frustrated. "It feels like we're just marking time."

He considered me seriously, knowing I was sincere about my frustration. "I think it's building blocks, Carla. For one thing, we can't rush it. That last piece we did with the Weaver was huge, and not all healing is that obviously large. Some of it is putting the smaller pieces in place so that if and when we need a structure or container that will hold more, we'll have it."

I sighed heavily, sinking in my chair. "All right, but I don't like it. I want to get done with this. I want a **life**."

He grinned, familiar with my crankiness. "I wouldn't have guessed. Come on, woman, let's check you out on the table." I groaned in mock protest, hauling my body up and out of my chair. Time to get to work.

Again, he scanned my energy field, seeing what he could find. Finally, he sat back on the stool, looking at me.

"What we have here is an implant, Carla. This one is designed to keep secrecy."

"Why?"

"We do have to remember that most cults are involved in criminal activity."

"As if torture and murder aren't." Still cranky.

"Yeah, I know. But today seems different. Didn't Richard say that he'd found some evidence of criminal activity?"

"Yes, he did." I stretched a bit on the table, loosening up the tension in my legs. "We've stumbled over this before."

"Well, it helps to remember that, in order to somewhat normalize what was going on. This was a bunch of crooks who had psychic abilities and were taken over by darker forces than they knew. But it's important to remember that they engaged in criminal activity and had a need to hide that."

I thought back to Richard and what we'd found. "Richard told me that cults raise money through prostitution, pornography and drugs."

"Um hm." He paused. "There seems to be an implant here which is designed to keep you from remembering, and specifically to keep you from talking. It was to protect them. It has also protected you from knowing, and so will likely be difficult for you when we work with it."

My energy was plummeting. He worked to fill me up again, and we returned to the implant work. Immediately my energy fell off again. Gabe sighed, then shook his head. "I get it. Now I understand." I looked at him, ready.

"Attached to the implant is the affect, or feeling, of hopelessness. The point is to get you into hopelessness and low energy, with a sense of there being no point in working on building energy, etc. That's to ensure that you won't build energy. Then you won't heal and run the risk of remembering which would be dangerous for them. It was first and foremost a way to keep you silent. They just did it in a more subtle way than the threats of common crooks. To normalize it somewhat, these were psychic crooks. But crooks, nonetheless."

I thought about the days and nights when hopelessness would stalk me like a thief, seeking ways to steal my fight, my drive, my will to keep going. "It's important then, not to misattribute the hopelessness, isn't it?"

"Yep. It's deliberate. It's straight ahead to keep you discouraged, not healing, and silent. Has nothing to do with who you are, your courage for healing, or any of that."

Preparing to take it out, Gabe paused once more. "I want you to understand the difference between full of energy and hopeless versus empty of energy and hopeless. So that you can distinguish this state that they have implanted. You may run into this again."

We worked on the different states until I was clear. I would recognize this one again, if I ran into it. This was about the cult, and I could better fight the hopelessness now. We spent the rest of our time together removing the implant and filling me up again, sealing the few leaks which were there.

Driving home was a pleasure. The sense of hopelessness which had dodged my steps and the miles getting to Gabe were gone. I could enjoy the changing scenery, study the clouds and the ways they shifted and danced. I had learned a multitude of ways to entertain myself for these long drives, learning the ways of the birds and animals, noting the farmlands, and watching the people. When all else failed, I always had my books on tape. The drive went quickly.

In the days and nights which followed, images began to surface, at first seeming hidden behind the gray mists of impossibility. Working with Richard, I heightened and clarified them, seeing myself as the small child I had been. Images of hiding in the woods and watching things being loaded into trucks, hiding behind stone walls as a two and three year old, watching meetings and clandestine exchanges. Hiding, and being dragged out of hiding and beaten. Hiding, and running through the woods with the older children hissing at me to run faster. Always the shortest legs, always at the rear and most vulnerable. No wonder I had learned to run so fast.

Somehow, in a twist of fate, even as a very young child, I took a perverse pleasure in hiding and watching the adults as they did things we weren't to see. It seemed we all did, running as a pack of children, trying to stay hidden and learn their secrets. It went right along with my father's injunctions to hide our real truth about ourselves, to blend in. Not in ways which he would have ever anticipated, of course. As children, it was our way of gaining personal power, the power of hidden knowledge even though we never talked about what we saw.

Deep in the Albuquerque barrio, I leaned back on the bed in the small white adobe home. The house, set back from the street and crowded by flowering bushes that were pouring floral scent into the air, was poor yet clean. Candles lit the room, their shadows dancing on the walls, while the fragrances of herbs designed for trance states filled the air, mixed with tobacco, chanting and rhythmic drumming. In my own trance state, I followed the shaman as he journeyed. My Life Journey. What was my life about, the meaning, the rhythm of my days? Why? How was I to get through and where was I going?

The ceremony completed, we talked for a long time before sharing his simple meal of beans and rice. His shamanic journey framed my life path as a climb up a steep mountain shrouded in billowing dark clouds. A difficult life, yet with protection from the forces of the natural world, and small intriguing, sparkling lights set on the trail just ahead of me, enticing, calling me forward in my curiosity. Lights to keep me going, to get through the journey, complete the quest. Healing on the other end. Twinkling lights placed there by spirit to encourage and draw forward in the darkest

of times. In retrospect, I saw those lights. At the time, only the
faintest shadow of something not yet learned, a mystery of spirit
which I had to learn, something more pulling me forward . . .

THE SOUL'S JOURNEY

Soul's Journey

The weeks and mont4hs edged by with a slow, muted rhythm. Persistently, I worked to clear trauma and add coping skills, the cult a constant backdrop to all my experiences. Jennie went to Germany for six months as an exchange student. Jack traveled extensively abroad for work. Both changed forever. I knew it when I saw them. I also knew that only time would show me the meaning of their changes. Nate, meanwhile, was in college. How our lives change as healing goes on.

Vacations came and went, and school was back upon us. My energy was slowly returning, allowing me to marginally increase my work load. Progress. It seemed as if eventually I'd have my caseload back up to full speed. Though I didn't know if I'd ever have the energy I once had. But did I need to be that driven? Some of it had been a way to not deal with memories. Gabe never tired of reminding me of when I had been working three jobs. I didn't want that back.

The air was crisp as I threw my overnight bag into the car for the trip north to Gabe's. The sky was low with clouds that looked pregnant with snow, causing me to sniff the air, checking for that snow scent. It felt on the verge this afternoon. I hoped I could make it all the way north before a storm really came. It was so unpredictable. Memories filled my mind of prior trips, hurtling through whiteouts with only the tail lights of the car ahead visible. Sections of the drive were treacherous. Quickly, I threw the rest of my things in, pulling out of the driveway.

As darkness fell, a few icy flakes scooted across the windshield, painting the highway with a thin layer of snowy frosting. On the riskier parts of the drive, the promised storm held off. Tension kept my breath shallow, only relaxing as I entered the city. Civilization had its benefits, feeling safer in a storm.

The next morning was bright and clear, the sun glaring off the scant remnants of the evening's snow. Even at Gabe's building, the world looked fresh in the brisk air.

"Dreams, Gabe. I'm into dreams." I was settling into my chair, having thrown my jacket on the one to my left beyond the table. Thoughtful and frustrated, I drew my legs up, sitting in a sloppy yoga position, trying to remember. He looked relaxed in his chair, coffee in hand, the office looking the same as always with random coffee mugs scattered among the papers and books, carryout containers in the trash and more stones on his table. Phones rang in the business office, and someone walked by the door. I was ready to go. I'd had questions for weeks now. He had on his blue shirt and sweater with his jeans, his dark eyes alert, showing him ready to go.

Patiently he smiled at me, noting my settling in for a discussion. "So, tell me." I had clearly decided on our starting point.

I went through several dreams, then came to the one that really confused me. "This one's about an evil woman. I just feel cold and gray inside when I think about her or talk about her."

He was watching my energy field as I talked. This dream, out of all of them, caught his interest the most, and he stayed with it. I noticed his listening pose, and paused while he checked with his guidance.

"They tell me that it's a signpost dream, rather than an actual memory. It's pointing us to something. Where do you feel it in your body?"

We continued tracking energetically, with his chronic reminder. "You know, your psychic ability includes your ability to pick up other people's feelings, both body and emotions, in your system. And then you think it's yours. You're always going to have to be careful about that, and learn to distinguish what's theirs and what's yours."

That had come up before. One of the hazards of having some psychic abilities. Again, we turned to the woman I had seen.

"You know, Gabe, the impression of her is so strong. It surprises me."

"She's more of a thought form to you than a dream now."

"So she's more like a gathering of energy, which means a force here in the room."

"In a manner of speaking, yes." He was listening to guidance again, and then looking. "I can see her as a thought form, Carla. How would you describe her?"

"Mostly my feeling about her is cold and gray. Like dark cotton batting. I can see her to your left." My tone had become dull and lifeless, reflecting the lifelessness of the image.

"Yes. And she is cold and gray. That cold and gray is the evil that she was accumulating. It hid the spark of spirit from her so that it could no longer inform her of her actions and what they meant. It's like she did evil, and now it was doing her. It was controlling her. It's not like she could even evaluate it."

I thought back to a man I knew who had a life after death experience. He had gone to "hell" and his experience of that was the absence of light. Everything was gradings of gray and black. This seemed comparable. I reminded Gabe of the story.

"Is it like that for her?"

"Similar," he noted. "Her light is tiny and surrounded by the gray and cold." He listened to guidance. "This is part of what the dream was pointing to. There's a lesson here." He returned to me.

"She was so far into the evil and consumed by the evil that she could no longer connect with her spark of life and re-decide about it. She will have to come back again and again, and it will take her a very long time to re-gather her light."

"But she can do it?" Do I have to worry about everyone?

"Yes, she can do it. It just will take a really long time." Smiling ruefully, he quipped, "It's not necessarily a compliment to be told that one is a very old soul." His smile and comment brought relief for my concern.

Serious once again, he continued. "Partly, it will take such a long time because no one could face all that evil that they had done in a short time. It could only be worked in small bits."

"Is her soul lost?"

He leaned back, fiddling now with his black coffee mug. "Listen to your heart, Carla. You so often listen to what others say to you. Now listen to your own heart on this one. Your life experience in this lifetime gives you more experience than most on this question. You can answer out of experience, while they are answering out of theory. What do you understand here?"

"No, she's not a lost soul. I would get that from others, because of the extreme evil that she did, but she's not. She can regain the light in her soul. It's just that she'll spend a long time doing it. That's not a punishment. It's just that it will take a long time to fully turn her direction around. She was so caught up in the darkness in this life, and lost so much light. It will take a long time to change and correct the course of her soul's journey."

I looked directly at him, eyes somber, thoughts turned inward, my feet on the floor now. He nodded agreement as I processed my thoughts. I continued.

"You know, part of my grieving has been for the souls that were sacrificed. I worry that they are gone to the dark side forever. Any thoughts there?"

Gabe listened carefully to his guidance, nodding slightly in the way that I had noticed before. "Guidance tells me that what was taken in most cases was their energy, rather than their soul. People were using the energy from the soul force to gather power." That much made sense to me. I could understand that.

"In a few cases, the souls were sacrificed. That's like a bargain. The sacrificer gives the soul of the sacrificee to the Dark side in return for something, like power of some kind. They assume that there is no karma and no consequences. However, there is a time when their debt comes due. It's like, buy in December and no payments until June. But June does come. When the time comes, the soul is released, and the sacrificer must pay up. We don't have to worry about how that is. That's not ours. The deal is that the soul is released."

I leaned back in my chair, breathing a sigh from my held breath. "Thanks for checking on that. It helps me let go of some of my grieving."

I reached down to take off my shoes. "Energy work?"

"Ready when you are."

The dream awoke me with a start. Horrified, weeping, wet with sweat, I realized that it was about myself as a child, holding my favorite kitten, dead and mutilated. It was early, but soon the house would be stirring. Getting up, I took an early shower, trying to clear myself of the feelings from the dream.

Jack and Jennie got up, quickly going their separate ways. Driving through light early morning traffic, I got to my office ahead of schedule, flipping on the lights, checking the answering service and watering my plants. That done, I was still restless. While I was putting my cup of hot water in the microwave, tea bag in hand, the phone rang. I rummaged among the papers to find it before the service picked up.

"Hello. This is Dr. Sorensen."

"Oh, hi, Dr. Sorensen. This is Kevin. My car won't start!"

I could hear the anxiety in his voice. He had never missed a session, so I felt pretty sure he wasn't faking it, although that was one of the classic bail-out excuses. Kevin, I trusted.

"It's OK, Kevin. What do you think is wrong?"

"I don't know, but my Dad's coming back to help me with it. He'll jump it if necessary. But I don't see how I can get in this morning."

We continued, rescheduling, and hung up. I now had another hour before I started seeing clients. Nervous as a cat on a hot tin roof, as I occasionally told Gabe, I needed to do something else about my nerves.

Closing and locking my inner office door, leaving the waiting room open for any early arrivals, I settled back in my chair. What to do? Dipping my tea bag in my oversized bright blue mug, I went over the options I had learned in my therapy work. Putting the tea bag in the trash, I sat back, settling myself for work.

Calling in my guidance for protection, I breathed deeply, inhaling relaxation and exhaling tension, slowly putting myself into a trance state. Not sure of what to do next, I visualized the southwest, land of my heart, seeing myself walking on a hillside. A few gnarled trees dotted the earth amongst the shrubs, dots of green and brown in a vast grey-green landscape.

Allowing the scene to develop on its own, I noticed that before me was a faint path. Following its invitation, I walked the path slowly, aware of the high altitude, the clarity of the air, and raptors circling overhead. I breathed in the crisp pine smell as the path led past a cluster of ponderosas. Crows called. As my awareness developed, I heard the distant sound of drums and rattles, the sound seeming to be all around me, keeping me company as I walked, yet I didn't see anyone.

The path turned left, and I followed it around the bend and up a slight rise. There, in a sheltered area, stood a figure, shimmering with light. I knew it was a woman, but the image was vague and fuzzy. Waiting quietly, I let my awareness build.

"She's an old woman," I thought to myself, focusing. "A Native American." Then I startled. "A Medicine Woman."

The woman, as if waiting for me to acknowledge her, motioned me over. Noticing the feather in her hair, I remembered my teaching, offering her a tobacco braid. Silently the woman accepted my offering, moving off behind a grouping of rocks.

Ever curious, I followed, finding her standing by a particular rock. Looking down, I noticed the hollow in the rock, filled now with water. Intuitively, I knew what was wanted.

Carefully I walked to the small fire behind the woman. There, picking up two green sticks, I lifted a coal from the fire, gently placing it in the water. Together we watched. Interestingly, I noticed that the images were forming, not in the water as my observing mind expected, but in the steam over it. As we watched, they began to form into shapes.

"It's a ceremony," I thought, watching, absorbed as though it were going on at the time. Then I realized that it was a cult ritual, quickly drawing back, reflexively. Yet I wanted to know. Needed to know. Leaning forward again with the Medicine Woman, we watched.

In this one, the sacrificial animals were cats, including my beloved kitten. Adults, cleaning up afterwards, thought to further taunt and traumatize two-year old Carla, placing her mutilated kitten's body in her hands. The child ran hysterical from the scene.

Together we watched her wandering, sobbing, in the woods and noticed another figure coming up and joining her. Her brother had found her and walked alongside, comforting her. I heard his words, typical even in adulthood.

"Now, that wasn't very nice of them." His classic understatement, yet meant as a way to calm the small child. We watched as slowly she calmed, absorbing his well-intentioned presence. As the steam drifted away, they faded from the scene. I understood that my dream that morning had been a memory.

With that understanding, I got up, thinking it was time to leave. The Medicine Woman motioned me back. There was more. The Medicine Woman retrieved the green sticks, dropping another hot coal into the shallow pool of water, and together we watched. Again, we saw the same scene, only this time I noticed the glow.

Around my child self there was a white light, glowing softly but clearly. I was completely surrounded with it. And as we looked, we saw several other light beings there with the child Carla. She was surrounded by light beings, protecting her mind and spirit, bringing her a sense of loving presence distant yet palpable. Clearly, the Medicine Woman wanted me to remember this protection, even in this present time. Again, the steam from the coal dissipated, leaving the clear desert air still, yet full with meaning. This time we were done.

Grateful, I thanked the Medicine Woman, turning reluctantly to leave. She nodded a farewell as I turned and walked back down the path, aware again of the fresh pine and sage-scented wind and the blue sky with a few high clouds leaving tracks across the expanse. Walking, I felt stronger with each step. I knew that the dream was a memory, that I was supported in the past and present, and that I could go on. I walked down the path, with the wind and the sky, breathing deeply, returning to a state of alertness in my office. A few more minutes and my therapy day would begin.

The March winds were fierce, whipping my coat open and hair into my face, as I pushed against their force towards the door to Gabe's office building. Pressing my purse to my side, I grabbed the door of the building and yanked, falling into the doorway with the next gust. The cold was actually invigorating after so long in the car, and I welcomed the briskness. Too soon I was caught up in the stale building air as I passed the pharmacy on my right where chocolate and nuts called to me, reminding me how good a junk snack would be. Ignoring temptation, I headed for the elevators. The elevators of the firemen, I reminded myself with a small smile.

Settling in, I told Gabe of my Medicine Woman meditation. "Is that where she went!" he exclaimed, sitting up suddenly in his chair, his coffee splashing out over the edge of the tilted mug and towards his sweater. Grabbing a paper towel, he returned his attention to me.

"She was with us when we did that work with her in this office about a year and a half ago. And I haven't seen her since."

I grinned at his astonishment, not realizing he'd lost track of her.

"Seriously, Carla. I had been wondering about that. I've been giving myself a hard time about her not being around. I just couldn't understand why she didn't come back. I had worked with her before, then we did the work with you, and then she disappeared. I thought maybe I had done something wrong. And here, she was with you!"

I chuckled lightly with his reaction, then jumped slightly as his meaning hit me. "Uh, Gabe. That was just a visualization. As in a meditation that I did with her. I'm not sure I'm following you."

Now he grinned full out at me. "Carla. That wasn't just a visualization. Do you know what the difference is? Like, how you tell if it's a visualization or if it's happening on the astral plane?"

"No. I didn't know there was a difference."

"Actually, it's fairly easy to discern. In most visualizations, we know what they are and where we're going and so forth. But in this one, she took charge of it and changed it."

"How do you mean?"

"Well, remember what you said. You were finished with the visualization, as you thought it was. Though I question even that part of it, as it sounds as if it was doing you, rather than you following a script of some kind. But when you were done, and ready to come back, she called you back to the fire, added a coal to the fire, and gave you more teaching. Her changing it was a clear indication that she was with you and in charge of what was happening, rather than you being in control of it."

I snuggled in my chair, grateful for the creature comfort of the chair and my tea, as I considered. I was getting the difference as I remembered the experience. I looked at him, waiting for what else was coming, knowing that he wasn't done yet.

"This was taking place on the astral realm. A higher spiritual plane. Did you notice the difference in the lighting?"

"Actually, I did. It was the Southwest, and yet the lighting had a different feel to it. A shimmering opaque hue. A very different quality."

"Um hm. And this was a teaching. She really wanted you to know about the presence of Spirit there, with and for you. It's an important lesson and one to remember."

Remembering the vision, a peacefulness settled over me. It helped as we moved into more healing work. This session became one of grief work, the grief of the small child Carla as she mourned the trauma done to the other children. The Medicine Woman came to assist once more.

The Native peoples were also there in the spirit realm to assist us. I was aware of being in two different realities at the same time. On the one hand, Gabe and I found the child Carla grieving and worked with my own unfinished grief work. In the other reality, with the Medicine Woman, I experienced the soft drumming of the Elders, the child dressed in buckskins with black paint on her face, the robes and skins which wrapped her in their shelter as they drummed her grief with wisdom and compassion. And the drumming went on for a long, long time.

In retrospect, this was hump time. A time of gathering. Finding strength, coping skills, support systems that needed to be upgraded for the work ahead. A time of frustration, as I felt so strongly that there was more ahead. Yet the Divine was in charge. Fortunately. My rashness and eagerness to be out of pain would have sunk my ship. This time was needed to build the foundation for the rest of the journey, a journey of healing, learning the action of faith and trust, and of creating a new life of love and vitality.

The illness period was mostly behind me now. It had taken two and a half years to come through that valley. Slowly I continued to recover strength. Over that hump, I was gathering for the last big push. A push to find the healing and meaning in the Sacred Wound.

A week later, Pia called. "Walk?"

"Sure, come on over." I was glad to hear from her.

That evening we walked my neighborhood, her slender form effortlessly moving along as we noted the homes and stepped around old tree roots interrupting the smooth flow of the concrete sidewalk. Her shoulders sagging, I wondered what was going on. Looking sideways, I gave her a quizzical look.

"My boss is getting me down," she admitted, frowning and grumbling as she stepped aside for a forgotten bike lying abandoned. "You know, he's always been a problem for me."

She'd looked up then. I knew he'd always been a problem, and I worried periodically about her. She seemed committed to her work in the clinic, but got significantly depressed with his autocratic ways. Quietly, we visited, walking through the mixed neighborhood, changing topics often. The early spring breeze carried a hint of warmth, accompanied by forsythia starting to bud and crocuses pushing up for the light of day. Promises of better days to come, I hoped. For both of us.

Soon we were laughing and giggling, enjoying two small girls as they played on a nearby swing set. The ordinary things, I thought, as the sky started to deepen with dusk, colors building in the west. Things that remind us of the cycles of life, and of going forward. Things like good friends.

Heart of God

The trip to Gabe's was nothing extraordinary, yet I found myself jumpy again, anxious, delaying the inevitable by stopping to shop in the morning. A later appointment, I needed lunch, but couldn't imagine keeping food down. I would have yogurt now, I decided, and eat something more substantial later.

In his office, I reviewed the dreams of the month and a trauma trance that had upset me. Nothing specific that we could get our hands on. Gabe sipped coffee and listened to me wander in my thoughts, curled up in my cushy chair, jacket on the floor on my right. Finally he straightened, putting his coffee on the stool beside him and leaning forward.

"Carla, it seems like there's a door between you and whatever the problem is, and something is seeping through, slipping around the door and under it. That's what's making you anxious. Something needs to be in the open now."

I definitely could have passed on that thought. I tuned in to the possible image, recognizing it's validity for me, too. "It feels like a mist creeping out from around the door."

"Exactly. So," he paused, "let's put a window in the door and maybe we can look through the window. Does that feel OK?"

Safety first. I liked the idea. I settled back, relaxing into a light trance state to look through the window in the door.

"It's a light colored mist, soft, no real substance at this point. Whatever is happening is pretty far away. It feels OK to go through the door," I reported cautiously.

Gabe nodded, tracking me, moving closer to be of support.

I walked through the door, and immediately startled. "The mist is turning dark, a murky black. Hard to see." I shivered.

"Leave the door wide open."

"No kidding. In fact, I'm making it bigger. I may have to run for that sucker," I added.

"Put a large exit sign over it, so you're sure you can get out," Gabe added.

"Neon." So I can find it in the dark, I thought to myself. Satisfied with the large door and its glowing neon exit sign, I sat down to wait, my back to the door molding, knowing something would change. Patience. There. I could begin to see it now, at the far edge. The candles, fire, figures moving. Dread settled.

"Make the mist into a large movie screen," Gabe told me, and I recognized the screen technique that I frequently used for trauma work in my therapy practice. Good idea. Big screen. Far away.

The screen cleared, showing dark figures and myself as a child of three or four wearing a white robe in the bleak inky night. Struggling and squirming, my child self was held against the altar, forced to watch, large men in black robes pinning my small arms, forcing me against the cold stone. Horrified, I realized what they were forcing the child to watch. Pain filled me as the tears rolled down my cheeks.

"Tell me, Carla," Gabe urged softly, watching.

"A small child, being tortured. They are drawing it out to increase the pain."

"I know. I see it, too." His voice was quiet, sad, compassionate.

I was aware of my child self, dizzy and sick with the pain of the other, nearly fainting from the forced watching, my little white robe marking me as the one chosen to be held responsible for the tragedy as the men held me there for punishment.

"It's old torture methods," Gabe spoke quietly, putting an intellectual frame around the anguish, giving needed distance. I could feel him pulling back, regaining his Warrior stance.

"What did you do then, Carla?"

I watched, becoming the little girl once more, feeling into her essence. Immediately, I knew.

"I took the pain into myself. It's the only way I knew to help her. It was so awful."

"Where did you take it?"

"Into my heart chakra." I opened my eyes, aware of Gabe, sad for the child, for my child self, for all the tragic deeds being done. Tears streaked my face.

"You can't carry that much pain, Carla. It's way too much."

"I know. But I don't know what to do with it." I saw myself, siphoning it off, soaking it in like a sponge, trying to relieve the little girl's pain, its weight unbearable.

"You can't carry it, and I can't either. You need to take it from your heart chakra, and give it to the heart of God."

"How do I do that?" It sounded like the impossible task.

Gabe moved his roller chair over until he was beside me on my right, carefully placing his left hand in back of my heart and his right hand in front, supporting my heart chakra and running energy.

"Let yourself go into your heart chakra. Go as far as you can. I'll track you. I'm with you."

With his reassurance, I turned my attention away from the cult and into my heart. Struggling with the concept at first, I found I really could go into my heart. With his hands to help me focus and maintain energy, I followed my attention deep within.

"Good. Now go further."

I went back as far as I could, back into a soft sweet cavern with smooth sides and a slight rosy half-light, opening for my passage, then narrowing. I was as far as I could go.

"That's good. There. Now, when you think you've gone as far as you can go, and you can't go any further, keep going."

It had become very narrow just then, but at his urging, I continued to persist. His voice supported me, as well as his hands, urging me forward, telling me that I really could do this. Suddenly the passage opened up. It's as if I were standing on the edge of a secret cliff on a starry night with the universe of God opening before me. The ground solid and damp beneath my feet, I knew myself to be secure as I looked out, speechless with the grandeur and vastness. It looked to be a magnificent night sky before me, pulsating with unending love, little lights twinkling, each sending its own radiance into the vastness. A view of eternity, yet so close I could touch it.

I looked again at the twinkling lights, seeing the stars, each a pinpoint of love for every living soul that ever existed. In awe I absorbed the love of God, from a place I never dreamed existed.

"It's full of love and goodness, and can take all the pain, Carla. Go back into your heart now, and collect all that pain, and bring it back out."

Reluctant to leave the abyss that emptied into Love itself, I did as Gabe suggested, turning back to my heart. Gathering the piercing, jagged red and black pain that I had stored there, I pulled it into a pulsing ball of energy, throbbing in my hands.

"Good." Gabe was tracking me, feeling the energy.

"Now, give that pain to the Heart of God. All the love that is there can take it and absorb it. You'll see, Carla."

My mind warred with the suggestion. I didn't want to despoil the Heart of God and all the Love that was present in this sacred place. Yet my trust in Gabe was strong, and I also knew that I couldn't manage that much pain myself. Holding it in my hands, I quietly opened them, allowing the pain to flow out.

My own heart wide open with love and compassion, I watched as the ragged red and black shards of energy flowed into the vastness, gently and sweetly absorbed, transformed as the colors lightened and spread out. The transforming love was powerful, tangible and clear, changing the pain into specks of white light as it was absorbed back into Love. The Heart of God was more than big enough to take this pain and ease the suffering, transforming it into the light of God. I watched in silent awe.

"Good. Good." Gabe's quiet voice encouraged me as I let it all go, until each sharp painful strand was gone.

Slowly then, I eased back into my own heart, automatically returning, my task done. From awareness of my own love and compassion, to my heart chakra, to my perception of Gabe's hands supporting me, I slowly returned, reluctant to let go of the vastness of eternal love. Remembering my exit sign, I sadly realized that I didn't need it. The danger was over. I could come home now.

A break, and then we sat again, my Diet Coke and Gabe's coffee providing some semblance of normalcy. I sighed deeply and looked up at him, his rangy form leaning back in his chair, now in its usual place.

"You took the pain on as your own."

"It was all that I knew to do. I had to do something. She was in too much pain, no thanks to their concerted efforts. What else is a small child to do?" I grinned weakly with that one, trying to lighten up. Then, adding, "I felt so guilty about it all, since it was my fault."

"It was another one of those set-ups. You were deliberately being blamed. Remember, Carla. Brain washing. Tying you irrevocably to the cult. How could you ever consider leaving? Typical trick for a group of thugs."

Well, that put it back in perspective, I thought to myself. They certainly were just that. Big bullies. Should pick on someone their own size.

"How old were you?" Gabe asked again.

"Three or four."

"Yeah, really. It was your fault. Come on, girl. Get with it." He paused then, thinking of something else. "Carla, who else was there?"

"I don't know."

"Go back into the scene. It's time you knew who else was involved and in what way."

Reluctantly, I leaned back and slipped into trance again, seeing the cult easily this time in my mind's eye. As usual, I couldn't see faces, yet I had come to realize that I had the ability to recognize people by their essence. A hard-won ability. Sensing, I felt my father on my right, an unknown man with a huge aura directly across from me, and my sister a bit further back on my right, all in enveloping black robes.

"Why did they have my sister there?" I questioned Gabe.

"They were grooming her for a role, something like a priestess," was his take on it.

I couldn't find anyone else that I recognized, letting go of the image and returning to the reality of Gabe's office. We relaxed into our chairs again as I focused into the office, taking in voices, the tapping of a computer next door, and the scent of coffee. Again I picked up my Diet Coke to fiddle with it, waiting for Gabe's observations.

"I could only find your father and sister, too," he affirmed. "If your brother and mother were there, they evidently weren't near the altar."

"Mm hmm," I nodded, sipping the Coke. "That was my feeling. Makes me wonder about my sister, though I do know that she's pretty psychic. I can understand they'd groom her for more."

"You looked angry as you realized who was there." Gabe let the comment drop softly, like the glove of a challenge. Immediately my eyes flashed at him.

"I don't get angry!" Oops. It didn't take long to reconsider that. Wonder why I had such a trigger defense about anger? But the past scene from the dojo was clear, Darlene hitting my nose by accident and my temper flashing on contact. Oh, man . . . more work to do. All this in silence while Gabe watched, a small grin close to a smirk. His right eyebrow raised in the unspoken question.

"Oh, all right. We'll think about it later. But Gabe," I turned serious again in a heartbeat, "what happens if I get triggered at home. Can I go to the Heart of God by myself?"

"I don't know if you could do it alone, Carla. I certainly couldn't. But you can always call me if you need me. And I want you to. That's part of taking good care of yourself."

I was reassured. The month had been a hard one, and I was still afraid of the triggers or flashbacks. I probably wouldn't call him, but it was very reassuring to remember that he made himself available for me. I realized we had a few more moments to consider possible problems in the coming month.

"Is there anything we can, or should, do for that child?"

Gabe considered, checking in with his guidance. "No, Carla, there's nothing. It was a tragedy." We went back to my anger flash.

"Yeah, it makes me mad. I probably shouldn't think this way, but there is part of me that does hope there is such a thing as divine retribution." Fury flashed in my gaze.

"I just want to take them out!" Gabe snapped. "I know it's not spiritual, but it makes me angry."

"Well, that's a relief. It's how I feel, but it's at war with my shame over the teachings of love and spirit and all."

"A time for everything," he sighed, checking his watch. It was time. I would miss him. What a huge healing it had been.

In my car, I spent time winding down before getting back on the interstate, watching a wild spring storm roll into town, winds blowing and heaving tree branches, throwing the few remaining crows into erratic patterns in the air. As quickly as it started, it was gone, leaving the ozone smell of freshness and a clean-washed feel behind it. Just like my life, I mused.

The session had been painful, desperately so, and yet ended with such a sense of love. The two feelings were able to co-exist, the Heart of God big enough and full enough to hold the terror, pain and evil of the cult. The love would stay with me, giving me peace in the dark hours.

In many ways, my health was improving. Thank God for large favors. I could now walk almost three-quarters of a mile, a huge improvement of my prior distance of about three houses.

"That's what Epstein barr and mono together will do to you," my homeopath Richard had told me when I had complained. "Not to mention your viruses, toxic metal poisoning . . ."

"OK, OK, I get the point," I had fussed back. It just didn't mean that I had to like it. I'd hated it. Now, two and a half years later, health was returning.

Back home, I was walking again in the mornings, loving the early spring days. Still dark which gave me the privacy that my introverted nature loved, yet I was usually out as the sun rose. The combination was perfect for this time as I contrasted the darkness of my experiences with the growing light in my life.

Jack was in England on business, and Nate was on the road, too. He was still doing well academically in college, yet he traveled constantly for his favorite concerts.

Their absence left Jennie and me baching it. Up early, realizing there was almost no food in the house, I grabbed my keys for a quick trip to the grocery. Coming back, Jennie met me at the door, a long frown playfully planted.

"Grocery, girl," I replied. "Gotta have food." Walking in I found the table set for breakfast, french toast on the stove. That had to be a first. Maybe this girl was going to make it after all. I turned, smiling appreciatively.

"Yeah, I figured french toast sounded good. So I tried my 'mommy location device' but I couldn't find you!"

I knew what that meant. She'd been yelling for me from one end of the house to the other, waiting for my shouted reply. Laughing, I gave her a quick hug.

The next night, Nate called in from California. There was trouble on the trip, kids not getting along with each other, fighting. I stayed rational, gave him support, did the parent thing. And when I hung up, fell apart.

Shaking and crying, I curled up on my bed. I was sure that my inadequate parenting had caused his problems. My lack of availability, my own abuse . . . On and on it went. A freight train in the mind, I was quickly heading for derailment.

Without Jack there, I slept fitfully, waking up from nightmares shivering with fear, tears streaking my face. Would Nate be all right? Had I done him harm by who I was? How I was?

By noon, I knew that I had to do something, fumbling through my planner in frustration, placing the call to Gabe. I hated doing it. He'd always been available, but I'd just seen him. The ranting at myself went on for a long time.

That evening he returned the call. Filling him in, I ranted some more. "I hate this. I hate myself for it. Yet I am afraid. Maybe I harmed him somehow. Maybe it is my fault. If only I hadn't been so distracted while he was growing up. But I had to do my healing work, or I might not have still been alive."

Gabe had heard enough. Who can blame him? A mind out of control is not a pretty thing. But his answer surprised me, expecting him to firmly tell me to get it together.

"Carla, take this seriously. Put it into context. This is not about you having a cult history and then you having your current life. Put them together, in context, and what do you get?"

"Huh?" The response of a distraught mind.

"Think about it. What was your experience? In the cult, if you thought you made one tiny mistake, tragedy followed. Someone was tortured or died. And you were blamed. Because of a tiny error of some kind. Which they were simply using to have a scapegoat and to program you. You think this is not connected?"

My heart rate calmed as I listened to him, hearing truth and absorbing it. My cult history bleeding into my current life, I understood that at times that I felt way overly responsible. Mistakes were devastating to me. Still.

"It's also about survivor's guilt," he continued. I knew about survivor's guilt and referred to it in my practice. Harder to apply to oneself.

"You know," I told him, holding the phone while I shifted on my bed, "this is just a really difficult time for me. I pray every morning to want to be alive. It's not that I'm actively suicidal. I'm not. I just don't want to be here. It's just too hard."

"I understand that, Carla," he replied gently. "It's like the concentration camps. People often had to do terrible things to survive. As a very small child, you had to choose between allowing yourself to be forced to do tragic things or to die. Or to watch others die because of your refusal to do harm. There was no way out. For you, similar to survivors of concentration camps, surviving was at a very high price. It's easy to wish you had died instead. It is hard."

His clarity and affirmation brought calmness as I took a big breath. He was right. But what to do? The here and now?

"You need a different prayer in the morning," he went on after a thoughtful pause. "You need to pray first, just after your walk, and ask for help from the big spirits. They've assisted you before and will again. Then pray to the spirits of those you were forced to harm and release those spirits from you.

"After that, you are to use your tingshas, the Tibetan bells you have, and release those spirits from your heart on the sound of the bell. So as you ring the bells, you release the spirits from you on that sound. Have you got that part?"

"Yeah. I can do that." Having a task was grounding, too.

"Good. Watch the process both as you do it and during the day afterwards. See how you're doing. When you feel that you are cleared, then ask that the bowl, your heart chakra, be filled with joy and love and the desire to be alive.

"Right now there is no room for that, because your heart is filled with the spirits of those you were forced to harm and those whom you were blamed for harming. You are consumed by those devastating mistakes. So first you have to clear your heart of that, and then ask for life. This whole thing may elicit more mourning for you, so be aware of that. But you need to clear your heart, before you can fill it with joy."

"And Nate?"

"In your rational mind, you know your fears are unfounded. But you need to let go of the cult programming and tragedies for this to really compute for you. So you can separate the cult experiences out from your current life in a clean way."

Our talk went on for a few minutes more, Gabe soothing, reaffirming and giving instructions. I understood how the past and present were interwoven into the one fabric of my life. I would do the work to separate them.

The next morning, outside at dawn after my walk, I found myself reluctant to work with the tingshas after all. I wasn't sure what the reluctance was about, but it was difficult to get going. My best guess in the end was that it was about letting go of the spirits. I had held them in my heart, to love and protect them and to ask for forgiveness. It would create a different kind of loss to let go of them. I put the tingshas down for that morning. I had to get more ready for this.

For the next couple of mornings, I walked quietly, planning my ceremony. The following Sunday morning, after my walk, I stood under the giant spreading oak in my backyard, the sun washing the sky fresh and clean in hues of pink, orange and rose. A new day.

"Grandmothers, Grandfathers, Powers of the Four Directions!" I opened the prayer as forcefully as I could. I needed help. "Hear my voice! Be with me, I pray!"

Then I addressed the spirits of those I had harmed that were still in my heart, as well as the spirits of the ones that I had been blamed for harming, as I knew I carried them in my heart.

"I ask that you be released on the sound of the tingshas to the Heart of God, where you will find welcome, love, care and healing." As my words faded in the morning light, I rang the tingshas, loudly and clearly, in front of my heart chakra. The clear, penetrating sound carried into the gently growing light, carrying my prayers with it. And with the sound, I had an awareness that I had kept the spirits with me to try to care for them, when of course, I couldn't. Releasing them to the Heart of God was releasing a burden I could not carry, and releasing them to love and healing.

I was surprised. Even the first time, I felt clearer and a real sense of relief. It was as if I felt lighter. Encouraged, I did it again that evening at dusk, again feeling relief.

The following morning, I repeated my ceremony, refining it more each time as I gained more clarity about it. Again, I felt the lifting of the pain I had carried. Yet that morning, the third time I did it, it was different. Just after sounding the tingshas, while the sound still faded into the air, I became incredibly aware of life itself. Feeling the slight breeze, and hearing the beginning sound of the early-morning birds, I felt the pulse of life even as it echoed within myself. My prayer changed along with the subtly shifting awareness.

"I pray that life, love, and the love of life itself fill my heart in the space that the spirits have emptied. That all space be refilled with God's love and a desire to be alive."

With that prayer, I became acutely aware of the fullness of nature around me, feeling even more completely the spring morning and all of life pulsing with the heartbeat of God. Spring had come, and it had entered my heart also. I could go on.

It was a clear morning when I placed the call. Bright, sunny and time for a new beginning.

"Hello," the voice answered, gruff and low.

"Hey. It's Carla." If you can hear a smile grow over a phone line, it was there.

"Hey," was the only response, yet the voice was completely different. Gone was the self-protective caution, replaced with a smile of pleasure energy. Warmth instead of the cautious chill. The note of a Sensei recognizing a friend and comrade.

"I think it's time." A simple statement that we had both waited a long time to hear. I had been increasing my walking times, even introducing brief periods of jogging. Often overdoing it, I'd had to regroup, take days off, then return and try to approach my goal of improved health a little more slowly and cautiously. Over the weeks and months, I'd gotten stronger, inch by inch. Now it was time for the test.

"Good, Carla!" He was as delighted as I was. "But you're going to have to be really careful. I know you." Yes, he did. The risk of my overdoing was high.

"I'm in the new school now," he reminded me.

Parkman's dojo was large, had been there for over twenty-five years. Too many black belts were a blessing and a curse. The time had come to thin the herd of too much testosterone. Parkman got tired of being challenged. My friends had left.

I would miss the old school. The delicate oriental garden hidden behind the wooden gate, the rice paper covered windows, the bar and kitchen where we used to hang out. Mostly, I would miss my friends in training.

But there were risks there, too. Parkman pushed the edge and his students did the same. I'd been hurt there a couple of times. I knew I was always safe from needless injury when training with Sensei. A bit wiser, I was going with safety.

Well, truth be told, safety **and** poetry in motion. Once you've studied with an artist, there's no substitute. The grace and delicacy of a dancer; the power of a street fighter. He knew the art and how to apply it in a safe way. I was going back.

I arrived the next evening just as the light of day was fading. He'd been drawn to teach in this inner-city high school, where he could recruit the underprivileged from the neighborhood, working with them to increase the children's self-esteem and abilities. Worthy goals. But not comfortable.

The after-school program was just letting out, creating a traffic jam in the parking lot at the top of a deceptively steep short drive. One lane only, drivers paused and took turns, trying to maneuver the cars without scrapes and bumps. At the top of the small hill, kids of all sizes and colors leaned against cars waiting for rides, sat on hoods or walked between the cars, calling to friends. In other '~ general chaos. I shivered in apprehension. Not my idea of a

ɪ the moderately-sized linoleum floored rec room. ʝ the old school. Yet my visits to Parkman's school had taught me that the most important part was the Sensei, not the building. He was waiting.

His welcoming glance, respectful bow, and following hug were warm . . . and evaluative. His deep, dark eyes and senses assessed my strengths and weaknesses, noting my weight, strength and posture. Then the smile and twinkle returned as he hugged me again before releasing me to Sherri, the other black-belt woman who had come with him to the new school. She was clearly glad to have another higher-ranking adult.

I took it slow, for once, only having to stop once as I bent over with my hands on my knees. Maybe I had aged as I'd been off? What a terrible thought. Sensei kept the class at a low pace, practicing basics to help me readjust.

Soaking wet, I was soon bowing out, having mastered a long-term goal. Getting back in training. Karate taught me so much. I slung my gym bag over my shoulder as I faced the floor and bowed. A good beginning.

Thread of Light

The dream felt soft, comforting in contrast to so many of them. Before me in the luminous light, I saw a large book full of pages which were gently turning. Pages which showed images of the cult, but somehow I wasn't afraid. The pages turned to show the last one, then I noticed three more pages shimmering to the right of the book. Softly they lifted and slipped into the book, one by one. With their addition, the large book closed and the dream faded.

The next day, Pia called. "What are you doing, Carla?"

"Nothing much. Why don't you come over?"

"I'll be there."

Fifteen minutes and she was at my door, laughing at Kanji, waving good-bye to Jennie as she flew through the house and out. Sitting out back, we sipped our ice tea and visited.

"Things going better, Pia?" I asked, noticing her lighter mood. Relationships at the clinic must be improving. Her smile reaffirmed ~ver, as she sat relaxed in her lawn chair, graceful body fitting ~ther we shared, while watching the birds play at the ʾutterfly in the garden. The full smell of rich, .ed us, calling us to search for four-leaf clovers.

Back in our chairs, Pia turned serious. "So how's it going, Carla? I worry about you, you know."

I smiled at her, grateful for her support. "You know, I had a dream that seems to me to indicate that I'm nearly done. Wouldn't that be wonderful. I've really wondered about it."

"What was the dream?"

I told her the images as she listened carefully, nodding, absorbing the feeling of it.

"It has the feeling of completion, certainly. Three more pages. What do you think that means?" She looked at me, sipping her tea, forehead creased in a frown.

"Well, maybe three more big episodes? That's how Gabe and I seem to be doing this. At least in terms of cult events that are especially difficult and significant to me. We have these large events where we do spiritual work, and then we spend many sessions doing the psychological and energetic healing work from those larger pieces. Makes me wonder if there are three more of those large events that need to be cleared from my system." I shifted my chair to face her more, and to have the sun at my side.

"Well, I hope that's it," she replied, sighing with her concern. "Another thing I've wondered."

"Yeah?"

"When you talk about it, you talk more about the spiritual. I know Gabe also does regular psychology. And you said that he does the energy work, too."

"Caught in the act," I laughed at her. "I plead guilty. You know, Pia, he's an excellent therapist, and we've done years of solid psychological work, starting clear back with my incest memories. And he's taught me so much about energy work. But my real passion seems to be with the spiritual lessons."

"Why do you think?"

"Because that's where the hope lies for me. That there's a wisdom and a meaning to all of this that transcends random suffering. I have to know that part to make it a meaningful experience, worth having suffered that much. Do you understand?"

"Umm. I think so. I kind of wonder about the whole picture with Sasha that way, too. Why was she born, nearly sold into prostitution, brought here? Then again, what's the meaning for each of us in what happens?"

"That's what captures my passion, Pia. It's like my quest for the meaning behind it, and I think it's a spiritual issue."

We talked some more, cherishing precious time with a friend. Too soon it was time to go, indicated by her cell phone ringing.

"Speaking of Sasha, she wants a ride. Gotta run, Carla."

The attack came swiftly, much quicker than I had anticipated. Startled, I grasped the hand thrusting the wooden knife at me, and twisted hard. Too quick and off balance, the man in the white gi flew up into the air. Turning mid-air, he plunged abruptly to the floor, landing knee first on top of my right foot, the wooden knife clattering away against a far wall. Smoothly done, he would have followed a more gradual trajectory to a safer landing, but my response had been in panic, and he landed with full force on my foot. The sharp pain was immediate, shooting through my body. I winced and pulled back.

Sensei had caught the unnatural movement as I jerked the hand in fear, and was immediately beside us. Surveying the damage, he didn't need to say it. He looked at me thoughtfully and left me to tend to my foot. My attacker shook himself out and moved on to his next practiced victim, waiting to make sure his new partner was ready and aware. Limping, I steadied myself for my new partner, reminding myself again of the need for awareness and focus. Regretfully, I watched my foot changing color and swelling. If ice didn't do it, maybe Gabe could help.

Sitting at the side icing my foot, my mind drifted back to my early teens. Lacking awareness of the cult then, I had possessed a fascination with knives. I remembered the night when I had stood in the gathering dusk, facing my opponent. Ready for the fight, I had hesitated, then reached down inside my sock and pulled it out. The switchblade flashed in the streetlight as my hand flicked it open. Immediately the on-lookers had pulled their circle back. I didn't know why I had done it, but the blade was out now.

Then suddenly there was a responding click and flash of light, as the glow from the streetlight glittered off another blade. A chill ran through me, as full awareness of the escalating danger finally filled me. Risking all, I had hesitated, then thrown mine to the side and waited. Relief had flooded me as the other knife also struck the ground at the edge of the gathering crowd, and we had closed to strike out our rage at life.

The fight had ended, but my fascination with knives had not. I needed to learn to conquer knives, and my fears. But that would be for another day. At the moment, I needed to ice my throbbing foot.

It was good to see Gabe again, though I worried a bit. You couldn't miss the lack of carpet in his office. I looked at him, query in my eyes.

"My allergies," he responded, as I noticed his flushed face and puffy eyes. "We think maybe it's the glue."

"Does look weird, I have to give it that," I muttered looking around at the concrete base with a few throw rugs. "Oh well, we can work in anything at this point."

Grinning ruefully as he took his seat, he shook his head. "Always something, you know? Just to keep you on your toes."

We settled, while I filled him in on my concerns. "You know, I had a lot of trouble with summer solstice again. It didn't seem as though I should as we've done so much work, but it was very hard." I went on to list symptoms and fears arising.

"I wonder if you're still connected to the cult in some way so that you're getting triggered by their current activity, rather than by memories. You know we've been working from the Post Traumatic Stress model, assuming that you're being triggered into anxiety and panic by memories coming up. I wonder if this is something different."

I thought about it. "We've done enough work to settle the holidays down. And this was bad. It makes sense, what you say, though I don't know how that could work. And I'm telling you, it makes me nervous as a cat."

His grin was spontaneous. I glared back. "What?"

"Carla. Nothing bad. I just get such a tickle out of your language sometimes." Laughter leaving his eyes, he got serious.

"I have another client with cult connections. But her connection is to the spirits behind the cult people. And that connection had to be broken."

I hadn't thought of that. Talk about a sobering thought. I didn't want yet another connection, another layer. I shivered.

"It's like, in that case, the spirits were pulling the strings, not the cult people. The powers in charge were those spirits that the cultists had invoked. It's kind of interesting because the people think they are so powerful, and in fact, they are being used. But it is a different force to reckon with."

I didn't like it. Not one bit. Maybe it wasn't true. Sitting up straight in my chair, I argued.

"Well, it may well not be true, Carla. We certainly don't know yet. But we do have to remember that you were consecrated to the cult. When we worked on that, we did the memory work, because that's all we knew to do. There may be more."

We sat quietly. There was a sense of work to be done, but no real direction for the work. All that I was aware of was my rapidly escalating anxiety. Slowly I drifted off.

"Where'd you go, Carla?" Gabe asked softly as I faded away.

I wasn't initially aware of having gone anywhere, but then realized that I had slipped into a trance state and was staring over his left shoulder.

"What am I staring at?" I wondered dimly. Then I noticed the white spot behind him. The spot shifted, growing into a slender white thread. As if from the depths of a thick fog, I told him of the thread. His voice came from far away, almost disembodied from a person.

"Follow it."

I stilled myself. Center, Carla. Awareness and focus, just like the dojo, I reminded myself, moving into warrior stance. I could focus on the white thread. Where did it go?

Surprised, I found I could follow it. Into the shimmering mist, I followed the slender thread, watching as it got more narrow. Frightened of losing it, I reminded myself to breath.

Startled, I suddenly realized what was happening. "It's going underground."

"Follow it there. See where it goes."

Carefully, I made the turn down, following the slender glowing thread. Stunned, I stopped in amazement.

"What?" Gabe's voice released me from a kind of paralysis, allowing me to think again.

"Gabe, this is finally proof. I have an overactive imagination."

His voice was steady, serious as he followed me, seeing what I saw. "Describe it to me, Carla. Put it in your own words."

I settled back into my trance state, able to start again where I'd fled in disbelief. This was a different breed of cat, as my family would say. Quietly, I told him, shivering.

"The thread went into an opening in the ground, so I went through and found myself in a tunnel of sorts."

"Um hmm." He was with me.

"It's dark. I can hardly see," I added, reaching warily to the side to steady myself. Jerking my hand back almost immediately, I gasped.

"What, Carla."

"It's OK. I was just surprised. It's damp and I didn't expect it." I took another breath, grounding myself. "The sides of the tunnel are rough-cut, sort of like a mining tunnel, and sloping down, with the rancid stench of stagnant water and things rotting. Yuck." I was getting sidetracked, and pulled myself back into focus.

"It's slippery," I squeaked, slipping on the slick mud from trickling water sliding down the dank walls.

"Be careful."

"I am. I'm following the thread forward and down. It's so **cold** in here Gabe. Deeply cold to the core." I paused, then continued. "This is where I bolted before. Just too weird."

"Describe it to me." He was quiet, close at hand.

"The tunnel slants down, the seeping rocky floor making it hard to walk. At the end, it opens out into a cavern. I stopped there, at the edge of the cavern."

"Good plan. Continue to describe it to me."

"The walls are rugged, jagged, barely reflecting the gray light and disclosing different qualities of darkness from inky and dead to glassy and reflecting. Water still seeps into this place, seemingly everywhere. And there's a deep, cold evil feeling that goes to the marrow of my bones," I added, shivering again.

Letting my breath out, I continued, shaking my head at the impossibility of the scene while I perched on the edge of the tunnel as it spilled into the cavern.

"There are beings here. Very dark, kind of blob-like seeming almost part human and part beast. Ugly." That as I moved cautiously back another step.

"Oh, man. They even have large velvety black wings. Gabe, I have to be making this up." I was close to whining. Not good.

"It's OK, Carla. I see them, too. And they are unnerving."

"There's a scent of arrogance in the air."

"Yes. The arrogance is a calling card."

I paused, watching the figures. "At the far end is a bigger one, more blob-shaped. I think he's the leader. The others seem more subordinate."

"Um hmm. See which one you're connected to, Carla."

"Connected to?" My voice rose. Oh, shit. Grounding, I sensed into the cavern, tracking through my kinesthetic senses.

Again I noticed the light thread, realizing that it was **my** thread of light, connected to me. I looked for the other end, continuing to describe the scene for Gabe.

"Actually, there are several central figures with the main one at the far end. They are all kind of lounging around, bragging and being arrogant with each other, the leader egging them on. Then there are a number of lesser figures along the side, subordinates from the size and position of them. My thread goes to one of those figures on the left. My left," I added.

"Yes. And how are you connected?"

I followed the thread to the figure's midsection, where I sensed a leathery substance. "A pouch. My thread went into it."

"Look into the pouch, and see what's there."

Taking a deep breath, I let it out and focused steadily. Zeroing in on the pouch, I felt as if my vision were x-ray, seeing inside to the jumbled items, examining them.

"There are stones in there." I paused, evaluating.

"What else?"

"Bits of things." I stopped, hair rising on the back of my neck, feeling my way into the substances. "Oh, I get it. Locks of hair. Fingernails."

"What does your thread of light connect to?"

I hated the thought. All of it. Focusing again, I felt my way along the thread, coming at last to a solid form. My trained warrior stance was serving me well. Examining the form, I knew.

"It's a piece of fingernail."

Gabe slowly moved his roller chair towards me, stopping at the square table on my left. Listening to guidance, he picked up a bundle of feathers, carefully selecting a large black one. Stroking the feather, he turned to me.

"Crow is going to fly in and get your thread. And then fly like hell, to coin a phrase," the last with the hint of a smile.

"Excuse me? What are you talking about? Crow can't come in here."

"This isn't the same as the vortex, Carla. There's no pull like that. Crow can fly in, get it and get the heck out. Now, hold the feather, stroke it, and follow the light thread."

I followed his directions, gently holding the feather, breathing a small prayer. What were we doing? God help us.

"Crow is following it down now, into the tunnel." Gabe paused. "There. He's in the cavern." I could see it, too.

"They can't see him because of the dark," I told Gabe. "He's following the thread. There! Oh! He's going for the whole pouch." I nearly shrieked in surprise and fear. Surely the cultists had a better chance of catching him with the pouch weighing him down. Surely that dark spirit will realize it much sooner.

Gabe caught my fear. "It's all right, Carla. He's taking the whole pouch so that way they won't know which connection has been broken."

Fear filled me, stopping my breathing. "Won't they know he's in there and going for it? Won't they get him?"

"They'll know when the pouch is gone . . . There! He got it! Now he's flying out. Look, Carla. There are 60 to 70 crows. It's pandemonium in there. With all those crows, they can't find him."

Tracking the scene, I jumped as it broke into sudden chaos. Surprise, outrage, pursuit all broke forth at once as the dark beings shouted, raged and fell over each other in recriminations, joining the chase.

"He's out of the tunnel!" Gabe exclaimed as Crow, amidst the flock, broke free of the tunnel entrance and soared. Then all was silent, and I lost sense of the action. Again, I waited, the other realm closed to me now. My last sense was of Crow and the others, exploding from the tunnel entrance, and the dark beings in close pursuit, raging, shouting and cursing each other.

The silence continued. Finally Gabe turned to me. "I sealed the tunnel." I didn't understand, but trusted him.

He slowly wheeled his chair over to me. Putting his left hand out above me, he reverently gathered something etheric in, handing it to me, placing it in my hand and covering it with my other hand. His hands completely covered mine, with mine holding something very important, very precious.

"Here. Hold this. It's a gift from Crow." I did as instructed, aware that this was a sacred gift. Carefully, I covered my left hand with my right and waited, a pulsing between my hands.

Gabe moved back to his earlier position across from me, and returned to a meditative state. I couldn't follow this time, so I waited quietly.

After a time and a deep sigh, he returned to me. Again he very carefully and seriously put his hands over mine. "Carla, this is your sacred connection. It has been taken and connected to the dark force, through no fault or cooperation of your own. Now it's time to reconnect it to the Source of all good. You are the only one who can do that. You are to take this thread, and decide what of the Sacred that you will reconnect to, and then you must say the words to reconnect. This **you** must do."

I thought long and hard. I was clear about the importance of it all, and determined to do it properly. It was ceremony, and must be done in a good and holy way. As it was my sacred thread, it was also critically important. Yet I paused.

"I'm not sure what to connect to." Various images flowed through my mind, leaving me uncertain.

"What are you considering?"

"I've thought about water. Water is very important to me. And I got an image of a raindrop. And another image of a six-pointed star."

"You need to reconnect to something sacred, yet something that is not in the physical realm. It has to be of the eternal world, not of the natural world."

The image came back to me from our work with the Heart of God. Once again, I could see the sacred points of light, each one a vibrant, shimmering point of God's Love. That was where I wanted to be connected. While it reminded me of a star, it was of the eternal and of Love.

"How do I say it?"

He taught me, coaching me in the Sacred words. With his guidance, I said them, and as I said them, I released the thread from my hands. Slowly I let my hands open, offering the thread and reverently asking that it be returned to the Sacred. In awe, I watched as it uncoiled from my hands, and began to gracefully flow outward. Ever outward. Free like a bird it flowed, knowing its destination, to be connected to that far away Light.

And then, it happened. I felt the connection as the thread arrived and was attached. To my amazement, I noticed something even more. Something completely unexpected. It was the sound of angelic singing. Beautiful beyond words. The singing continued jubilantly, echoing both out there in the universe and within me. The closest and only comparison that I had was the cherished Alleluia Chorus and its exuberance. Joy filled my heart as I listened, aware of the celebration as Light welcomed me Home. Slowly, and softly, it faded, until I turned at last to Gabe.

"I heard it, too," he smiled. No words could fully express the beauty of what we had just witnessed, and together we sat in silence, awe and appreciation.

Then he shared his experience. "It was like the angels rejoicing. One of their souls has been returned to them. It was like they talk about the heavenly host and the rejoicing." It was a warm moment, to be shared and remembered.

Slowly then, we moved our attention back to the present, and Gabe became serious once again. He considered carefully, then turned to me. "I'd like to tell you what happened when I sealed the tunnel."

I had forgotten. Of course. The tunnel with all the dark spirits rushing to capture Crow. I knew he had done something, and I had to let it go at that moment. Not trusting anyone else, I had come to trust him implicitly. Now I could tell that there was more.

Actually, I considered and realized that his sealing the tunnel had come quite quickly, and that I wouldn't have thought to do it. In retrospect, I was fervently glad that he had done it. The thought of those enraged spirits storming out, chasing Crow and whoever else, was not one I cherished. I was grateful that he'd had the presence of mind to close it. But clearly there was more to it.

Gabe continued. "I don't usually talk about these things. There's no point in giving more attention and energy to the evil. But this was pretty amazing." His face glowed in awe.

"When Crow and the other crows were escaping, I saw the evil spirits coming up the tunnel after Crow, so I put a cover, like a man hole cover, over the tunnel." I thought again about this evil rushing up. To this world. Not a pretty thought.

"Then I went to follow Crow and be with you. When things were settled down, I returned to the cover to check it. What I found when I got there was that the evil ones had rushed up the tunnel, and were furious. They were there, banging on the inside of the cover, enraged and trying to break it open."

He paused, looking again at the sight he had seen. "I was worried about it. I didn't want them flooding through into this world. So I said something over it. It was a Cabalistic phrase that I have just recently learned. It invokes God's name, in other phrases, something like the Lord's prayer does. I wasn't sure what would happen. I was just trying to seal the cover more securely."

I watched him, aware of a sense of innocence in his work. He had been concerned and had done the best he knew in the moment. There was no ego in this tale, only honesty and a sense of humility. Then he looked more directly at me, this time with sheer amazement in his eyes.

"When I said the Words, a light began to glow there just above the cover. Then the cover began to glow. I could hear them in there, and the pounding on the inside of the cover slowed down with their confusion about it, too. Then the light began to glow in intensity around that cover, and this astonishing Light began to emanate from it, coming out but also going in."

He paused, then continued again, eyes wide with astonishment. "Their cries of rage turned to confusion, then to pure terror. I've never heard anything like it. Just pure terror. They turned and ran, fleeing back down the tunnel, trying desperately to outrun the Light. The Light grew and grew in intensity, filling the tunnel and flowing towards them until it overwhelmed them completely—and I could hear them no more."

"Here we sit," I thought, "two rather ordinary people, involved in the magnitude of the battle of Light versus Darkness, and we just witnessed the Light win out." Awe and amazement were the only possible responses.

Finally the scene faded a bit in its intensity, and I recovered with the question that had been niggling at the back of my mind. "Gabe, what about the others, the other ones that were connected in the pouch, the souls that had been taken by the cult? What happened to the pouch and what will happen to them?"

Gabe smiled, again, listening to the answer of his guidance. "Crow gave the pouch to **someone who knows** what to do with it."

The answer satisfied me. I knew it to be true.

We had some time left as we finished the session, so we turned to light table work. Nothing intense. Gabe looked at my injured foot. It was continuing to hurt a lot, and I had been limping. My worry was whether I had broken a small bone in there.

"What did you do to it?" he queried.

"I dropped a guy on it." I smiled my most innocent smile. As a martialist, he would understand. Again he smiled and shook his head.

"Got to be more careful about throwing these guys around."

"I know."

"Well, it's not broken. You did damage the connective tissue, though, so we'll need to work on that. And the impact flattened the arch of your foot." Quietly we worked, still in a muted state from our experiences. Shortly, we finished.

On the road again, with long driving hours before me, I considered our time together. Again the current world collided with those other realms where the impossible and the unbelievable occurred. Driving, I carefully balanced my chicken pita in my lap, trying to take occasional notes as I thought of things to continue mulling over. Gabe hated my driving. Oh, well.

Traveling down the interstate, it occurred to me that my brother's and sister's threads were most likely in that pouch also. Quietly I prayed for them, that the day's work would help free them of their bondage. Gabe and I had done so very much that day. Clearly we had "closed a file," as Ruth's spirit had told me.

Slowly, I relaxed back into my present world, admiring the blue sky, filmy clouds and wheeling crows.

I had more energy after the session with Gabe, a sense of the world put right once again. Gradually, I found myself moving back into daily life. Jennie was a high school senior. She'd be gone next year. I wondered what life with Jack, and no kids, would be like. Right now I wanted to catch the present time.

Sunday morning found me in the kitchen, an increasingly rare event. Bacon and scrambled eggs nearly done, Jennie staggered down the stairs.

"What are you doing, Mom?"

"Breakfast?" I looked at her, feigning innocence.

"Sounds good to me," Jack announced, wandering into the kitchen from his computer. "Want juice?" He prepared to make it in the blender, our favorite way.

It was a good morning, one I remembered years afterwards. A hiatus in my therapy work, precious moments with Jennie and Jack. My mind no longer focused like a laser on what might happen next, or grieving for what had just occurred. Peace had found me for the first time in months. Two pages to go in my book of trauma and recovery? Maybe I'd make it.

The Void of Darkness

Karate class sped by. The workout had been a good one, and I was wringing wet, as usual. The sign that we had really worked. The four months of training had gotten me back in shape, and I loved it. Bowing out, I headed for my bag and day clothes, ready to dry off, change and head home.

"Carla!" I turned at the command.

"Yes, Sensei," I replied with a bow. He clearly wasn't done with me for today. Motioning, we lined up side by side to continue our practice. Occasionally we worked out together after class, practicing the higher katas and giving him a time to work, also.

"Kiotske! Rei." He called the commands as together we came to attention, then bowed. Working with him was usually pure pleasure, as our energy fields joined and worked through the movements. Working with someone over the years builds a flow to the movements, a kinesthetic knowing where and how the other is, how to move in harmony. Together we reviewed two katas in synchrony.

Side by side at attention, he called the next.

"Chinto! Rei," and bowed.

My eyes opened wide in astonishment. Stunned, I looked sideways from my bow, meeting his gleeful, laughing dark eyes as he peered sideways back. My black belt kata. I had been a brown belt for years. I was back in physical shape. Time to get to work.

Dreams filled my nights. Rambling work sites under construction, a new office with no waiting room, bullies counting on people not telling about their actions. One night I dreamed of something hidden way in the back, shrouded in deep shadows, waiting to be brought to light. Random pieces resonating their juxtaposed messages, rousing me to restlessness, wondering what was left to work.

Once again, I lay on Gabe's massage table, while he scanned my field. I'd had a rough trip up, feeling sad when I saw a thin young man, long brown hair, t-shirt and blue jeans, being harassed by a police officer. I recognized so much in the quick glimpse as I drove by, feeling his dejection as the wind blew his hair around his drooping shoulders. The image had stayed with me, sorrow with it.

Now Gabe sat back on his stool, left hand supporting his right elbow as he propped his foot on the stool rung. "What are you aware of, Carla?"

I hated the question. Usually, not a lot. Not if I could help it. Giving up my reluctance, I tuned into my body.

"Not much. Just a sense of heartache, I think. And that started with seeing the boy I told you about. It makes my heart hurt, a real pain. And it feels mostly like falling into a desperate black hole. I really don't like it." That with a discouraged sigh. This cult work was getting old. What a drag.

Gabe's voice came back to me as he watched my energy field. "Does it start in the heart, or below the heart and come up?"

Weird question. I checked in, then startled with surprise. "Huh. It does start below the heart and come up. Like starting in the solar plexus. That's how I sleep at night you know, with my hand over my solar plexus."

Lying there, I kept my awareness open. By force of will. Again surprise overtook me. "You know what? There's a thread again.

And it goes somewhere. But it doesn't seem likely since we just had a thread in that other session, and I've never known us to repeat a theme."

"Just stay with it and see what happens. Follow the thread." He moved to my feet, running energy to help me stay focused. I watched him go into his meditative state with me, and returned my attention to the thread.

"Drats. It goes along for a short while, and then seems to come to a barrier. I can't get past it." I felt apologetic. We probably needed this information.

He waited quietly, running energy, while I remembered the power of thought. In my mind, I decided I could do this if I set my intention to it. Focusing, I found the barrier and willed myself beyond it. Immediately, I was on the other side.

"Keep talking, Carla." I was slipping deeper into trance, losing contact with him. With an effort of will, I kept both realities open, talking to him.

"I'm in a tunnel again, though it doesn't seem the same as before." I paused. Uncertainty assailed me as I hesitated.

"Just stay with what you experience, and keep talking."

"All right. It's a dark, cold tunnel with an empty, desperate feel to it. A dull metallic gray lighting lets me see. A flat feeling, like hopelessness. I'm following the thread in the tunnel." Gaining confidence, led by my curiosity, I strode briskly along the tunnel, wanting to see where it went, seeking the secrets of this mysterious cold place.

Suddenly, I jerked back, an inner sense warning me as I stopped my forward motion, teetering, nearly losing my balance, as the earth beneath my feet fell away into nothingness. Gasping, I stepped back several steps, reaching for the damp rugged wall for balance. My heart pounded furiously in my chest, relaying the fright signals to the rest of my body. Shaking, supporting myself with my right hand on the side of the tunnel, I felt the emptiness drop away immediately in front of my feet. Dismayed, knees weak, I slid to a seated position to keep myself from toppling over the edge.

There, spread out limitlessly before me, was a Void. In its unending vastness, it reminded me of the Heart of God. There the similarity stopped. This was the opposite. Empty, dark and desperate, it was a Void of Darkness. I could sense the desperate souls, suffering in their agony and hopelessness. Frozen in place, I lost all ability to talk, to communicate with Gabe. Mesmerized by the wretched darkness, I was paralyzed in its terrible fascination.

Dragging my attention to try to find Gabe, I realized he was working on another plane, tracking what I was seeing. Remembering that my job was to keep the pathways open so that he could do his work, I settled on the edge of the emptiness, holding myself there by force of will.

This is hell, I thought to myself. I had always kind of wondered what hell really was like, although I didn't think of it much as I didn't want to give it real credence. This was it.

Finally I could tolerate the despair and hopelessness no longer, and began to back up in the tunnel, finally turning and finding my way back. Counting myself back to three, I opened my eyes in his office where I still lay, cold and shivering on the massage table. Gabe was silent, in the meditative state, still working. Patiently, I waited until his eyes opened. The look was deep and sober.

"Well?"

"I followed you into the tunnel, and then somehow lost you in there. You got ahead of me or something. So I called on Wolf to come help me. I've been working with Wolf recently and, it's been helpful."

I remembered my eager anticipation to find out where the tunnel had led, and how I had strode along, confident. Not good to leave your partner behind, given the places I tended to go.

"I followed Wolf, and we went through a tunnel, the thread with us. We came to a great empty space full of suffering and evil. I called on the Spirit World for help. I think that's about when you must have begun backing out."

He looked to me for confirmation. It fit. Our work was separate but similar, confirming our experiences.

"In the Spirit World, a shield of light was formed. It was round and formed of two moon-like slivers." Again, he turned to me, showing me the shape and formation of the shield.

"I'm just realizing now that it was a shield formed of all the different phases of the moon. A shield formed from the proper use of the power of the moon. The moon was so misused in the cults. This moon shield was to correct that misuse.

"This work restored Moon Mother to her proper place of power, love and healing." Carefully he further described the shield, the phases, and the symbology of Moon Mother. It was deeply satisfying to us both, to see Moon Mother used properly in all her power, using her light to conquer evil and despair.

"The shield was used to seal you off from this terrible place. Then I gathered the thread and Spirit returned it to you. That thread of your essence was taken back into yourself. You're no longer connected to that place."

I thought of the Void. "There's so much suffering there."

"It's why you've been so especially sensitive to suffering, Carla. Like the young man you saw today. Most people would have a glimpse of feeling about it. You were devastated. It was because that kind of event connected you once again to the Void, and you experienced overwhelming suffering. You felt both, the event and the Void, making it much harder for you. My guess is that this happened often for you, which is why you are so exquisitely sensitive to the suffering of others."

I realized he was right. My sadness more nearly reflected what I felt in the Void than an appropriate sadness about the young man. Other examples flitted through my mind, all similar in my experience of suffering out of proportion. It was about each incident combined with the Void. That would do it.

"I know this is redundant, but am I free of that now?"

"Yes. You'll be all right now. Moon Mother has sealed that place off from you. Our work today was also about restoring the beauty of Moon Mother. Anything can be used for good or evil, and the cults used the moon for evil. That has been rebalanced today, and I think you'll always see the moon now for her beauty once more."

I liked the thought and would watch and see how it went. Our time was nearly up. Together we put the table back. I started getting my shoes on as Gabe replaced the stool, sitting again for a brief review of the rest of my life.

"Things going ok at home, Carla?"

"Yeah," as I shifted gears to look at the rest of my life. Then I glanced up abruptly, tying the last shoe as a thought struck me.

"You know, I've been thinking of getting some training in mediumship. I saw it really help one of my clients. What do you think?"

He shifted back in his chair, rocking slightly as it adjusted to his weight change. Thoughtful, he then smiled.

"Somehow, it doesn't surprise me."

"Yeah?"

"You've always liked the spirit realm. And you can make contact. We've shown that. I expect it's a natural for you. Where would you train?"

"Um. A friend brought it up to me. He trained on the east coast with the Spiritualist National Union."

Gabe rose, our time now up. Green coffee mug in hand, he walked me to the door. "I've heard they are very good. I'd look into it."

"Thanks, I will," as I gave him a parting hug. We always had so much to cover in our sessions, I mused as I walked down the inner hall. Pulling myself back to the present, I reminded myself to pick up the gold parking token from its woven straw basket as I made my left turn to the exit door. Practicalities, girl, don't forget, echoing in my mind.

Two months went by as Gabe and I continued our work. I realized that I was definitely improving. My distress level was way down, flashbacks seemed to be nearly gone, nightmares mellowing back to the status of dreams, and physical symptoms resolving. There was no sense of connection to the dark void. Life was about today.

Walking in the evening, I smiled as I thought of my dream of the book showing three pages left. Maybe I only had one more really difficult session, with the rest being processing. That would certainly be wonderful.

The next evening, fixing dinner, I realized that time had flown. The food ready, I called out to the family. Jennie and Jack materialized, and we sat down. At the last minute, Nate, home from college, burst in.

I looked at him, eyebrows up, seeking the explanation. We'd planned on dinner together, and he was rarely late for food.

"Sorry. I got caught in organized religion traffic," he grinned as he pulled his chair in, reaching for the potatoes.

"Huh?" Jack verbalized with the rest of us agreeing. "What's that?"

"St. John's was just letting out from some service. I could hardly get through." He passed the potatoes and reached for veggies, as Jennie handed them to him. I chuckled. Our brand of normalcy in a recovering family.

The next night I had karate, and was racing around, running late yet once more. My last client had been a talker, and wanted to ask more questions as he left the office. Finally I had closed the door, written my notes, locked my desk and turned off all the gadgets. Rushing, I headed home.

Changing into my gi, I grabbed my bag, heading out the door.

"Where you going, Mom?" Jennie was watching.

"Karate. Be back in a bit." I flew out the door.

Bowing as I entered the workout room, I immediately noticed the difference. The emotional climate was cold. Looking around, I sought the cause, my breath shallow and senses alert.

No one was speaking. Sensei was up in front of the room, stretching out alone. Sherri and Sensei's son, Ramon, both black belts, were in the back, silently stretching against the wall. It was unusual to have three black belts there at once. I glanced at the kids, scattered against the far wall. They were also quiet, silent even with each other. Maybe the black belts had intimidated them.

Or maybe the kids were sensing something. I quickly registered, and moved to stretch out.

"Line up!" So much for stretching. "Kiotski! Rei." We came to attention, bowed and knelt for opening meditation. That done, Sensei nodded to Sherri. "Warm them up. Carla, go to the back and stretch out."

The uneasiness still filled the room, a faint cloud of static keeping everyone on edge. I watched and waited. Warm-ups over, he bowed Sherri out and resumed leadership of the class. "Carla, please wait outside the class."

A prickle ran up my spine, lodging at the back of my neck. What was going on? Soon Sherri came for me. Wordless, she nodded and I followed her to the second, far right door to the class. Entering we bowed, and my eyes flew wide open. The room separator was drawn. The test board set up.

My black belt test.

Driving home, I thought of the moment when the test board of black belts had me turn my back to them. Turning around to confront them on command, I'd been faced with the bricks and boards. We rarely practiced with them, so that it would really count when we did. I had to break. He'd not told me about that. Focus, concentration and sheer willpower, I determined to break the first time. It had to be then.

Afterwards, the test board had risen as one, bowing and excusing me. Returning, Sensei remained stern, as a chill raced through me. Then his smile broke.

"Congratulations, Sensei." He bowed. I was a black belt.

A week later, I drove the long miles to Chicago once again, eager to tell Gabe about my black belt. Sharing news, we played and laughed together before starting the work of the day. Yet dread had been following me, and I knew we had to get to it.

Soon, I was fairly seething with frustration. There was clearly something we needed to take care of, something just above my heart, but I could not, would not, see it. It had been hard enough just to get into my body.

"It's as if we're clear back to the beginning," I grumbled to Gabe.

"I know. This is hard."

It was equinox full moon, and I had been in deep despair again. I hated it. I should be nearly done. Not drowning.

"You know, it's like I can see my child self, just sitting there, arms folded across my chest, my feet pulled up and crossed under me. There's a part of me that's in total rebellion at this scene. That child is **not** going to look. It's just too much somehow." Prickles went up my spine. I knew I'd spoken a truth, dormant, lying in wait to ambush me. It felt like the presence of the icy ghost who had followed me all the days of my life, long skeletal fingers reaching in the dark for me.

"What if we add some light? Will that help?

"Maybe." I was feeling **very** stubborn.

He added light. I felt it grow around me. By then we had rearranged ourselves. Gabe sat behind me, left hand behind my heart chakra and the right over my solar plexus. Comfort. Trying to hold against unreasoning terror. Add energy to the system. Amp up to match the need.

In my image, the little girl took one peek as there was more light. Her response was immediate and definite.

"Nope!"

She turned around and faced away from the area.

"What if I look for you?" Any way will do, just so we get there, was the unspoken message. And, we'll take any route that provides sufficient support to manage the problem.

"OK." That would do. Just don't ask me to look.

He looked at the scene unfolding, ran more energy, more light, and with my eyes closed, I heard him sigh.

"What?"

"It's not a pretty picture." He paused. "What if I look now with you?"

For some reason, I gave in, asked for courage and agreed.

"Can you look?"

"I think so." Part of me wanted to get beyond this, so I pushed myself, trying to over-ride the child part and look.

"I can't see. My eyes are open, but it's like I'm frozen. I just can't see."

"Can you allow yourself to hear what is happening? To enter the scene with your hearing?"

Well, maybe. That's a route. I finally relented. I could hear. I was just sort of thinking that if I denied it, it wouldn't be real. And besides, maybe I was making it up . . .

Later, I regretted agreeing to hear.

"I hear shouts, and some chanting, and screaming. Lots of screaming that is more clear than I've ever had." That, shuddering.

"Yes, screaming. Is it an adult or child?"

"It's a child." My heart sank.

Together, we put the picture together. In pieces, through the session.

A cult torn asunder by mad, out of-control demands for blind obedience. Demands made on a family in the higher tier. An equinox celebration. A refusal. The leaders' rage gone wild with horrible consequences.

The high priest and his followers, always teetering on the thin edge of sanity, had lost all semblance of control in their wrath. This was impulsive revenge against a highly placed member for lacking blind obedience. Unheard of, it was the act of petty tyrants gone mad, loosing all their pathology in one wild act to try to regain power.

Storming into the room where we children were kept, they grabbed the daughter of the disobedient man, dragging her screaming from the room, the rest of us frozen in fear and terror. I wanted to reach out for my small friend, my playmate. Scenes of us running through the woods, laughing together, fighting over snacks sped through my mind in a flash. My friend, they were taking her. Knowing there was nothing I could do, I stood frozen, knowing if any of us moved, we too would be taken. The sounds told us the story. A rage gone wild, beyond all limits of control or reason. Cruelty. Torture. Murder. I huddled the children together in the bedroom. As the oldest, I tried to keep them safe, putting hands over the ears of the smaller children. Pain, torture, and sacrifice assaulted our senses against a terrifying backdrop of unpredictability. What would happen next?

Finally, it was quiet. Eventually, we children fell asleep clustered in a corner, comforting each other with our warm bodies, slowly calming the trembling in each other. Silence with each other. If we were totally quiet, maybe nothing more would happen. We clung together.

My heart dropped to the deepest part of my soul with the remembering, a tragic feel creating a hollow spot inside. I had experienced a lot; thought I knew grief. This was the worst. Somehow, it was the most real. I had kept the other parts we had dealt with at some distance, but this was right there. More than ever before. Maybe it was her screams. Other sacrifices had always been drugged. I couldn't understand, just floated awash in sorrow.

Gabe was silent as I finished my tale, sorrow lining his face, his head bent. Braver than I, he had looked. I had resolutely kept my view to the bedroom. It was all that I could bear. Finally, he looked up. "Anything else, Carla?"

"I need some spiritual help with this one, Gabe."

We moved to the massage table, worked energetically, listening. Silence met us. We struggled to find something to bring balance to the experience.

"There's a thought form associated with this, Carla. We can undo it. And instead of releasing it, use it to empower you and sanctify that energy to your use. To the use of power rightly wielded. To be able to stand your ground against the misuse of power as you encounter it. This will help you be stronger in the face of tyranny, rather than being frozen as you were at the time of the trauma."

I nodded my agreement, lost, numb. As he worked with the energy, an old memory returned, a glowing pool of sunlight.

I told Gabe. "The next morning, after this had happened, I sat in a small, golden pool of sunlight. Placed there by my parents, it's the one memory I have always had. The sun gleamed on the hardwood floor, showing the little rubber toys of farm animals and implements, gifts from my uncle and his work, special to that place alone. My parents had placed them there for me to play with, and to keep me in view. I was five and numb with grief. Toys meant nothing."

"Go on, Carla," as I faltered.

"Six adults, my parents among them, sat at an old wooden table nearby, talking in low hushed voices. Even as a child, I knew that a deep sadness pulsated the air in the room, a sadness I had never understood when the memory had come."

Gabe nodded, tracking me as I talked.

"My five-year old self had puzzled over the problems and finally risen. Standing by my mother's side, my chin just even with the table, I had looked at her. 'Why didn't you do something?' I had asked."

"'We didn't know. We had no idea that was going to happen,' was her only response. It made no sense to me. I was shepherded back to my pool of sunlight and the toys. I knew they wanted me to be quiet. I sat, still and limp, grieving in my own way. In hushed tones, they had continued the adult discussion.

"Now I understand, Gabe. They were stunned and helpless. I've always known their grief from the feelings I could recover when I tapped into that time and place," I told him. "We never returned to the farm." That, somewhat sadly. "I had missed the toys as they were unique, not something that were ever sold on the market. And the freedom was wonderful. Amazing how we can partition off parts of an experience."

"It's how the mind works," was his quiet reply.

"As a child, I didn't understand never returning. That farm was the place where all the relatives gathered. No wonder we didn't go back, now that I know the story. I remember asking several times as a child, and was always brushed off. But we didn't have many friends, and these people, crazy as they were, were all I knew. Now they were out of my life. Permanently."

"A big change." He was staying with my reflections, letting me tell him about it. I needed to talk. To explain all the missing pieces that had never made sense.

"Over time, I have researched the place enough to know that it was what we called the 'little house' on my aunt and uncle's farm. The house where my aunt's lover lived. Weird, isn't it."

"We could redefine weird," he soberly replied.

"We never went back," I repeated, trying to sort it out.

"Your father was a powerful man, Carla. He misused that power repeatedly in the cult. But for once, he used it well when he took your family out. Cults don't take kindly to that behavior."

He paused, considering. "But you know, that's how some of those cults ended. Someone went too far in their pathology, and it abruptly brought people to their senses. They could no longer deny the sheer brutality and pathology of what was going on. It was generational in your family, and therefore harder to break, but it happens this way. Someone goes berserk with the lust for total power and goes too far for the tolerance of the members."

I could understand it. No wonder we never went back to the farm again.

Gabe continued. "Your father also must have come to his senses about the risks to your own family. While the leaders were under control, you weren't at risk because he was high enough in the hierarchy. But with them losing control in rage and retaliation, you were all in imminent peril. What had once been 'them,' or the feeling that it was other people who could get hurt, was now 'us.' Your family was in danger, and he finally saw that. Even if he didn't appear to understand how wrong the whole thing was, this at least propelled him to get out."

Quietly we considered the tragedy, and the outcome for my family. Because of the tragedy of the child's brutal death, we had been freed. My father knew that it could have been me, I was sure. The lust for total power had split the cult asunder. Richard, my psychic homeopath, had told me that the cult had died out. I was sure that was true. And in my work, this was the last page.

"What was your father like after he left the cult, Carla?" Gabe asked, sipping his refilled addiction.

I thought about it, searching the memory banks. "Overall, I would say he continued to have an irrational and sudden temper. It would particularly flare if he thought I was in any physical danger. Man, would he get mad." That as images flashed through my mind of his rages.

"But where did he put the rest of that energy and aggression?"

"It's a good question. So far as I know, he turned it to his work. He rose high in an oil company, becoming the assistant to the vice president. He was to become a vice president when one died, but he died first. A heart attack at 49. But there was no clear replacement for his cult activities that I know of."

"Hmm." Gabe took it all in, pondering the complexities of human nature. Then I watched as his eyes took on a softer look, clearly shifting to yet something else.

"Carla, I want us to go back to the scene of the cult for one last time. I think there's something there we need to see."

I sighed, reluctantly agreeing.

"Look at that place again, and tell me what you see."

Looking back at the farm, I watched. Surprise filled my voice as I turned to Gabe. "I see the land. I see the land where all this happened, and all the people are gone. It's just the land."

"The land was traumatized, too."

After a pause, I looked up at him and smiled softly. "It's changing. It's like it was frozen. It wasn't healthy land when I first saw it. Just sort of there. Like a still picture, in black, white and gray, but empty of life and vitality. As if it had stopped having any life force from all the tragedies there. As if Mother Earth was grieving."

I watched as a glow filled the air, creating light and shadows, giving depth and the beginning of color to the scene. "Now it's as if there is light coming back to the land. And life coming back. It's wonderful."

Gabe watched, smiling. "It's a process whereby your unfreezing of your experiences of that time has helped release something about the place and the land."

I watched as the trees and grasses took on deeper hues, flowers bloomed, and the birds and butterflies returned. Gabe sat back, considering it further.

"It's the clearest I've been about this. As we have healing taking place on one plane, it takes place simultaneously on other planes. Life exists on many planes, and they affect each other."

Our time was up. Later, driving home, I had a renewed awareness of the land, the colors and life force. It comforted me as I drove, still bereft, grieving. Rather than leaving with a sense of resolution to the events, I left still feeling devastated. This time the trauma remained open. I needed something more.

The next day, I had an experience which startled me. Sitting alone, drifting, watching the rain slide down the windowpanes and my grief filling me, an awareness flooded me. It was as if I knew. The girl had made a decision on a soul level to make that sacrifice. It was her chosen task for that lifetime.

The teachings say we know how we will die when we choose our life on this plane. And that must have also included her. A sacrifice made in hopes that it would break the cult. A terrible way to die. I had to remind myself that we don't know the whole picture and all the reasons from the limited perspective of this lifetime and this plane of existence.

Yet of this, I felt certain. For her, it was a soul choice. With the awareness, my grief ebbed ever so slightly, moving now into the more bearable realm.

Looking back, I wondered why it took so much longer that time. What was so much worse, in a cult where atrocities were the norm and the experience of the day. Meditation showed clues.

One day while lying in my healing room and wrestling with the questions of why that event had happened, where were the guides, why didn't they stop it, I remembered. The statement of Robert Gerson.

"Evil exists."

This is, indeed, a world where evil exists. The guides are there, supporting us in our difficulties, but they don't force anyone to act differently. It is our choice. And, in fact, evil does exit and will continue to do so.

Another day, I remembered that I'd been told my task in this lifetime was to heal myself, that I might be a healer of others. I was aware of the circle of elders around me in my meditation, supporting me as I struggled with the questions. Evil did exist, and my task was to heal and learn from it. That as I searched for meaning in the meaningless.

Another day I realized that I had been in shock since Gabe and I had done the work. The first stage of deep grieving. No wonder I had been feeling so numb and hopeless. I was beginning to come out of it, returning to a life with kids, husband and work to do. But I recognized the signs of shock, and knew I'd been there.

So what was the shock about? Weren't there other more shocking things in my life, with previous events of the cult? Mulling this over in meditation once more, the answers came like echoes bouncing back to me, transformed to answers from beyond myself.

I understood that even in a cult, there is a sense of order. A timing, a calendar, a ritual. Who dies and who doesn't. Some order that provides a predictability. Which in itself, provides a minimal sense of security. A sacrifice will not happen on Wednesday when my father's at work. And on and on.

The shock was the randomness of it, the disruption of an order that had been established, rules of conduct even in the darkest of places. A child tortured for revenge, no drugs to numb her pain, leaders out of control, chaos erupting which destroyed any elusive sense of order or safety, my family awakened from their stupor and distraught. Suddenly, anything could happen and did.

With understanding, the shock wore off and the grief process continued as it should. I realized that I was grieving for the entire cult experience. Often I sat, staring into nothingness as those grieving are wont to do. Only over a long time, did it soften, like the soil in the spring rains, bringing room for new hope and growth.

Hearts of Fire

Days and weeks passed by, as I integrated that last, tragic session. Gabe and I continued our sessions, dealing with energetic and psychological concerns. My grieving continued to be intense, and I brought it up to Gabe.

"Why am I still grieving so much? I don't remember grieving this much at other times in our work?"

He leaned back in his chair, dark hair held back now by a ponytail with a small earring in his left ear. The man was changing right before my eyes. Bagels littered the desk from a hasty breakfast, and coffee cooled on his stool beside him. His inward look was going over his own store of research, looking back to me with his understanding.

"It's the pattern of grieving, Carla. You studied it when you began to teach professionals about grief work. Remember the process?"

Grumbling to myself, I acknowledged that I did. Shock and disorganization, followed by all the other emotions in any order, and finally followed by resolution. Didn't mean I liked it.

"But why is this still going on? The grieving from our other sessions seemed to resolve much more quickly. I did finally work out that I was in shock. Did that at home. But it does seem more extensive."

"I think you are grieving now for the whole cult experience. We have finished the direct work, and that's allowed you to let yourself do the grieving for the whole picture. You couldn't let go and do that before you felt we were done."

"I can understand that." I nodded and reached for my Coke. Putting it down on the small table, I looked at him again.

"And so," thinking out loud, "we also do different things in the different stages of recovery therapy, don't we, Gabe."

"Yes, we do. First, we establish supports to handle the shock of discovery and the journey ahead. Then we work on personal self skills to get through the trauma work while still using the supports. Doing the trauma work requires all the support and self skills we can get. The most intense grieving is part of the reorganization or the last stage. It all fits into a pattern, really."

"That's ok. I like it. I like tidy. But I did grieving earlier, too."

"Yes. We do each of the kinds of therapy work all the time. It's just that there are particular areas of emphasis as we go through the process. Don't worry, Carla. You are in the reorganization phase now, and doing well. I do think we've done all the trauma work, and now it's about building a better life in the present. This grieving will lift."

"Thanks. I just needed to know that."

A final thought filled my mind as I shrugged into my light jacket.

"I did some research lately, Gabe. I've been looking into astrology, and I ran my father's chart as closely as I could figure it.

His eyes lit up, bright intelligence investigating a personality making them sparkle. "What did it say?"

"A lot of things that unfortunately fit quite well. He may have been a double Scorpio. Says he wanted to have power over others, was drawn to the occult and he had a hard, ambitious nature." I paused, remembering.

"That's true, isn't it?"

"You bet. He would be secretive and was born with a strong inclination for all sorts of strange and unfavorable adventures which would involved serious danger."

"No kidding. Wow, what a chart."

"Yeah. Really. It also said he would struggle between the positive and negative poles of the occult and power, his life very tragic *or* very fortunate. He had a choice. He needed to exert control in his involvement in any esoteric or occult activities and organizations. So he could have done it differently, but didn't. The whole thing really amazed me."

He shook his head. "I'm not an astrology expert, but it sure sounds like your father."

"It had another thing that interested me, too. Said there would be a major and dramatic event, and that after that his ego would change entirely."

"Seemed to, didn't it?"

"Yes, it did. We talked about that last time, and he still had his temper and drive, but I don't have any indications of the interest in the occult continuing."

"So, has it helped you to find the astrology?"

"Absolutely. I can't be sure since I don't have the birth time, but this feels close. And I just have to remember that he had choices."

"Um hmm."

"OK. I gotta run, kiddo. I want to beat that Chicago rush hour as much as I can."

"Good luck." He smiled at the effort in futility. "Maybe it will be a bit less now than later."

I stood, zipping my jacket before heading out. A quick hug, and I was gone.

Would he ever really know how much his help had meant to me? Could any words convey it? How do you give thanks for a life returned? Somber but softer thoughts followed me as I drove the freeways, exited on the ramps and finally got out of the heavy traffic where I could relax a bit more.

A month later, I walked briskly down the sidewalk, passing the long line of fashionable cars parked at the meters, until I turned into the door on my left. The Thai restaurant was a more recent find and immediate love.

Inside at the cash register, my attention registered the diners, picking out Pia's smiling face waiting for me. She waved, and I wound between tables and the welcome scents of assorted Thai food, sinking gratefully to my seat. Pia's drinks and clutter already filled the glass-covered small table as I added my two books, dropping my own purse and schedule book on the floor by the wall to my left.

The noise was just beginning to build in the small place, as the lunch crowd flowed in, but Pia was not deterred.

"So, how **are** you?" Her usual enthusiasm spilled over, as she leaned over the table to smile and welcome me even more. I returned the smile, loving her spark again and again.

"I'm good. Really good. And you?"

Soon we settled back to the business of ordering, and clearing the immediate mess for more drinks. The waitresses were quick, knew me, and left us to our talk.

And talk we did. The usual combination of love, life and our work of heart. I told her about applying for mediumship training, and my client who had been so helped by it. She smiled, not surprised.

Talk turned to Pia's father, and his recent move to hospice as she began to push her food around her plate. Her head down more, she talked of the issues it evoked for her whole family, the dynamics of dying. Here was the issue again. Making the transition. Plates were removed, and we switched topics again.

"So, tell me," she began, "are you really doing all right? You seem a bit reserved."

"I've been having trouble with self-esteem again, Pia," I explained. "Just been thinking more about the cult, and processing my feelings about it. And it leaves me disturbed."

"What part of it?" Pia listened, her eyes watching every word, as our tabletop was reduced to glasses of Coke and water. Tables were emptying near us, and the pace slowing. I felt the calmness and acceptance in her body as I talked.

"You know, the hardest part, Pia, is not the having been victimized. It's being forced to be a perpetrator. Sure, I had a knife at my throat, but I still did terrible things."

She leaned forward. "I want to tell you about one of my best friends in my yoga training that I did in California." Her voice was steady, eyes clear and obviously present to me. This woman was not afraid or repelled by my past.

"She was also a cult survivor. And I know what you're talking about. We talked long hours. She's the first one to really explain all this to me. And she also told me about being forced, as an innocent child, to be a perpetrator.

"You do remember, Carla, that it's the perfect way to bind a child to the cult and to the dark side, for a lifetime in some ways. I think because the self esteem is so low."

Once relaxed, she leaned forward once again, muscles taut, intensity in every fiber of her body. "And I want you to know, that is the most ultimate form of child abuse. It's not being assaulted. It's being forced to be a perpetrator. That's the one we haven't even begun to address yet."

I drew back in my chair, then sipped on my water, carefully taking the new thought in, tasting it like a new foreign food. "I never thought of being forced to be a perpetrator as child abuse."

"But it is. Don't you see?"

I put the water down, finger playing in the wet rings on the table. Finally I looked up at Pia, clarity in my eyes.

"You're right. I hadn't seen it that way. And no, we haven't addressed it professionally, and the shame and other feelings it causes. It is profoundly and deeply abusive."

"And there's one other thing to consider."

I looked up again. "What's that?" Thoughts were already swimming in my mind.

"We all have regrets and shame about some of the things we've done. And done as adults. That is, if we have any sensitivity. We know we've messed up and when, and we have shame about that. In our own ways, we've all been perpetrators. Good people, people who want to be whole, will recognize that."

I knew it to be true. Smiling at Pia, relieved at her help and love, I noted the time. The meters would run out soon. Finding the check, we got our credit cards out and collected our things.

I handed the bill and credit cards to the waitress. Quickly we were done. "Pia?"

"Yeah?" The small glass door slowly closed behind us, as we felt the outdoor heat melt our clothes against us.

"I'm going to write the book that I've told you about. And teach about this. It's time we confront it. It's not OK to keep cult abuse a secret. We need to continue to teach the healers and therapists, and find new and more powerful ways to bring healing."

"I know." Pia smiled, waved and turned to walk up the street.

Back at my office, I slid into my computer chair, rolling it up into place, cold water in hand. There I sat, pensively lost in thought as the computer came up. Watching the letters blink and flash, changing colors and back again, I absentmindedly reached to the right for the desk drawer. Suddenly I realized what I was reaching for. The little long slim piece of paper, that nestled in its home over the years at the bottom of the clutter.

I knew it was there somewhere, as I more urgently sifted through the pencils, pens, paper clips and scraps of undoubtedly important notes. Every few years I read it, soaking in its meaning. A faded pink color caught my attention, while with my other hand I advanced the computer screen, preparing to write.

The screen in place, I pulled on the faded paper corner, extracting the slip. Long ago I had cut it from the back of a church bulletin. Now I read it again, while the summer breeze blew in the window and the birds talked to me once more from a nearby maple tree.

The initial line of the benediction was familiar. "May the Lord make His face to shine upon you and be gracious unto you." Then came the part that had been added, attributed to the teacher I had known from so long ago, the anti-war activist of the 70s, the man who insisted we stand up for what was right, what was good, even if it was hard. Very hard.

"May God give you grace never to sell yourself short; grace to risk something big for something good; grace to remember that the world now is too dangerous for anything but truth, and too small for anything but love. So may God take your minds and think through them; may God take your lips and speak through them; may God take your hearts and set them on fire. Amen."

It was time. So be it.

I would write. Contribute. Reach back for the healing of others.

The weeks passed and the months. My life settled into what one might consider a normal routine, without the interruption of terrifying nightmares, deep periods of grieving, or ill-formed anxiety. While I retained the memories of the cult, it wasn't forefront in my life. It was a new experience, and one I was savoring as I walked through the seasons, connecting to the rhythms of the earth and moon.

I was improving, and I knew it. Tentatively, like new sprouts in spring, I tested my new life, free of cult memories and intrusions.

In karate, I continued to train, working now towards my second degree black belt. Lots of people drop out after their black belts, having proved to themselves that they could do it. My goal was one higher. That I was serious about it.

Walking into class one night, I smiled to myself, remembering my first hesitant classes and my inability to do a pushup. The night the green belt woman hit me in the nose and I nearly started a fight. All the tests and lessons learned. I'd come a long way, I thought again, as I stood dripping with sweat at the end of the class. I had regained some boundaries, and learned lessons about life and family there. I would always cherish it, as I bowed to Sensei. We'd spent years together, and I'd grown in the process.

Jennie went on to college, leaving Jack and I to adjust to each other. I suspect we did it about as well as many couples when the last child leaves, which wasn't very well. He immersed himself more and more in his work to fill the gap she left, and I'm sure I did the same. Slowly we were growing apart.

Yet over the months, I began to feel a restlessness, a sense of something yet to be done. Something unfinished. Eventually, I identified it as a wondering once more about karma. And past lives. And patterns. Was there any bigger picture to this? The small question began to grow like a snowball rolling down a hill, becoming larger and larger until I knew I had to do something. There was a past life related to my being in the cult, I felt sure. The picture didn't seem complete. Perhaps this would bring it full circle.

I had been studying past lives, and working with them increasingly in my practice. And I knew how to do my own with the help of the one tape I had finally found that helped me. I just had to find out.

I waited for a deep winter night when Jack was out of town for the weekend on business. I wanted time to integrate any material I might get. Carefully, I prepared, setting up my altar in my healing room. As an extra precaution, I called Pia.

"I'm going to do the past life regression that I told you about, Pia. Like, tonight."

"Will you be all right?" Her voice sounded worried, and with some good cause. I could get into deep water here.

"Call me in two hours. If I'm still in trance and don't answer, I'm in trouble. Then you can come over."

"You sure that's enough? You want me to come now and sit with you?"

I smiled at her offer. Friends are great. "No, thanks. I think I'll be OK. Just give me a call as backup. That all right?"

"Of course. Two hours." She reminded me as she hung up. I knew she'd be true to her word.

Carefully, I lit my candles, got grounded and called in my spiritual protection. With the tape recorder beside me, and my notebook for later, I lay down to begin the work.

Turning the tape on, I allowed it to lead me into a trance state as I willed my body into a deep relaxation, followed by a technique to help me get out of my body.

Setting my intention to finding the past life which most related to my experience with the cult, I let myself move through time and space, my spirit guides with me. The tape played the instruction: "You are now there. Look down, and see your feet. Are you wearing shoes? What do they look like? Or are you barefoot?"

Slowly the images came into view, and I relaxed even more deeply into trance to let the story unfold. I saw myself as a young girl, maybe eight or nine, standing by a fence, left hand on the top of it. Just beyond it was a cottage. Tracking back, I knew that I had been born a psychic child to gentle farmers. They recognized my skill, and my father took me across the spring fields to the village, where I would be raised and trained by the village healer. She became the only mother I could remember.

I returned to the scene where I had entered the past life, finding myself standing, scanning with my psychic sight. Something had caught my attention, and I had automatically tracked the disturbance.

My mind reeled back, as if hit by a strong force, while my psychic vision took in a group of men, riding hard, long black capes flowing behind them as they careened recklessly through the muddy, narrow road through the woods. In a split second, I knew their destination and their task, while struck almost physically with their malice, hatred and underlying fear.

Shock struck my body. A sweet and gentle soul, always protected, I had never even been to the city. I had only known love and kindness, as I learned my tasks and searched the countryside for herbs and healing plants, assisting in the care of the villagers.

My child self gasping with the assault of the vision, I stood paralyzed at the gate, then turned, fleeing into the cottage to the woman, the healer and my substitute mother.

"They are coming for me, child." She stooped down to briefly hold me. We had both seen what was to become of her, the brutality and the fires. Yet her first concern was for me. "You must hide. Go. Upstairs to the loft. Hide there."

Terrified, eyes frozen with fear and mind unraveling like a large rope with too heavy a load, I panicked and ran for the door, fleeing into the yard. Hiding myself behind a large barrel I watched as the men plunged out of the woods and to our doorway, pulling rein with rearing horses and shouting.

Pulling her from her cottage, they lashed her to a horse, angry and shouting. She didn't fight them, resigned to her fate. Slashing the horses, they rode towards the woods with its path to the city, waiting with its fires for the proclaimed witches. Soon they were out of sight. My vision saw what was to come. Despair filled me like thick black smoke. Terrified, I ran for the forest, losing myself in its deep silence, dappled shadows and sheltering depths.

Watching the events, I knew that I had lived for a short time only, eating berries and finding water, hiding as much as possible like a stalked animal, mind gone mad, heart broken. The villagers had searched for me. I could see them walking the soft leaf-strewn paths, calling my name, as I crouched down, hiding from those who would have saved me. I died soon after, broken in heart and soul.

A sad tale, I reviewed it in my mind. Anything else I needed to know? I didn't think so, allowing myself to begin the slow journey back to present time and place. With the candle burning low, I thanked my guides for their help, then rested. Later, I wrote it all out, my mind seeing the images over and over.

Pia called and was reassured that I was all right. But I was drained, physically and emotionally. The next day, she arrived quietly at my door.

"Hey, Pia," I greeted her, still subdued, noticing something in her hands.

"Chicken soup," she announced with a smile. "I thought you might need something while you recover." She gave it to me and left, allowing me more time to ponder, write and put the pieces together.

By Monday I was back on my feet again, if slowly, and a few more days brought me back up to speed. Yet the regression left powerful footprints in my life. This current life was one of healing. I'd been told that before. And I knew of a number of other solitary, challenging lives where I stayed detached from others. Now, in the fullness of time, I understood that this was a time of healing many lifetimes. Of that time long ago. And the many lifetimes in between when I wandered the earth, facing a bit more evil each life, and becoming a bit stronger for the experience.

Over time I had gained the strength I needed to face the evil once more on that same level of intensity. The Sacred Wound is not healed by being handed to us on a platter, I reminded myself. It is again presented as a wound, and we are given the strength and resources to heal it, if we but will. Will we choose healing or bitterness, is often the question. The wound is presented so that we might have the option for healing.

And my family? Did I need to be bitter about the traumas I and others had suffered? A big question. Yet I knew the answer. I would have picked a family which would have allowed me to continue in my own soul's path. One which would have enabled me to face the same level of evil and despair that I'd had in that other lifetime long ago. It was time to heal the full cycle of lives. It would take a lifetime such as this one to do it.

And so, how could I be bitter about the man who had set the stage for my ultimate healing? I would have picked someone to do it, for my own soul's growth.

And so in my morning prayers by the medicine wheel, I prayed for my parents. My father was the most difficult, as he was the most involved. I wished him to find his way back to the light. My prayer was simple.

"Please keep him in the light with the love and compassion he needs to face this lifetime, and to grow from it on his soul's journey. A ho." With that, I let it go.

Time marched on. Spring came with a joyous burst of color that I hadn't seen for years. It was April and I was on my way to Mediumship training.

My anxiety followed me as I walked into the small bedroom with Rebecca to carry out our mediumship assignment. The window looked out over the rural New York landscape, rolling land with great oaks, maples and pines. The Catholic convent and retreat center had the usual plain rooms, I thought, as we seated ourselves in our straight-backed wooden chairs.

"I'll go first," Rebecca offered. I breathed a sigh of relief. I hated being on the spot with these assignments, even though they were necessary.

Seated across from me, I smiled at the picture she presented. A sturdy woman in bright, loose clothes with thick blond hair which reached to the middle of her back, she moved with the grace of the ballerina of her youth that she still carried within. She smiled reassuringly to me with her usual encouragement. Experienced and a practicing medium, she was in this training to improve her skills. I was in it to find mine. I was glad she was going first.

It went along as expected for the first few minutes as she described two people she had in spirit. Then she paused.

"I have your father here in spirit."

I startled, frozen in place, my eyes fixed on her face as she kept her attention in the spirit world. This woman knew nothing of my history. What would she say? My father had shown up only once before, from far away, afraid of my reaction if he came closer. Why was he here? Was it him?

She frowned, trying to understand. "Your father had a strong mind. He was a very mental person."

I nodded, confirming. That was correct.

"He believed that if you had a strong mind, you wouldn't get emotionally sick. He saw the emotional as causing sickness and he didn't want to deal with people who were emotional. Yet he had a soft spot, an unspoken appreciation of his daughter, though he put her through many trials to get her mentally focused."

I thought back to the rest of my childhood, and it was consistently true. He had emphasized repeatedly the importance of being mentally sharp and focused. I had often credited my business sense and success to him. He gave me that kind of mind.

"Correct," I responded. It was the only feedback we were allowed to give. Correct or not correct. With a sigh, she went on, searching for the words.

"He didn't let you be as emotionally free as you could have been as a child." She paused, then picked it up again. "There was a cottage by the lake."

I nodded. This could be easily verified. I had loved it.

"There's one more thing. He's heard your prayers and wants to thank you for them. Your prayers for his soul's growth." Rebecca frowned, concentrating on the unfamiliar terms that I used as a part of my life.

"He's very grateful for your prayers. He understands his mistakes. And he had never actually believed that there would ever be a bridge back to this world for him. Your prayers have created that bridge, allowing him to work on his soul's growth once again. He sends you thanks."

I was speechless, only nodded. We weren't to give what we termed "messages" but this one had come, and she had repeated it to me. I was more than grateful. Confirmation that our prayers are heard. That we are known by those on the other side. An understanding that those who have walked a misguided path can come to see the error of their ways. That we can all grow. Bitterness or an agenda on my part was unnecessary and irrelevant. I was glad I hadn't taken that path.

We finished our work, and the class. On my long drive back home, I reflected. My cult work really felt done now. Hearing from my father had somehow created a sense of completion. It was time to move into this new part of my life. There was so much to look forward to. Challenges and growth, to be sure. And spirits with me on both sides of the veil.

Days, months and years continued to roll on by, as my life changed slowly and subtly. Spring came again, vibrant and alive. I walked the land of a farm with my friends Luke and Sharon. My black lab mix from the pound, Ollie, ran ahead of us, bounding through the grasses and chasing anything that moved.

Luke, tall, dark and muscular, and Sharon, his short brunette wife, were wonderful friends, and I loved them. They knew my past, but it rarely came up. That part of my life truly felt like a past existence.

The farm was pulsing with new life, lilac fragrance hanging heavy in the air, redbuds and dogwoods sprinkling the woods with new color. We walked in knee-deep grasses and wildflowers, land and people released from the bondage of winter. The farm, Luke and Sharon's home, was turning into meadows and forest, full of hidden delights with new growth. It had been a quick spring, in a hurry. Summer seemed to be coming immediately on its heels.

Luke smiled at me as I lifted my face to the sun. "You're looking great today, Carla. Life going well?"

"Yep!" I smiled back at him, while fleetingly comparing internally. Long years of therapy, my life changing from terror and nightmares to contentment. Sharon caught my look. "Thinking about the changes, Carla?"

"Um hmm." I nodded, while laughing at Ollie out ahead of us, leaping up through the grasses. His pleasure reflected my own. The changes in my life had been immense.

"You know, I feel like I used to walk in a black cloud all the time. Now, here I am, walking in sunshine, joy and pleasure with good friends."

I smiled genuinely at them. They were good companions for me. My thoughts turned briefly to Pia. Missing her. The move had taken her far away. Friends changed, ebbing and flowing, like life itself it seemed. Luke and Sharon were wonderful in their own way. A real blessing.

"How long did your cult therapy take, Carla?" Her question brought me back. She rarely asked me these questions, and now I seemed ready to talk.

"You know, my guess is ten to twelve years," I answered, counting to myself. "And then there was my prior incest work. It was three to five years, I'm sure. A long time," I smiled back at her, responding as her arm wrapped around my waist in a warm hug.

"You saw Gabe for some time after that last difficult session where the cult came apart."

"Um hmm. There were still things to clean up. Thought forms. Old patterns. Energy blocks. It did take some time. I'm just really grateful we worked with energy, too. I'm sure that shortened the time."

"Why?" Sharon, just starting her work as an energy healer, was searching for the applications.

"It cleared the dark energy from my energy field. Removed the thought forms. Gave me the strength to keep going through the painful times. It was really transforming work. I'm grateful that Gabe knew it so well."

"Worth it?" Luke's question, as he bent to pull thistles from his pant leg.

"You bet! Gabe and I talked with one of his guides one time. I was complaining about how long it was all taking. So his guide asked me, 'Is it worth reclaiming yourself?' The answer to that was easy. Though I still didn't like the time factor, of course."

I slipped my arm around Sharon in an answering hug, then let go as we nearly fell in a hole. Luke laughed at our antics.

"So what's next?" he wanted to know, as we wandered down the hill to the pond, Ollie leaping ahead of us.

"I asked Gabe that. His guide helped us on that one, too, and it's a tall order. My quest is to reclaim my power. It's now an act of power instead of coming from a victim stance."

"You had to do the other first, though."

"Absolutely. I had to do my healing, so I can reclaim my own power. And I think I'm on the front edge of cult survivors healing. As some of us do it, it won't take as long. We had the same learning curve with incest. I'm glad it should be quicker with the ones behind me. But now, my sights are ahead of me."

I grinned at them. "And on good friends."

They gave me a playful shove as we slid on down the hill, coming to a seat by the pond, Ollie leaping in with full abandon. I was grateful, aware of the long journey from terror to peace.

Life had come again to my soul, songs sang, enthusiasm found its home. I had new passions, joy in friends, love for nature. There were down moments, of course. That was part of life. But it was balanced, and there were logical reasons for the dips. And today was a good day, with the sun shining and the future full of promise. It was a new day, and I loved it. We stood up, and walked back to the house together.